For

NELSON —

A GREAT MEMBER
= OF THE BSO FAMILY.

ALL BEST WISHES   HALL, BOSTON

FROM SYMPHONY

Ron Della Chiesa   CHIESA

NOV. 2011

RADIO MY WAY

FEATURING CELEBRITY PROFILES FROM JAZZ, OPERA, THE AMERICAN SONGBOOK AND MORE

By

Ron Della Chiesa

With

Erica Ferencik

PEARSON

Boston Columbus Indianapolis New York San Francisco Upper Saddle River
Amsterdam Cape Town Dubai London Madrid Milan Munich Paris Montréal Toronto
Delhi Mexico City São Paulo Sydney Hong Kong Seoul Singapore Taipei Tokyo

Editorial Director: Daryl Fox
Editor-in-Chief, Communication: Karon Bowers
Editor: Ziki Dekel
Development Editor: Kay Ueno
Assistant Editor: Stephanie Chaisson
Associate Managing Editor: Bayani Mendoza de Leon
Executive Marketing Manager: Wendy Gordon
Marketing Manager: Phil Olvey
Project Coordination, Text Design, and Electronic Page Makeup: Integra
Manufacturing Buyer: Mary Ann Gloriande
Senior Cover Design Manager/Cover Designer: Nancy Danahy
Cover Images: Top, © Charlies Giuliano; bottom and author photo on the
flap, © Fred Collins; co-author photo on the flap © Nina Huber

Credits and acknowledgments borrowed from other sources and reproduced,
with permission, in this textbook appear on page 290.

Library of Congress Cataloging-in-Publication Data

Della Chiesa, Ron.
   Radio my way/Ron Della Chiesa; with Erica Ferencik.
      p. cm.
   Includes bibliographical references.
   ISBN-13: 978-0-205-19078-2
   ISBN-10: 0-205-19078-2
      1. Della Chiesa, Ron.   2. Radio broadcasters—United States—Biography.
   3. Radio and music—United States.   I. Ferencik, Erica.   II. Title.
   ML429.D46A3 2011
   791.44092—dc23
   [B]   2011031836

---

1 2 3 4 5 6 7 8 9 10—STP-Courier—15 14 13 12

ISBN-10:   0-205-25270-2
ISBN-13: 978-0-205-25270-1

To Joyce: you're all the world to me.

table of contents

Let me begin with a warning: if you can plow past this foreword, you won't want to put this book down. Here he is, for once without a microphone, as breezy, informative, and witty as you've heard him all these years. If you like Ron Della Chiesa, and who doesn't, you're going to love this book.

I've known Ron Della Chiesa since I began as a production assistant at WGBH in 1985. I remember the first time I was asked to work with him. It was to direct fundraising on *MusicAmerica*; and with this assignment came a warning: he doesn't take direction, and he doesn't follow the fundraising mandates—including time limits on pitching segments. Somehow I sensed, correctly as it turned out, that there was more of a problem with the fundraising directive than with the host in question.

Having experienced successful fundraising drives at other stations, I knew that the "accepted" techniques didn't always fill the coffers. With Ron I sensed the opportunity to go for a humorous approach. In no time we had worked up a shtick where I was giving "updates" from Fundraising Central (our term), with a recording of an old-style teletype chomping in the background. Even though I was in the same room with him, we'd pretend that it was difficult for us to hear each other, or to know if I was on the air. What was the goal of the fundraising campaign? Were we close? How much closer? We were breaking each other up and having a ball. The phones would not stop ringing with callers eager to pledge large donations.

It may be difficult for some to believe that Ron's enthusiasm is genuine. But it is. Countless times he's burst out of the sound booth after a Boston Symphony broadcast pouring out his excitement, even more than what he conveyed on the air. He loves what he hears, his passion undiminished even after listening to thousands upon thousands of hours of musical performances from every genre imaginable. Most of us would be jaded over time. That is not Ron Della Chiesa.

Many books of this nature contain more than a dollop of correcting past wrongs for posterity. That isn't Ron Della Chiesa either. If you're reading this now only to see if you are the worthy victim of a score-settling, you may as well put this back down. It isn't here.

It's a good bet that if you are mentioned, you have a place of honor. And if you have a section of this book devoted to you, you have a vaulted place in

Ron's vast pantheon of musicians and personalities that have enriched his generation, and I trust, generations to come. My congratulations!

—Brian Bell

Brian Bell produced the Boston Symphony radio broadcasts beginning in the fall of 1991, and wrote every script Ron Della Chiesa read for those programs, as well as concert presentations by the Boston Pops, the Handel and Haydn Society, the Boston Philharmonic, and OperaBoston.

CHAPTER 1

Radio Kid

THERE ARE TIMES WHEN I LOOK BACK AT MY LIFE TO DISCOVER where this passion for radio began, only to realize there's no mystery at all. My beginnings were storybook-perfect to grow the seeds of an obsession for broadcasting. Ever since that first day I sat in awe in front of a radio, I wondered how I could become part of the magic of the voices inside the box.

I was born on February 18, 1938, in Quincy, Massachusetts, a city known as the birthplace of two presidents (John Adams and John Quincy Adams, both of whom had lived just a mile from our home on High Street) and for its stone quarries, where my grandfather toiled many long hours. In my neighborhood, the two most important things to kids after school were sandlot baseball and getting home in time to listen to their favorite radio programs. After all, this was the

First dip in the ocean, Nantasket Beach, 1939.

Author's collection.

Author's collection.

Golden Age of Radio, a time when radio was the focus of entertainment right up through the advent of television in 1948.

We would race home to listen to the *Lone Ranger, Superman, Captain Midnight, Duffy's Tavern, Tom Mix and the Ralston Straight Shooters,* and *The Shadow.* These wondrous programs filled our afternoons and evenings with entertainment. Everything happened in our minds: that was the magic and the mystery of radio. Our charged imaginations kept us hooked day after day. Who did Captain Midnight look like? What about his evil enemy, Ivan Shark? And Tom Mix, the cowboy? We could send away for a picture, but we were too busy building our own movie sets in our minds, conjuring the faces of our heroes, their loves, and their arch enemies. Each program would end on a cliffhanger, leaving us breathless from one day to the next. I'd lie in bed staring in the dark worrying about Superman: Would kryptonite trip him up and keep him from springing Lois Lane from the evil clutches of those who were terrorizing the city?

Most of the shows were sponsored by drinks or cereals: Ovaltine sponsored *Captain Midnight,* Ralston and Farina backed *Tom Mix.* So many labels from Ovaltine got you the Captain Midnight secret decoder ring. But when you finally got a ring, the message was always the same: "Buy Ovaltine!"

I confess I still have my ring and an embarrassing number of premiums in an envelope somewhere. To this day I get excited when I see a lumpy envelope in the mail! Hell, it might be a decoder ring or prize. A pair of glow-in-the-dark Tom Mix spurs, anything's possible. It boiled down to scoring boxtops, labels, and premiums;

so I had my mom, a very Catholic woman, stealing Ovaltine labels in the store. But that's what it was like being an only child for me.

My parents would go to hell and back to make me happy.

■ ■ ■

My mother, Florence, and my father, Aldo, had been married a good thirteen years before I was born. As an only child, I became the focus of their life. They both grew up in Quincy and became schoolteachers. My earliest memories of my father, however, really begin at the end of World War II, in 1946. I didn't see much of him before that time because he was called up from the reserves shortly after Pearl Harbor in 1941.

My mother described the day my father caught the train to report for active duty. We went with him to South Station. This was in 1942, and I was just four years old. Crying, I begged my father not to leave and ran after him into the train. It was not an easy day. A kind-hearted couple who'd been watching approached and offered to drive us home or help us in whatever way we needed, but my mom declined the offer and just thanked them. We went home, just the two of us, where we had to build our lives together until he returned.

Those early days were a bittersweet mix of missing my dad and enjoying a quintessential New England childhood that was tinged with all that World War II brought to the populace. People tightened their belts; Rosie the Riveter rolled up her sleeves. I remember lying in bed listening to the sounds of destroyers being built in the Quincy shipyard nearby, a rhythmic pounding that went on all night long. I'd gaze out my window at a sky lit ghostly white from the factories below. We'd ration stamps, buy savings bonds, and save scrap metal. A star was displayed in the windows of the families who had a brother or a father serving overseas.

My mother, Florence Della Chiesa, 1922.

Author's collection.

We sat in the dark for air raids, waiting for the all-clear to turn our lights back on again. I remember my photograph being taken in a little army uniform, then gazing at it the next week in the newspaper where my mother had proudly sent it.

Though times were hard for my mom, she definitely knew how to take care of business. She handled all the practical matters: the finances, the shopping, everything required of a World War II housewife. I think she tried to keep things as "normal" as possible for me, but we both missed Dad.

Meanwhile, I'd listen to the radio.

■ ■ ■

Our radio was the centerpiece, the beating heart of the living room, in fact, of the whole house. At seven years old I became a regular listener of the Metropolitan Opera on Saturday afternoons. My mother would be cooking in the kitchen on snowy winter days when you couldn't get out, while thundering, passionate voices filled the rooms, warming us. As young as I was, I would have given anything to see an actual opera.

The voice of Milton Cross was magic to me. He had a way of telling the story of the opera and describing the action on stage that brought it fully alive. He would capture the colors of the costumes, the way the great gold curtain parted to magnificent scenery, the way the singers moved, and the reaction of the audience. The bravos, the pageantry, all the romantic or wrenching drama were forever etched in the theater of my mind. I thought at the time that it would be the best sort of life to be an opera singer. I eventually realized that I didn't have the voice. But from those earliest childhood days, I felt that someday I just had to be on the radio.

I was so inspired by radio programs that one day I built a fake radio station in my bedroom. I had a turntable, 78 rpm records, and a little cardboard microphone. I'd write my own scripts, create my own shows, commercials, and man, did I impress myself!

I had the radio bug, and I had it bad.

■ ■ ■

My dad came home in 1946; I was eight years old. It was then that I really began to get to know him. The truth was, my father was a dreamer. A graduate of Massachusetts College of Art in the twenties, he thought only of painting, travel, and the beautiful places in the world he wanted to visit someday. For him, it was all about aesthetics. My father really was one of these inherently gifted Renaissance men; he certainly wasn't someone out to make a lot of money or change the world. He lived in his own world of art, music, drawing, paintings, sunsets, and beauty in general. When he wasn't teaching art and mechanical drawing at Braintree High School, he'd be painting or drawing or indulging his love of art by visiting museums. He told me he once spied John Singer Sargent walking along Huntington Avenue and followed him all day, though he was so in awe of the man that he couldn't bring himself to approach him or say a word.

Author's collection.

As young as I was, it was hard to understand the notion of my father at war and his necessary transition to civilian life. I now know that part of his recovery from the trauma of what he had seen those past four years was to immerse himself back into his world, especially that of music and painting. He also couldn't wait to be a father and husband again.

On Saturday afternoons the radio would always be tuned to the Metropolitan Opera, but now my dad added a whole new dimension to the experience. Not only could he paint, he could sing all the arias from the operas even though he couldn't read a note of music. He had a collection of 78 rpm records that he played on our wonderful cherrywood Victrola; his parents had brought it with them from Italy. To this day I listen to Caruso recordings on that very same turntable—incredible how the sound fills the room!

Dad would sing while he was shaving, sing at the breakfast table, sing as he got dressed for work. He'd put on a record and belt out arias from Verdi, from Puccini, and sing along with all the great tenor voices from Italian opera: Caruso, Gigli, and Di Stefano. In a way he was like my dear friend Tony Bennett: when he wasn't painting he would sing; when he wasn't singing he was sketching or painting.

My father began to take me into Boston on Sundays. First stop was always art supplies, his brushes and paints, followed by a museum, after which I would beg him to take me to radio stations. I was obsessed with wanting to know how a radio station looked, how it was all laid out, who did what, and how everything came together to create shows. Usually he'd give in to my pleading, and we'd go visit one of them. Many of the stations at that time were in hotels. WBZ was in the Hotel Bradford in the theater district; WNAC was in the Hotel Buckminster in Kenmore Square near Fenway Park. A radio station in a hotel was such a romantic notion; tourists would be checking in on one floor, while the floor above would be dedicated to a station. A plate glass window was the only thing separating an orchestra with a live studio audience from the broadcast booth, an announcer, and gaggles of wide-eyed tourists and visitors.

It was my father who took me to my first opera, *La Boheme*, in 1946, at the old Boston Opera House on Huntington Avenue, not far from Symphony Hall. It was a beautiful building, patterned after the great opera houses in Europe. It has since been torn down, but there remains a little street called Opera Place, its original home.

This is where it all started for me, on that hot June afternoon in Boston, where the sounds that moved me while listening to the radio and my father's records finally became wed to a live performance. We sat way up and far in the back on one of the several balconies that hugged a horseshoe-shaped stage, peering down at the performers through binoculars. My ears vibrated from the sheer power of their voices; even at that young age I was stirred by the dramatic emotion behind the words. I sat in awe as love, betrayal, suffering, and joy seemed to explode all around me.

Soon after this day we took a trip to New York City, venturing past the old Metropolitan Opera house where so many greats had sung—Lilly Pons, Beniamino Gigli, and Rosa Ponselle. From there we went backstage on 7th Avenue where all the scenery was stored. The back door to the stage was open, and I turned to my dad and asked if we could go in. He found one of the stage hands and got permission to walk out on the stage. We passed through a dark, musty hallway to the back entrance. Finally, I stood there on the well traveled blond wood—it seemed to go on endlessly until it disappeared into darkness at the back of the house. It was magic. My father grinned at me and said, "Come on, Ronnie, why don't you sing a few notes?"

My heart pounded as I gazed up at the famous golden horseshoe, but I think I sang a little bit of Pagliacci. The great hall seemed to hold my voice in its giant hands, echoing it softly back at me. Now I can say that I sang on the stage of the old Metropolitan Opera house, the same stage graced by the great Caruso.

What a nice way for a Quincy boy to begin a relationship with opera.

CHAPTER 2

Finding My Voice

FANTASIZING ABOUT A CAREER IN BROADCASTING COULD DISTRACT me for hours, but eventually I had to get outside and play ball, literally. And I found that real life was different out on the sandlot. Don't get me wrong—I had all the baseball cards, and I loved the Red Sox. The truth was, I was a terrible baseball player. It wasn't for lack of trying, or for lack of love of everything about the game, especially the getup for the catcher, but baseball greatness was like

Can't run, can't hit, love Red Sox.

Author's collection.

7

girls: unattainable. I loved nothing better than the crack of the bat, skidding into bases, sun in my eyes and the mound under my feet, but you see, I lacked speed. I'd field a groundball, but without fail it bounced back up and hit me in the face. It drove me flipping crazy. As a kid, my arm just wasn't strong enough, and there was no one around to really show me the ropes. Remember, there was no Little League back then. I recently complained about my problem to an old friend, former Red Sox great Sam Mele. He said, "How'd you like to have a ball coming at your head at ninety-eight miles an hour? No, seriously, you need someone to coach you, end of story. Every day I was out there I had my brothers to teach me." In any case, I could count on one hand the number of times I got a piece of that baseball. And I didn't have a clue about football—except that football players really did get all the girls.

How to get the girls: now *there* was an enigma that took years to decipher...

As I was screwing up in right field or brooding in the dugout, I'd picture one of my favorite Red Sox players, Dom DiMaggio, Joe DiMaggio's younger brother. I liked him because he seemed as if he should have nothing to do with playing baseball. He was this scholarly looking guy they called "The Little Professor," not at all rough and tumble or even very big at 5'9", playing out there in center field with his glasses and glove, holding his own, and a great ball player. He had real style. He actually answered a letter I'd sent him when I was ten years old, saying how much *he* appreciated hearing from *me*.

It was a day I'll never forget.

■ ■ ■

Childhood memories become especially precious for most of us as we grow older. Mine flit through my mind, often unbidden:

The comfortable cape house my dad built for the grand sum of five thousand dollars; the steam engines that chugged by the playing fields after school; the pet parakeet that got a weird growth and died but sang his tail off for the five years we had him; the canary that didn't sing, but for some reason we named Perry Como; bowling at Kippy's Candlepins in Quincy; building a tree house with stolen lumber and installing a makeshift stove with a pipe; dropping a sheet from the branches and showing movies with a five-cent "entrance fee"; being confounded by algebra and geometry but entranced by Richard Halliburton's *Book of Marvels*; starting a "hamster club" and, unfortunately, baking a few of them in the hot summer sun; eating my mom's great desserts: apple pie, corn muffins, lemon meringue pie, fruitcake, Toll House cookies; and my mom calling me home in the evenings for dinner. Yes, they really did stuff like that back then, just as in the *Henry Aldrich* radio show. The thing was to play it at least a little bit cool and not run back home right away....

As it turned out, I can't mourn my days on the baseball field too much. I mean, I was a different sort of a kid. How many eleven-year-olds in my neighborhood had seen their first opera and daydreamed about singing arias in front

First business venture, July 1947. L–R: John Ross, David Maglio, Charles Ross, me.

of thousands? I was seriously out of the mainstream on that count. What sort of pre-teen hangs out at the Public Library Music Room listening to Puccini, Verdi, Bjoerling, and Lanza for hours on end? I used to go to the one in Quincy. They had two or three booths where I could dig in and listen to all the opera and classical recordings we didn't have in our collection at home. I'd sit there and pour over the notes on the back of the album: the history of the composer, the story of the opera, the Libretto. Often I'd sitting there in the dark, gorgeous voices soaring in my head, until someone tapped me on the shoulder and told me the library was closing and it was time to go home.

Even my friendships were based on a shared love of music. By my teens, a small circle of friends had developed and drew quite close. Bob Buccini and I were thirteen, hanging at his place when we heard Paul Antonelli belt out this mindblowing rendition of "Old Man River." Here was this kid our age with this mature, full baritone operatic voice. I was slackjawed. His dad, Guido, was a teacher and prominent violinist who played Broadway music in pit orchestras, very well known in Boston music circles. We bonded over a passion for music, his Italian-American background, and the fact that he was an only child too, also with musical ambitions. Bob, who at age twelve had already lost both parents and lived with an elderly Italian aunt, used to come over to our house all the time to hang out and listen to music and, more often than not, sit down to dinner with us. My mother and father became a sort of surrogate set of parents for him. The three of us boys not only huddled around the Victrola listening to opera, but we did the usual kid things: get in trouble and chase girls. Even today we're in touch;

though I have to say they can find me, but I can't always find them. They'll hear me on the radio or see me on TV, and they'll call or email me. So wonderful to hear from friends I've been blessed with for over sixty years.

■ ■ ■

In the 1940s and '50s it was all about discovery and "firsts." There are so many I will never forget: my first animated film, *Pinocchio*; and my first live action, *Lassie Come Home*, which I saw with my mom at Camp Lee in Virginia where my Dad was based. I bawled my eyes out watching that film, because of Lassie, of course, but also no doubt because it was such an emotional time seeing my dad between his deployments all over the world.

Movies were huge in the early forties, especially since this was before television. Not only was it a big deal when a movie came out, but each showing was a major production. After you settled in with your popcorn and soda, things would kick off with a cartoon or newsreel, then a B movie, the coming attractions, and *finally* the feature. Imagine seeing all of this for just a quarter. It was a whole afternoon or a whole morning's worth of entertainment. You could really lose yourself in there; I know I did. At that time Quincy had four movie theaters: the Adams, the Strand, the Capitol, and the Art. We loved the Adams Theater most of all because that's where the weekly serials ran, each episode leaving you with a cliffhanger: someone jumping out of a building or holding a knife to the hero's neck. You could hardly wait to return the following week for the next episode.

Watching *Fantasia* was a profound experience for me, mainly because of the unprecedented way Disney matched great animation with music. *The Three Caballeros* (1944) took things even further: it was one of the first films that mixed animation with live action. Donald Duck himself ventured down to Brazil and danced the Samba with Conchita. *Song of the South* impressed me the same way.

Disney characters inspire and delight me to this day, possibly because the very first album given to me for Christmas was the soundtrack to *Pinocchio*. A lot of great music came out of that, including "When You Wish Upon A Star." I became enamored of movie musicals: *Singing in the Rain, Bandwagon, Oklahoma!,* and *Carousel,* as well as the tough guy films. Who could forget Bogart in *Casablanca, Key Largo,* and *Treasure of Sierra Madre*? I discovered sound tracks for movies, as well as film composers such as Bernard Herrmann, who cranked up the suspense in 1960s movies like Hitchcock's *Psycho, North by Northwest*, and *Rear Window*. There was Max Steiner, who almost painted the brooding skies above Tara with his score for the 1930s film *Gone with the Wind*, and Franz Waxman's heart wrenching music for *A Place in the Sun*. Dimetri Tiomkin created the moving score for *The Robe*, and Eric Wolfgang Korngold composed the rollicking music for swashbuckler films such as *The Sea Hawk,* starring Errol Flynn. Many of these composers had fled Europe because they were Jewish, and the Nazis were coming into power in the 1930s. The youngest at that time was André Previn, who came to Hollywood when he was a teenager.

■ ■ ■

My father took me to my first concert at Boston's Symphony Hall when I was thirteen. Charles Munch was conducting, and I was blown away by the sound. Dad also introduced me to my first Boston Pops concert with the legendary Arthur Fiedler, a quintessential conductor and charismatic man who conducted the Pops for fifty years. I remember one day walking outside of Symphony Hall when Fiedler himself stepped out of his car. Two kids riding by on their bikes screeched to a stop and pointed, saying, "Look, it's Beethoven!"

Little did I dream that one day I would be up in the broadcast booth as the voice of the Boston Symphony, or have the chance to interview not only André Previn, but John Williams, who would become the most popular film composer of all time.

Another first from that era was my introduction to New York City through visits with my aunt and uncle who lived in Scotch Plains, New Jersey. My lifelong love affair with New York began with those one-hour trips from their home into the city with my dad. In the late forties the city had a whole different look: automats that dropped a wax-paper-wrapped sandwich down a chute for a quarter, women and men in sharp suits, and everyone in hats. A bus tour took us by the old Met opera house on 39th and Broadway, through the Bowery, uptown to Harlem, and midtown to the Empire State Building, the tallest building in the world at the time. A visit to the live television show *Broadway Open House,* hosted by Jerry Lester, really opened my eyes, as did the RCA–NBC tour, where I stood at the very podium where the great Toscanini conducted concerts.

It was on our way home from one of these trips that I begged my dad for a TV. There weren't too many television sets around in Quincy in 1948, when they were just starting to be commercially available, but I just had to have one. He finally took me to a trade show put on by RCA Victor in the old Mechanics Hall on Huntington Avenue in Boston, where you could see an actual television. We walked around the hall gaping at these big black and white boxes with screens only seven or ten inches wide. It was magical. The first person we saw on television was in fact Arturo Toscanini, all dressed in black, with his mane of white hair flying as he conducted the NBC Symphony Orchestra.

Two years later, after untold begging, we finally got a TV, a twelve-inch GE. The first show I saw was the *Ed Sullivan Show*, which I loved, but I really howled watching *The Show of Shows* with Sid Caesar and Imogene Coca, who brilliantly satirized Italian opera and movies by mixing Italian with all kinds of nonsensical words. *Playhouse 90* showed live plays, and it was quite a revelation to see what radio stars Jack Benny, George Burns, and Gracie Allen actually looked like.

TV got me so excited that I got together with a group of friends and built a mini-television studio in a friend's garage in Quincy. Empty cartons morphed into video cameras; soup cans became camera lenses. We made a boom micro- phone with a long stick and a can rubberbanded on. I'd sit behind a desk and announce the news of the day, introduce guests, pitch toilet paper and Supersuds. My buddy, cameraman Glen McGee, claims it all started in that old garage. We even took the show on the road—to the baseball park where we did a play-by-play in front of all sorts of confused passersby.

Girls, as I recall, were not intrigued by our efforts. This may have had some- thing to do with my entertaining the thought of becoming a priest, especially in my mid-teen years.

■ ■ ■

I was confirmed by Cardinal Cushing, an Irish, Boston-born man with a good heart. I admired him, and I became an impassioned Catholic, though I never went to Catholic school or was an altar boy. When I was much younger I even made a little shoebox with curtains with a cup inside, crushed bread for wafers. With a prayer book off to the side, I'd genuflect to my heart's content. When I look back on it, I realize I was in love with the whole ritual of it: the mass, the mystique of the altar, the tabernacle, the chalice, how the priest would raise it to the heavens, but not so much the theology. It was that primo acting role that really got me: the ritual of the bells and the incense. Certainly the chalice-raising scene in *Parsifal* hovered somewhere in my subconscious mind. Regardless, to this day it all intoxicates me each time I visit the Cathedral of the Holy Cross, a magnificent Vatican-like edifice in the South End.

The teen years—around the time hormones really hit—can be a rocky time. I for one didn't quite know what to do with them. I certainly felt different from a lot of my peers. Instead of being out in the streets stealing hubcaps like other teens, I was home listening to Enrico Caruso. Not a great way to meet girls, plus there was my physique: I was on the skinny side, no matter what I ate.

I remember preparing myself for weeks to ask a stunning Sandra Dee look- alike to dance at a high school record hop. How you can actually plan for some- thing like that I don't know, but I practiced every verbal and logistic scenario humanly possible before that night, hoping to make failure an impossibility by leaving nothing to chance. "Would you like to dance?" "How does a dance sound?" "Feel like dancing?" Or pretty much just yank her up onto the floor. This girl was *mine*. Arriving early, I scouted the room, finding the best possible places to hang out, look casual, and maintain my Tony Curtis hairstyle.

And there she was, sitting alone, which was perfect. I didn't want to have to ask her in front of her giggling, smirking friends. She looked gorgeous under the glittering lights of the high school gymnasium. But still I waited; I wanted a nice, slow ballad so I could make my intentions clear.

The moment came. The song was "The Great Pretender," by The Platters. I approached and she gave me this coy look. I thought I even detected a smile creeping up one side of her face.

"Would you like to dance?"

"No," she said, and looked away.

All the air left my body and my face froze. I walked away out of the gym into the beautiful spring night. What the hell did I do wrong? I felt like an ass. I must be wearing the wrong kind of jacket. My tie was stupid. The pricey suede shoes looked suddenly ridiculous.

It all put me into a deep funk for a good three weeks: taking apart those moments and putting them back together, hearing that "No" in my head a thousand times over, my undignified, silent exit. It didn't help that in the following week I got into a fist fight with this kid who'd been bullying me for a year, losing in a big way. To this day I'll indulge in the occasional daydream about getting even.

■ ■ ■

Between striking out with girls and baseball, I started to get obsessed with swing music and playing the trumpet. My friend Dick Hayes had a Zenith console radio with a turntable that played 33 1/3 rpms—a huge deal at the time. We'd hang at his house listening for hours to Benny Goodman, Les Brown, and Ted Heath, but mostly to the Glenn Miller orchestra. "In the Mood," "String of Pearls," "Chattanooga Choo Choo," "Moonlight Serenade"—we couldn't get enough of that big band sound. We also watched *Sun Valley Serenade* and *Orchestra Wives* more times that I care to recall. I loved the big brassy sound and became convinced I could play the trumpet.

I really gave it my best shot. How could I not try to play an instrument when I was steeped and stewed in music, both through my own hours of listening but also with my dad belting out arias over breakfast or jumping up at a party to sing.

My cousin gave me a trumpet, and I started to take lessons from an old big band trumpeter in Quincy named Joe DiBona who charged just two bucks a lesson. I started my research in a record store, also in Quincy, called Jason's. They had booths where you could listen to the records before you bought them. I wallowed in Miller, Goodman, Count Basie, and Duke Ellington, segueing into Sinatra, Mario Lanza, Peggy Lee, and Ella Fitzgerald. I bought what I could and played along with the records at home.

I was starting to develop my sound, but after many months realized I didn't quite have it. I wanted to play so badly, but I pushed to make it happen faster than I could. Impatient, I guess. So I quit, even though the high school band director asked me to join the band. I guess I didn't have the confidence. Little did I know that later in life that brief acquaintance with the trumpet would come in very handy. As far as my own future as a musician, it didn't look promising, but I knew I had to be involved with music somehow. So I went back to my cardboard broadcasting booth. That's where I really felt comfortable—writing my own commercials, delivering them, and playing DJ: "Here is a wonderful recording by Mario Lanza. He's got a big hit with 'Be My Love'…"

■ ■ ■

As much fun as I was having playing broadcaster, I had a growing awareness that I didn't know what the hell I sounded like. I needed a tape recorder, which wasn't cheap back in the early fifties. They cost around fifty dollars—a lot of money for my parents, both teachers, to spend on anything, much less something so strange as a tape recorder. Undaunted, however, I kept begging my dad for one. After about the tenth or eleventh "no," I realized I needed a new tactic.

We were driving to Wollaston Beach in Quincy on a beautiful summer day.

"Dad," I said, "I just gotta have a tape recorder."

My mother rolled her eyes and folded her arms, staring at the beach out the window.

"We've talked about this," my dad said.

"You hear me upstairs, I know you do. Talking into a cardboard mic."

"That is a problem."

"Look, I can't hear what I sound like. Really hear my voice. I don't know what I'm doing wrong, I'm just talking to myself like an idiot. Talking to the wall. I have to be able to record my own radio shows and play them back—"

"Christmas is coming," he replied, as the hot July winds blew.

"I can't wait till Christmas. This can be my Christmas present, okay? I don't care about anything else."

He pulled over to the side of the road, got out of the car, slammed the door, and started walking, steam pouring out of the top of his head. A little way off he stood with his arms folded. My mom said, "Well, now you've done it."

I got out of the car and ran over to him. "Dad—"

"Ron, I can't get you everything you ask for."

"I know."

"It's not possible now. Wait a few months."

"But Dad, you know how you feel about your painting? And your singing?"

He looked at me for the first time since this discussion began. The look in his eyes made me remember the kind of pain he was in when he first got back from the war, and I almost couldn't continue.

"That's how I feel about being in broadcasting someday. Being on the radio, having my own show."

He looked away again. "Why don't you just go back to the car."

Defeated, I did what he said, calculating all the way how many months or even years it would take me to save that much money. Nobody said a word to each other all the way home.

The next day, I'd stowed away the fake microphone and was lying on my bed, daydreaming about serenading my latest crush with my trumpet, then quickly substituting that with a fantasy tenor saxophone.

Dad appeared in the doorway. "Okay, let's go get you your tape recorder."

CHAPTER 3

Steppin' Out

My FUTURE IN RADIO TRULY BEGAN WITH THAT FIRST, RELATIVELY gigantic tape recorder. It was a reel-to-reel VM, or "Voice of Music." At first I was ecstatic, following my parents around and recording them, my cat, my friends, crazy stuff off the radio. That feeling soon ebbed. I started taping my own shows, one after the other, playing them back for hours, and trying to pin down what was wrong. After a while it became pretty obvious: I'd been cursed with a horrible speaking voice. I couldn't believe how high and whiny I sounded, but to add to my own personal hell, there was something else terribly, eerily wrong that I couldn't quite put my finger on.

WJDA, established in 1947, was the first radio station in Quincy. So, of course, I was obsessed with it. When I was ten years old I drew a sketch of what I thought the inside of the station looked like and sent it in. My uncle Amilio, the first Italian Mayor of Quincy, did his nephew a favor and called the manager and owner of the station, James D. Asher. He told Mr. Asher that I was interested in radio and wanted one of my taped shows to be critiqued. I was invited for a tour of the place, even did a little spot on a kid's show. Still no word from Mr. Asher about my tape, however, so I started bugging my dad to follow up with another phone call. In the end, I got my wish.

I don't think I've ever labored so hard on anything as I did on that demo tape, and I don't think I've ever sweated quite so much in anyone's office as I did in James Asher's office on that sweltering September day.

After directing me to what seemed like an enormous leather chair opposite him, he took my precious tape, put it in his recorder, and pressed "play." He put his chin in his hands and stared at the machine as we both listened. Heart pounding, I watched his face as if it were the shroud of Turin and someone had told me they'd seen it move.

He frowned and turned off the recorder. "Son," he said, "I don't think you're quite ready to work in radio yet."

"Yet." I was hanging on to the "yet" for dear life. "But, what do you—"

"You're not bad, but you have a real diction problem."

"Diction?"

"You've got a real heavy Boston accent."

"I do?"

"You don't pronounce your 'r's."

"I don't?"

He rewound the tape and played it through. Not one "r" in the entire reel. Talk about a light bulb going off. I thanked the man and couldn't get out of there fast enough to get home and listen to my tapes with fresh ears.

I listened to Milton Cross introduce the Metropolitan Opera with his perfect diction, then I played myself doing the same thing. Holy *paahk yaah caah in Haahvahhd Yahhd*—did I sound like a Bostonian!

I knew that in order to be on the radio I had to get rid of my Boston accent; I had to have a neutral accent. Beyond all that, Mr. Asher stressed before I left that day that I would need to know how to use phrases and inflection to deliver copy and sell, because in radio you're always selling. I became keenly aware that I hoped my audience would be the entire United States, not just Boston. I listened incessantly to all the announcers: Hugh James, Don Wilson (the announcer on the Jack Benny show), Don Amici and his brother Jim; Orson Welles, and Ben Grauer who used to do the NBC broadcast with Toscanini.

I sat down and made a list of all the problem words I could think of. All the poor, helpless words I was flattening and murdering with my accent: car, bar, later, never, over, dark; or as I was saying them: *cahh, bah, latah, nevah, ovah, dahk*. The list grew daily, and daily I repeated the words over and over until I had officially welcomed the letter "r" into my life and made peace with it. But changing how I spoke wasn't easy, especially when I was hanging out with friends who wouldn't have known what to do with me if I started speaking in a completely different way. They may have even started kicking my ass. Thankfully I was able to speak one way "upstairs" as well as "normally" in real life.

All in all it took me years to lose that accent. In fact, I still get called on it, most recently during a BSO broadcast. Sometimes I'll slip after a couple of beers with friends who won't hesitate to clue me in. But keep in mind, I live in Dorchester, a wonderful neighborhood, but one where r's are nonexistent. It's so easy to just relax, walk out my door, and fall back into an "r"-less life.

■ ■ ■

My first job was at the Alhambra Tea Room in Quincy Center. It was a restaurant with a soda fountain, and they made their own candy in the basement. The place was a landmark; my mother had worked her way through high school there in the twenties. When I was sixteen, she introduced me to the owner, a kindly Greek gentleman. I'll never forget her saying, "This is my son. Hire him, you'll like him."

The next day the manager, Al, taught me the finer points of making sodas, sundaes, and sandwiches. My first day on the job is still seared into my brain: a blur of ice cream and blenders, take-out orders, fries, burgers, and milkshakes—a thousand different things happening all at once. I was at the register, learning how to make change for the very first time, when my second or third customer, a woman in a scarf and sunglasses, bought coffee and skittered out of the store. Minutes later she burst back in and charged right up to the manager, saying, "That young man at the register, he cheated me! Look, I gave him twenty dollars for coffee, and I only got two back!" Well, I knew she didn't give me twenty dollars, and I got very upset, close to hysterical. My newness was so obvious—it was written all over me. Al stared at me as I insisted on my innocence, then turned to the woman. With a stone-cold look he told her he'd check the register and receipts. After a minute that felt like days, he looked up from the register and told her to get lost.

Things smoothed out after that, and I really got into the rhythm of being a soda jerk; in fact I worked there straight through high school to support my pricey LP habit. There were other benefits to being the guy behind the counter slinging hash and fizzing the drinks: I started to feel comfortable in my own skin. I began to realize that I had a personality, a sense of humor. Kids who'd knock me around as soon as look at me showed new respect or at least acknowledged me, sometimes even tried to pal up to me. Besides, the Alhambra was not just a social hangout, it was *the* place to be. On top of all that, the jukebox was jumping with the greats all day long: Nat King Cole, Ella Fitzgerald, Stan Getz, Billie Holiday, whatever you wanted to hear.

■ ■ ■

Around that time I stumbled on some muscle mags. I still wasn't happy with my build. Steve Reeves on the cover of *Strength and Health* with his 28" waist, 45" chest, chiseled features, and bulging biceps looked like a god to me. He was one great specimen of physical prowess. I asked my dad if he'd help me set up a bench in the garage with a mirror. He said sure, and that he'd tack a couple pictures of my hero on the wall to boot.

I ordered my weights from the York Barbell Company in York, Pennsylvania, and the mailman nearly blew his knees out lugging them up the steps. I flipped through the pictures of Steve, posing and puffing, then looked at my thin arms, back to the weights. I have to say I had some serious doubts at that point, but then I thought to myself, just open the box and set the thing up, for crying out loud.

I did the first curl and felt the blood rushing through every single vein and capillary in my arm. It was this whoosh of feeling alive, this reminder that I had a body. I looked through the book of exercises that came with the weights: bench, leg, and overhead presses, deltoid pulls, and bicep curls. I was out of control—it felt so good. As the days and weeks went by I'd look in the mirror and think, shazam! Something very good is happening here. I ordered more weights and set new goals, but after a while I needed more weights than it made sense to buy, so I joined Jack Donovan's Health Club.

At this point, I was looking forward to getting a little more one-on-one attention. Jack must have been in his sixties, but he looked fantastic, maybe because he never ever stopped lifting weights. A legend in the Quincy bodybuilding world, Jack was an old-time musclehead who ran the gym on his own. I'd come to lift and he'd be alone in the gym benching two-fifty. As I let myself in, he'd squeak out,

"Come on in and get set up, kid, you can do it. I'll talk you through it."

I'd say, "Jack, how much should I lift?"

"Yaaarghh...arghhh...two-twenty!" Clang bang of the barbell back in the rack.

So I'd go ahead and do my thing as he did his, gathering pointers here and there as he deadlifted, straining and squatting and groaning all around me.

As I finished up he'd call out, "Yeeeaaaaaah! Lock that door on the way out, wouldja, buddy?"

Sometimes I'd come in and he'd be locked in this little steam cabinet with only his head sticking out, a towel wrapped around his thick neck. I guess he got into the thing through a secret side entrance of some kind; in any case he was always smiling in there and I used to wonder what he was doing with his hands, although I never asked and I never got in the thing myself.

The point was, I wasn't scrawny any more, my voice was changing, and it felt like things were coming together. Girls weren't exactly all over me, but there were hopeful signs here and there.

■ ■ ■

I made my second foray into the real world of radio when I was sixteen years old at WPLM in downtown Plymouth, a station that had only been on the air for two years. Again I sat there sweating through every pore in my body as station owner Jack Campbell, a WWII vet, listened to my tape. Again the serious look and snap of the button as he turned off the player. Except this time I heard, "When would you like to start?"

My first challenge was how to get to work. I'd copped a ride with my dad to the station for the interview, but I didn't have my driver's license yet, and there was no way he could drive me there and back each day. All so strange because there I would be, fifty years later, broadcasting on WPLM! Regardless, at the time it was a much needed boost to my ego.

First a radio job, and then, out of nowhere, I fell in love for the very first time. On my way to the Alhambra I'd have to walk by Dorothy Murial's Bakery, and each time I did my heart would do a flip in my chest. This Kim Novak look-alike would be at the counter wrapping up a cake, fixing me with these doe eyes, an enigmatic little smile on her lips. Each time I went in to see her she lit right up; she made my teenage boy head spin. Gerri Robbins from Hough's Neck; I'll never forget her!

Luckily Gerri loved music, too. In fact, her dad turned me on to Sinatra; up until that time it had been strictly jazz, big band, opera, and classical. He put "Songs for Swinging Lovers" on the turntable and that was it for me. Gerri and I used to hit the Neponset Drive-in movies on the weekend, steaming up the windows so bad we had to turn the windshield wipers on. There were even a couple of times we drove away practically dragging the whole drive-in with us because we forgot to unlatch the speakers from the windows...

I may have been a teenager in love, but I didn't feel like a teenager when I took Gerri to the Newport Jazz Festival in Newport, Rhode Island, the granddaddy of jazz festivals. That's where we first saw Duke Ellington's Orchestra, Count Basie, Dinah Washington, Erroll Garner, and Billie Holiday.

Norman Granz was the gentleman who created Jazz at the Philharmonic, or JATP, as it came to be known. Granz initially organized desegregated jam sessions in Los Angeles in the early 1940s. These jam sessions evolved into the JATP concerts, which eventually went on tour. He was committed to the notion that black and white performers should be able to play together and that they deserved equal pay. From this belief grew the innovative idea of bringing together and taking on tour some of the greatest jazz musicians of the time, artists who up until then played mostly in smoke-filled clubs and dives, and often under segregated circumstances. Granz would open the evening with a jam session, after which each artist would emerge and play his favorite tune.

When the JATP came to Boston, there I was, a kid from Quincy High, with my first serious girlfriend, sitting smack in the second row of Symphony Hall. We sat rapt, listening to Flip Phillips, Illinois Jacquet, Ray Brown, and Buddy Rich; the list was endless. We sat so close we watched the beads of sweat rolling down their faces, saw the dents and scratches on their instruments, sometimes even heard their witty or sarcastic asides to one another. One by one a spotlight would shine on a different soloist: Dizzy blowing "I Can't Get Started"; Coleman Hawkin's classic rendition of "Body and Soul"; Lester Young, nicknamed the "Prez" by Billie Holiday, strutting out in a little porkpie hat playing "Polka Dots and MoonBeams." I said, "Gerri, look at Lester, you can only see the whites of his eyes." He was playing beautifully, but he was very, very stoned.

Meanwhile, jazz was exploding in clubs all over Boston. The level of artistry was so high I believe I became spoiled forever. Here were the stylists, the homegrown soloists and bands everybody else followed. Missing any of it was inconceivable to me. I had a parallel life going on: school, work, and home were all one thing, and then there was music.

The Jazz Workshop on Boylston Street across from the Prudential Center was run by Fred Taylor, "The Jazz Guy," who had been promoting jazz longer than anyone in the city. Downstairs in this dark, subterranean club, we soaked up the sounds of pianist Bill Evans, Stan Getz, and Thelonius Monk.

Adjacent to this club was Paul's Mall, also headed up by Fred Taylor. He brought in pop acts as well as Jose Greco. Today, he's busy booking acts at Sculler's in the Doubletree Guest Suites in Boston.

The Stables, a club on Huntington Avenue near Symphony Hall, showcased some of the most innovative jazz, especially between 1955 and 1959. That was where I first met Herb Pomeroy, who became one of the America's leading jazz musicians. His Herb Pomeroy big band, one of the most original ensembles of its time, included Charlie Mariano, Joe Gordon, Lenny Johnson, Ray Santisi, and Dick Johnson, among others. When Herb was teaching at the Berklee College of Music, he kept the band going and they performed extensively throughout New England and the United States.

Like many young jazz fans, I was a member of the Teenage Jazz Club, which met at a venue called Storyville on Massachusetts Avenue in Copley Square. George Wein, another great jazz impresario, some say the greatest, and the founder of the Newport Jazz Festival, opened the club in 1950, advertising it as "Boston's Original Home of Jazz." Though it was a humble setup, a long narrow room with the stage jammed into the right hand corner, a pantheon of greats glorified that space. Drinking nothing stronger than cold Coca Cola on a Sunday afternoon, I'd hear Duke Ellington's orchestra, Sarah Vaughan, the Four Freshman, Johnny Mathis, Billie Holiday, Charles Mingus, Lee Wiley, Ella Fitzgerald, Dave Brubeck, Paul Desmond, Erroll Garner, and Pee Wee Russell, among so many others.

So Gerri and I discovered jazz together, both of us just seventeen and out in the real world of smoky dance bars and dives, no longer at home sitting in front of a record player. Instead we were present as living, breathing jazz was being created on stages before us.

For me, it was a time of discovery, of venturing farther and farther out into the world and being astounded by the ever growing beauty I found in it. In his stunning book, *Jazz Is*, Nat Hentoff evokes this feeling of awe when, as a teenager in Boston walking by the Savoy, he recalls:

> ...a slow blues curls out into the sunlight and pulls me indoors. Count Basie, hat on, with a half smile, is floating the beat with Jo Jones's brushes whispering behind him. Out on the floor, sitting on a chair, which is leaning back against a table, Coleman Hawkins fills the room with big, deep bursting sounds, conjugating the blues with the rhapsodic sweep and fervor he so loves in the opera singers whose recordings he plays by the hour at home.
>
> The blues goes on and on as the players turn it round and round and inside out and back again, showing more of its faces than I had ever thought existed. I stand, just inside the door, careful not to move and break the priceless sound. In a way, I am still standing there.[1]

My decision to attend Boston University in 1958 was determined not only by the fact that they had one of the best communication departments around, but because they had their own student-run radio station, WBUR. One of my earliest assignments was to go out and interview whomever I could get to say, "Sure, kid, I've got fifteen minutes. Shoot." At first I was a bit apprehensive, but I soon learned the first law of the physical universe: people love to talk about themselves.

This proved true for the not-so-famous as well as the famous, people who I was sure would slam down the phone as soon as I stuttered out my request. Stunning me to momentary silence, Howard Hanson, renowned composer and dean of the prestigious Eastman School of Music for over forty years, gave me the thumbs up. So I trucked off to the Copley Plaza Hotel with my LP of his second symphony, the *Romantic*, which he was happy to sign. He told me that one of its themes is performed at the conclusion of all concerts at the Interlochen Center for the Arts in Michigan, and that his opera, *Merry Mount*, received a still unbroken record of fifty curtain calls. Think about that a moment: *fifty curtain calls*. Hours must have gone by. I think my favorite story, however, is the one he shared about proposing to his wife by dedicating *Serenade for Flute, Harp and Strings* to her because he was unable to find the spoken words to form the question.

Among my first interviews was the delightfully salty-tongued American soprano, Eileen Farrell, daughter of the singing O'Farrells. Again, I started off a bit intimidated, but I relaxed a bit more with every frank, irreverent answer she gave to my scripted interview questions. A major opera singer who also created a career in popular music, Eileen called herself the "Queen of Crossover." When we met, she'd been singing at Boston College after a major blowout with Rudolph Bing, general manager of the Metropolitan.

I asked her, "Wasn't it wonderful to sing at the Met?"

She said, "Not if they give you crap you don't want to sing. I want to sing Wagner."

No beating around the bush with her. All I know is, she had her good six years at the Met and went on from there to sing all over the world.

As part of my program at Boston University, I worked at WBUR. I was pretty much handed the position of Director of Public Affairs, which meant I had to manage a department. I soon saw that in radio you were either in sales, management, or talent. Quite quickly I learned that nothing about managing anything appealed to me, and I could stomach sales only if I was primarily talent.

My repeated requests were finally answered with *The Sound of Jazz*, a show I hosted once a week. I was on the air for the very first time. Of course it was the sound of jazz, but it was also the sound of twenty-year-old Ron Della Chiesa, a person and persona I was still trying to get to know and develop. On one hand I was starting to enjoy a bit more confidence about my appearance: learning how to dress, making sure I had the right little Tony Curtis curl on my forehead, and hell, maybe even take the time to glance at myself in the mirror before I left the house in the morning. All this seemed to make a difference with my image around campus, and women, in particular. But who was Ron Della Chiesa, really, as an announcer on the air? With this question in my mind, I did what I do to this day: listened to everything I could get my hands on, from network radio to local talent; from announcers at the end of their game to obscure voices who somehow drew me in. I was open to everything and everyone.

I used to marvel at Jess Cain, an announcer with an acting background who choreographed a unique morning show for over thirty-five years at WHDH in Boston. During three o'clock in the morning commutes from Hingham to Boston, he created skits, riffs, song parodies, and dead-on impressions complete with sound effects that he'd throw on the air the minute he got to the studio. "What you're trying to do," he told the Boston *Herald American* in 1974, "is jolly people into facing the day."[2]

Symphony Sid was another great talent and influence on me. He was famous for his hipster lingo, love of bebop, and knowledge of the black music scene. Sid was the top jazz DJ at the time, broadcasting live nightly from the all-glass studio at the High-Hat, which was on the corner of Columbus and Massachusetts Avenue in Boston. The great tenor saxophonist Lester Young, "The Prez," even wrote a theme song for him called "Jumpin' with Symphony Sid":

Jumpin' with my boy Sid in the city
Mr. President of the DJ Committee

Many of Sid's commercial sponsors granted him wide artistic license even though he tended to get increasingly stoned as the night went on, at times forgetting where he was. Here's an ad for "Solray Soap," as only Sid could pitch it: "It'll make your skin the grooviest *and* pimple free, baby." He even bebopped his

Boston radio legend Jess Cain and me, 2005.

Author's collection.

way through a commercial for a funeral home: "There comes a time for every hep cat on this earth to cut out from this world. My good friends at Samuel's Funeral Parlor have got you covered. When you split the scene, they'll lay you out in style. So remember, make your arrangements early, 'cause when you're gone, baby, you're *gone*."

Bill Marlowe, who Frankie Dee in his web-tribute named "The Baron of the Airwaves," was another icon of Boston radio I listened to incessantly. His real name was William Moglia but he changed it for a radio career that spanned over fifty-five years, beginning at age nine when he performed a soliloquy from *Hamlet* over WEEI. Bill would personalize every show with dedications, and he was a passionate advocate of the Great American Songbook, passing that torch on to me in many respects. He began the Frank Sinatra Show in Boston, even taking me aside one day and imploring me to continue this tradition.

Though Bill had a weakness for the horses and a barstool—he was no stranger at either Suffolk Downs or Jimmy Mag's in East Boston—he'd get right on the air after spending an entire night doing his thing with no sign of a hangover, a skill I soon learned was no small accomplishment. A tall, good-looking guy, Bill could talk his way out of any situation. He especially loved creating wild commercials for restaurants. In a voice as smooth as hot Velveeta, he could make a second rate restaurant sound like the Waldorf:

> *You know, friends, Pasquale's Pasta Palace on Route 1 in Revere is really special to me. Why? It's the pasta, my friend. These people* understand *al dente. It's not just a word to them, this is the pasta your mother made, this is the pasta your grandmother made, this is the pasta from the homeland; it's the pasta you dream about when you're far from home and* dreaming *about pasta . . .*

William Pierce, who hosted more than three thousand Boston Symphony Orchestra broadcasts at WGBH over a span of thirty-eight years, had the following suggestion about being on the air: "Always act as if you're a guest in someone's home; they've invited you to dinner, so behave appropriately." His words made a lot of sense to me then, perhaps even more so these days when so much of radio is angry, mean spirited, and negative, which is not my style. With his warm, calm, assuring delivery, Bill was the original voice of the BSO, creating a style many symphonic music announcers employ to this day.

Another radio giant on the dial during my BU years was Norm Nathan, known for his all-night jazz show *Sounds in the Night,* as well as for his motto: "(my goal is to) try to leave the world a little sillier than I found it."[3] His largest stage came in the mid-1980s, when he joined WBZ and did an all-night talk show that never had a real topic. In fact, he liked to "keep it light" by avoiding politics or social issues of any kind. Nathan's specialty was leading listeners down his own imagination's winding path, convincing one caller that Athol, a town in Western Massachusetts, was originally a town in Africa that was so beloved it was reconstructed, brick by brick, on Route 2. I'm asking you, what's not to love?

Early radio idol Milton Cross on the air at the Met Opera House, early '30s.

I also tuned in to Tony Cennamo, who started *New Morning* at WBUR in the late 1960s, a five-hour show of pure jazz that ran for fifteen years, a one-man revival of jazz in Boston. And, of course, I listened to all I could of the perennial Milton Cross, a class act who still introduced the Metropolitan Opera every Saturday afternoon, bringing opera alive for me and millions of others.

One day I was wrapping up my show at WBUR when I saw a guy with thick, horn-rimmed glasses step into the control room behind the glass. I'd heard of Arnie "Woo Woo" Ginsberg, but I was floored when he pretty much hired me on the spot to be an announcer for a variety of programs at WBOS.

Arnie, a radio engineer turned disc jockey, had one of the biggest followings in Boston, and he was one of the first rock-and-roll DJs in the city. I'll never forget his on-air voice—a continual adolescent crack mixed in with a cacophony of buzzers, Bermuda bells, kazoos, car horns, oogahs, and train whistles. It seemed to capture teen angst with a kind of knowing wink, and even turn it into a sort of victory. Regardless, he was hyper as all get out, a fast-talking mic artist who knew his music backwards and forwards, and I was thrilled to be working my first commercial job for him.

The station was located on Commonwealth Avenue near Boston University. From six o'clock to midnight during my last year of college, I ran the board, opened the microphones, spun the records, and did commercials. Arnie appointed me as announcer and English host for a series of ethnic programs: the *Irish Hour with Tommy*; the *Polish Variety Hour with Karl*; the *Boston Greek Hour with George*; *Music of the Near East with Michelle*; *Italian Melody Hour with Gino*; and *Songtime* with the Reverend John Debrine from the Ruggles Street Baptist Church. Suddenly, I was very *busy*.

On the very first day and the very first time I opened my mic, I introduced Reverend John DeBrine and his show. We enjoyed a brief repartee, and I thought everything was going along amazingly well. It almost made me nervous—how well everything was going—so after a while I checked on what was actually being broadcast and found his sermon was completely muffled, the Word of God under a giant pile of laundry. I realized his mic had not been on for about fifteen minutes. I'd like to say I coolly assessed the situation, calmly found the right button and pushed it, but instead I started to panic. Considering that a ten-second screwup on the radio feels like a century of hellfire, imagine what a quarter of an hour of garbling the Good News of the Gospel of Jesus will do. After a few frantic phone calls—nobody was around—I finally found the right switch and collapsed in my chair, praying for the Reverend's and the Lord's forgiveness.

With the ethnic shows I was really thrown into the fire and tested. At times I felt like Lucy at the chocolate factory, stuffing her face as the assembly line speeds faster and faster and out of control. I just couldn't keep up with who needed what, when, and for how long. There were times my life was actually threatened, but hey, I had fun.

First day at my first radio gig, WBOS, 1959.

Author's collection.

Here's the deal. The show hosts would do their commercials in their native language then cue me since I had to repeat the commercials in English. It was all live: no room for error, no seven-second delay, nothing. I controlled both our mics and all the music. Even though my guests were sitting right across from me, keep in mind that they were speaking in another language; so if they would forget to cue me in English instead of their native language, I had no time to react.

The hosts would just stop talking and hand me things to play. Shows ran back to back, and the music and programming would change radically. There was a lot of passion in those shows, not only about pride of content, but about the ticking clock. You had to be very careful not to go over your allotted time, even by a few seconds. These guys bought their own time and sold it. Heated arguments, actual fights, broke out nightly about this: George the Greek would start screaming to Gino, who did the Italian hour, "You bastard! You went over! That's *my* time. You owe me ten seconds, you son of a bitch!" Meanwhile Karl would be saying something to me in Polish as I tried to cue up the first record for the Irish hour.

Karl, who did the Polish hour, looked like Nikita Khrushchev, never smiled, and was always pissed off. He glared at me across the desk as he hammered away in Polish, flinging records at me. It was just a matter of time before I screwed up his show. Finally, it happened. One night after his show wrapped up he walked me into a corner in the studio, spitting, "You put on the wrong record. You made me sound like a fool. So now I am going to wring your neck." Luckily George the Greek hadn't gone home yet and pulled him off me.

George had his own excitement one night during the Greek Hour. For five dollars each he did funeral announcements for families of local Greeks who'd passed away. Somberly and slowly he read the names of the dead while I played a sad dirge in the background. One night I answered the phone as he was doing his thing. It was this hysterical guy speaking half in Greek, half English. I just handed the phone to George and cut in with a commercial to give him a chance to talk. In seconds he grabbed me and said, "Oh my God, the guy's not dead!" I handed him the mic and backed off. It was the guy's brother instead who had died, so George had to correct that on the air. I was kind of thrilled that for once something wasn't my fault.

And then there was Tommy Shields' Irish Hour, sponsored by Irish Airlines. I had the chance to do the commercial for this program because it was all in English. A tailor by day, Tommy was on every night from eight to nine o'clock. All of the Irish pols would come up and be interviewed on the show, and we'd feature the popular Irish performers of the time—John Feeney, Connie Foley, and Ruby Murray.

Irish Airlines wanted us to do more to promote them, so they sent Tommy and me out to visit Cardinal Cushing in Brighton, who had just returned via the airline from a trip to Ireland. I'm sure they had high hopes that the Cardinal would say something positive about his trip. Regardless, Tommy and

I were nervous about the whole thing. I'm not sure what his reservations were, but for me, to extract a commercial from the man who had confirmed me a few years back at St. John's Church in Quincy felt a wee bit off.

Tommy and I stood outside the Cardinal's residence in Brighton on a cold, rainy November night. Shivering, we looked at each other, shrugged, and lifted the huge brass knocker. Both of us jumped when the Cardinal himself answered the door.

He was disarmingly casual. After asking us if we wanted anything to drink—we both passed—he led us into his library, a stunning room with floor to ceiling bookshelves on each wall and the biggest desk I've ever seen.

"So, where are you boys from?"

"The Irish Hour on WBOS, your Eminence," I said. "We called earlier…"

"Well, you've got to give my best to that Woo Woo Ginsberg. What a great guy. He's my engineer for the rosary. Did you boys know that?"

"We listen to you recite the rosary every night," Tommy said. "It's wonderful."

I put the reel-to-reel recorder down on the table and pressed "Record."

"So, how was your trip to Ireland?" I prodded.

He waved away the question and sat on the edge of the desk. "Pure misery. Never seen such rain. The coldest wettest four days of my life—couldn't wait to get home. And the Irish priests!" He paused and shook his head. "What a bunch of lazy do-nothings." He pointed at me, then Tom. I believe I was shaking at that point. "It's not enough, you know, to preach two sermons on Sundays and take the rest of the week off. Ignore the flock completely. Did *God* do that?"

"No, uh, your Eminence."

"No, God put in six and *then* put his feet up."

Beads of sweat broke out on Tommy's brow. "So how was the flight, sir?"

"The what?"

"Your transportation, sir."

"You mean the plane?"

Tommy nodded vigorously.

The Cardinal took on a faraway look. "You know…flight…flight is a miracle. Don't you think so? I don't understand how airplanes actually fly, but there must be some element of the divine at work. But the flight itself? A nightmare. Screaming babies, no air—*zero* leg room—I had to fold my knees up under my chin. Plus, we were two hours late getting in."

He finally glanced over at the tape recorder, watching it for full revolution. "Well, did you get enough?"

After some discussion on the ride home, Tommy and I agreed: some interviews were simply never meant to make it to the airwaves.

At WBOS I was introduced to John Henning—a dear friend since the day we met in 1960, who has since, sadly, passed away. John had his first job in broadcasting at WBOS, going on to become one of the foremost television news broadcasters in the country. Robert MacLean of the *Boston Globe* called him "one of the best street reporters in the history of Boston TV news."[4]

John Henning and
me, Copley Plaza
Hotel, early '70s.

Author's collection.

When WBOS moved to the top floor of the Somerset Hotel on Commonwealth Avenue in Kenmore Square, there was a whole new glamour to my job. The view of the skyline from the studios on the seventh floor was unbeatable, especially combined with the steaks and martinis you could have sent up from the restaurant below. Between shows, John and I would head down to the Keyboard Lounge on the first floor, hang out, and listen to Bob Winter at the piano bar. A brilliant musician, Bob would put together a medley of themes from old radio shows, and we'd play a trivia game. The waitress at that time, a Boston University theater major, was Faye Dunaway.

Years later Faye and I met again over dinner at the Via Matta in Park Square with my wife Joyce and Faye's former husband, Peter Wolf of the Jay Geils band. She had just appeared as Maria Callas in the play *Master Class,* by Terence McNally. It took a little prompting, but finally she remembered hanging out with us those many years ago at the Keyboard Lounge.

I had kept working nights at WBOS after graduation from BU in 1959, but I also had taken a full time job at the shipyard in Quincy owned at that time by Bethlehem Steel. Being a night owl, the 6:00 AM to 3:00 PM shift took some getting used to, as did the earcracking sounds of steel being cut and shaped by huge machinery into parts of ships.

As a runner, my job was to deliver orders of all kinds of parts from the pipe-fitting shop to the plate yard to the basins where the ships were pieced together. Before my eyes, fantastically huge tankers and passenger ships rose up, looming like giants over us as we ran under their shadows, putting together their inner workings. There seemed to be a bottomless demand for ships at the time.

Though the work was tedious in many ways, I did meet my share of guys I'll never forget. I kept hearing about this one character, the "Butterfly," until finally my boss Red and I stopped him long enough to get his story.

Red, not looking up from pounding a pipe, said, "Hey Butterfly, Ron here wants to know how you got your name."

Butterfly unzipped his pants, and there it was: a monarch tattooed on his Johnson. With no small pride he flipped it back in, saying, "Yah, did that when I was stoned out of my mind in the navy. Didn't hurt till the next day, but then the motherfu—(shriek of ship's whistle)—hurt for a year."

Another guy, Dudley, worked in the plate yard. Red said to me one day, "I don't envy you going to see Dudley."

"Why?"

"You'll find out."

Regardless, I had to deliver orders to Dudley, so off I went. Dudley was bent over a pile of steel, tossing things behind him like he was looking for something. "Beautiful day out today, Mr. Dudley," I said.

He looked up at me with a murderous glint in his eye. "What the hell is good about it? For chrissakes, it's miserable. Give me the damn order and get out of here." Then he picked up a thick section of pipe and threw it at me, missing my ear by a centimeter.

Dudley might have been an extreme example, but there were a lot of disgruntled people working there. After a couple of years at the shipyard it was clear that this was not my career. I wanted full time radio or nothing.

The world, however, had a few other plans for me. At Boston University, I had been in the ROTC (Reserve Officer Training Corps Program.) Once you got out of college, you were vulnerable for the draft and your name got on the list. My choices were either be drafted, join up as an enlisted man for four years, or be an officer. I wasn't anxious to repeat what my dad had been through; in fact we talked it over, and he said if you're going to be in the army, be an officer; it'll be easier for you. In the end, I dropped out of ROTC after graduation and joined the Army Reserves, which was a six-year obligation: six months active duty and six years in the reserve, which is how I ended up a sergeant. I figured I'd stick it out for the six months and pray for the next six years. You had to go to a meeting once a week and Camp Drum for two weeks every summer. Camp: I figured hmmm, I could handle camp, though I suspected roasting marshmallows and singing around the fire were not part of the regimen.

Turned out, I was lucky in a sense; my service fell between the Korean War and the Vietnam War—a relatively quiet period, though Vietnam was escalating. My basic training began at Fort Dix, New Jersey, where most of the guys were a bit older and had been in Korea. I looked up to them and felt comfortable around them, but I was thrilled to run into Paul Antonelli, the crooner friend I grew up with in Quincy. He had gone to the BU School of Music and started up a group called "The Chariots." Just as I was starting basic training, he was getting out, so I got a lot of tips from him.

I know it sounds like a cliché, but basic training did put hair on my chest in a certain sense. I was a guy who loved to be home—my meals cooked for me, my laundry done, the smell of homebaked cookies wafting up to my room. I mean, what's not to love? I liked being home. I liked it then; I like it today. As I lay there in my bunk under my scratchy blankets, clothes folded at the ready for 4:00 AM wake-up call, guys exhausted and snoring all around me, I wondered if I could deal with this. But when someone is screaming in your ear to get moving—*you*, not the guy next to you or someone in a movie—you pretty soon realize it's all up to you now. You want breakfast? Get up before dawn and make the bed. Assemble and disassemble a rifle, then do it again. You want dinner? Go on a twenty-mile march. Dig a foxhole in ten minutes. Put up a tent in five. I missed my home, but I got it done.

In my second week of basic training during early morning formation—we're talking 4:30 AM, dark, raw, and cold—the company commander asked if anybody could play an instrument.

Actually, what he said was, "ANYONE WHO CAN PLAY AN INSTRUMENT, STEP FORWARD."

Some primitive part of my brain, disconnected from any past trauma from playing the trumpet, and perhaps—who knows—connected to the part that knew this might do something for me said, "Yes, Ron, you play an instrument," as my foot took a step forward. A few other half-asleep liars stepped forward too, I was happy to see.

The sergeant stopped in front of me, turned, then lasered into me with his stare. I looked just past his left ear like a good soldier.

"*You* play an instrument?" he barked.

"I do, sir!"

"And what might that be, soldier?" he asked as if he could hear me practicing, off-key in my room.

"The trumpet, sir!"

Again the long stare. As if already disgusted by my playing, he shook his head and resumed pacing in front of us. "All right. Musicians." He spat on the dry ground. "You're going to go home this weekend. Get your instruments and bring them back. We're putting together the company band."

That weekend I got my pass and grabbed the bus home, dug out my book of marches and banged-up old horn, valves all stuck shut, and woodshedded for forty-eight hours straight. No drinking, no girlfriends, just honking on that thing like a crazy man all weekend. My mom brought meals up to me, by ten in the evening begging me to stop so she could sleep. Dad just said, "Son, go do what you gotta do."

Back at Fort Dix the following week we had our first rehearsal. The band leader was this short chubby guy with a chronically pained expression. I honestly couldn't tell if he was laughing his ass off at me or if he was deeply impressed. It didn't matter. That forty-eight-hour cram session turned out to be the best damned move I could have made. That gig in the army band made the rest of my basic training a piece of cake. No more K.P., no digging foxholes, no latrine duty, passes *every* weekend, and the crowning glory, a chance to sleep till eight in the morning on occasion—nirvana for a night owl like me, and unheard of in Uncle Sam's army.

So even though that old horn never got me fame, money, or girls, it got my head out of the toilet, and for that I will be forever grateful.

CHAPTER 4

Nice Work If You Can Get It

AROUND 1960 MY CAREER TOOK ANOTHER TURN. I'D BEEN SENDING out my tapes with WBOS behind me as a reference if my phone rang with an offer. One day, it did. WBCN successfully lured me over to their offices, then located at 171 Newbury Street in the Back Bay.

WBCN stood for Boston Concert Network, and it was founded by electronics genius T. Mitchell Hastings, who also owned WNCN in New York, WXCN in Providence, and WHCN in Hartford. Mitch was a visionary mentored by

Radio innovator T. Mitchell Hastings and me at WBCN, early '60s.

Author's collection.

Major Edward Armstrong, a pioneer who developed the technology for FM radio. Mitch invented one of the first FM transistor radios, the Hastings Junior, which was named after him. Passionate about keeping classical music alive, he created WBCN in hopes of forming a nationwide system of classical music stations.

Don Otto, program director and another BU alum, was the guy who hired me and put together our playlist. My first day on the job was Christmas morning, and I did my own classical music show. I was on the air five days a week, mornings and late nights, but the station was twenty-four-hour classical music at the time.

It was the perfect gig. WBCN was a powerful station, and we had long leashes to do some great, innovative things. I met Nat Johnson there, and he became another one of my dearest friends who ended up taking a similar path to WGBH in the end.

But at WBCN we bonded over a love of opera. Nat and I would record operas for the legendary Sarah Caldwell, founder of the Opera Company of Boston and the first woman to conduct at the Met. Her office was right across the street at the time, so we found every excuse to be over there and learn all we could from her. Sarah became known for not only putting together complex works under pressure, but for reimagining standard operas with fantastic staging and costumes. These fresh, provocative productions are remembered to this day, and include the American premieres of *Moses und Aron* by Arnold Schoenberg, new interpretations of *Don Giovanni, Otello,* and *A Trip to the Moon,* using some of the most incredible talent of the time who were just as eager to work with her: Renata Tebaldi, Placido Domingo, Beverly Sills, Marilyn Horne, Boris Christoff, and Donald Graham, among others. One quote captures her spirit perfectly: "If you approach an opera as though it were something that always went a certain way, that's what you get. I approach an opera as though I didn't know it."[5]

I'll never forget meeting a young Placido Domingo, fresh from singing *La Boheme* with soprano great Renata Tebaldi, who at the time was approaching the end of her career and retirement. Since the elevator was broken, Domingo climbed the three flights to our attic studio, asking on the way if we had a piano. We didn't, but if we had, I would have had one of the first recordings of Domingo singing.

My kingdom for a piano! Oh, well.

At one point during the 1960s, I decided to do an all-Toscanini show. I wrote to Walter Toscanini, telling him who I was and about my passion for his father Arturo's work and its association with my very young childhood. I was shocked when actual reel-to-reel tapes started showing up in my mailbox at WBCN, steadily, week after week. I pictured this elderly, dignified gentleman standing in line at the post office every Friday, sending me, a complete stranger, live performances of his father conducting the NBC Symphony Orchestra. Many of these tapes had not even been released yet.

I took them home and listened to them over the weekend. The energy in these performances knocked me out! I was able to put together and broadcast two or three weekly shows until the station stopped playing classical, at which point I had to write Walter a letter to let him know the bad news. His reaction was to invite me to the Toscanini homestead in New York for a visit. When I arrived he invited me downstairs where he'd converted the area into a studio which housed all his father's recordings. He asked me what I wanted to hear; I suggested Wagner. In the middle of a rehearsal of *Siegfried*, Arturo lost his temper and started screaming like a wild man at the orchestra: "Vergogna!" (Shame) or "Infamia!" (This is an infamy!) I was quite literally blown back in my seat. What an amazing opportunity to get some insight into the maestro himself. Known for getting the most out of his orchestra, it became clear how much he demanded not only of himself but of his musicians.

Arturo Toscanini lived to age ninety and conducted up until his death in 1957. Years later, Nat Johnson at RCA was instrumental in working to reissue and re-release Toscanini recordings on compact disc (from LPs). In the end, both Nat and I had the pleasure of knowing and interviewing both Walter Toscanini and his son Alfredo.

Since WBCN was the flagship station, we'd tape our programs and send them to the other stations, which could work out fine or, just as often, *not fine*. There could be some monumental screwups. During one scorching hot July day on a drive through Hartford to New York City, I tuned in to our sister station, WHCN, looking forward to hearing one of my shows. Instead I heard "Oh Little Town of Bethlehem," "Silent Night," and other holiday favorites. Nobody was there. The station was on automatic pilot. Unintentional Christmas in July.

At the time we played LP records: you know, those ancient, hat-sized pieces of vinyl. In any case, there were times I might report for duty in the morning after, let's say, a lively night on the town. Head throbbing, four hours' sleep. And I was there alone. The goal on days like these was to hunt down one of the longer recordings, such as one of Beethoven's or Mahler's symphonies that clocked in at well over an hour. This allowed plenty of time for a jaunt (or maybe a crawl) down to Hayes Bickford or the Schrafft's Coffee Shop four stories below our studios. Two over-easy with bacon and links, maybe a small stack with homemade syrup, several cups of coffee enjoyed over the Lifestyle section did wonders for me one morning before I leisurely made my way back to the studio where I heard Beethoven's Fifth, which had never progressed past the first eight beats for the past fifteen minutes:

BA BA BA BAAAAHHHHH . . . BA BA BA BAAAAHHHHH. . . . BA BA BA BAAAAHHHH . . .

. . . and so on. Not my most shining moment in radio, I have to say.

I would like to imply that this happened only once. I really would. But I can't. The call of Schraffts was so strong that over the course of ten years at WBCN

I took the plunge downstairs a few more times. There aren't many ugly expressions in radio, but here's one: "Dead Air." Before we figured out it might be a good idea to bring a portable radio down with us, I had made the miscalculation of overestimating the length of Ravel's *Bolero*: 15 minutes, 50 seconds. My breakfast and scanning the sports section: 21 minutes, 34 seconds. The sound of a record turning in the groove is horrible. People called in thinking the station was off the air or that the show was cancelled. Mr. Hastings certainly had some choice words for me. Sponsors didn't love it either.

On another day I got back in time from a lightning fast lunch to find I was locked out of the building. The words "despair" and "panic" jumped alive for me as I banged on the filthy windows of the snoring super's dank basement apartment, screaming, "Joe, wake up! There's *dead air*!!"

■ ■ ■

Though a man ahead of his time in many ways, Mitch Hastings was not the consummate businessman. He had a lot of trade agreements in place of real advertising revenue, and all of his stations employed the same format, which turned out to be, in the end, not a profitable concept.

He was also a wildly eccentric gentleman, a disciple of the self-described psychic Edgar Cayce, who claimed to be in touch with the citizens of the lost continent of Atlantis. A Harvard grad from an established Boston family, Mitch espoused a variety of philosophies and topics, but as the years went on and the station started to teeter financially, the philosophies and topics just got weirder and weirder.

Keep in mind the world was changing dramatically. I was twenty-five, it was 1963, and the Vietnam War was escalating; American protesters exploded in number, marching in Harvard Square and across the country. And I will always remember, like everyone alive at that time, where I was when I learned about the assassination of John F. Kennedy. My dad and I had plans to see the symphony together that day, and stopped for lunch at a restaurant across the street from Symphony Hall. Above the deep fryer a soap opera was droning on. Walter Cronkite broke in. We watched his shattered face: "Shots were fired in Dallas, Texas..."

We walked across the street to Symphony Hall, where many had not yet learned about the awful news we'd just witnessed. The Boston Symphony opened with their first piece, which was followed by a long intermission. The conductor, Erich Leinsdorf, came out and announced that the President of the United States had been assassinated. A huge gasp, crying. When the crowd quieted, he announced that they would play the funeral march from Beethoven's *Eroica* Symphony.

I had seen President Kennedy just a few weeks before, on the steps of the Copley Plaza hotel during a visit to Boston for the Harvard–Yale game. We made eye contact and smiled at each other; there was a brief sense of recognition. His charisma was such that I could feel it from clear across the street where I stood.

The world was rocking on its axis in so many ways, including musically. The tide of rock 'n' roll was building against the relatively still oceans of symphony, jazz, American Songbook, and other established traditions. WBCN was there: the calm beach sunning itself as the tsunami of rock gathered strength.

As our sponsors started to bail and ratings dipped, Mitch's behavior progressed from odd to simply inexplicable. But he had a good heart and, no matter what happened, always had faith that everything would be fine.

One day I came to work to discover he'd hired a new program director who wanted to implement a crazy system for the playlist involving wheels and charts. The theory being that if we could mix our tempos a bit, maybe this would spice things up. Actually, it's hard to believe the absurdity of these words even as I am relating them, but here are some more: all the records were marked "Slow," "Medium," or "Fast," and were stored in bins labeled as such. No more playing three "Slow" records in a row! Even though symphonies have, ahem, things called *movements*, which often range in tempo, we'd have to follow this bizarre chart that told us when to choose records from the three different bins.

At least *that* strategy didn't last long.

Maybe because of his intimacy with radio waves in general, Mitch came to believe that he could communicate with spirits. Not a problem if all was going well, but it wasn't. Many a day I'd show up at work and find Mitch standing in his office in his underwear, shaving, and conversing with himself in the mirror. Again, not a problem in and of itself, but one morning I noticed the studio clock, a huge expensive piece that showed the time around the world, was missing.

"Um, Mitch...?"

"Ron! Good morning, my friend. Glad you're here. I was just thinking about the lost continent of Atlantis—"

"Mitch, the clock is missing. They must have repossessed it after we left last night—"

"Ahh," he said, carefully shaving his neck. "Time. What a concept! I'm so glad you brought it up. What is the past, really, and who can know the future? It's all about the present, Ronnie. I am a parishioner at the Church of *Right Now*; have you heard of it?"

"But how will we..."

He glanced at my wrist. "What's that on your arm, but humanity's way of keeping time?"

I sadly looked at my watch. Unpaid bills danced before my eyes; the studio's and my own.

The next day I found him again in his underwear, this time eating a doughnut at his desk and tinkering with a radio, the parts scattered all over its surface as if the radio had exploded. Behind us, big grunting bruisers were dismantling our AP and UPI teletype machines which brought us news from around the world. Mitch had skipped paying the bills that month.

"Mr. Hastings, the AP guys are here! They're pulling the wires! They're taking the machines!"

He snapped a tiny part of the radio back in place and took a big powdery bite of doughnut. "That's okay, Ronnie, have faith. These earthly matters always have a way of working themselves out."

"But how will we do the news?"

"Just read from the newspaper, my friend, if you even care to do that."

"The *newspaper?*"

He cocked his head. "You make a good point. Newspapers are absurd. Irrelevant. Tomorrow will be the same thing, different parties involved. But the same old stories: love, war, strife, poverty, suffering, mixed with the occasional bright spot: a new bridge, or perhaps your favorite sports hero makes the touchdown to win the game. I just can't concern myself with it."

The next day, although I was pleased to find Mitch wearing pants and a shirt, I also found a notice taped to the door saying the power would be shut off by nightfall if we didn't pay the bill.

I said, "Mitch, they're gonna cut the juice. We're going to go off the air."

He looked at the notice. "What a bunch of soreheads. A bunch of bureaucratic slaves. Have faith," he said, and left. "I'll go scare us up some funds."

The really crazy thing is, he always did. Yes, we were off the air for twenty-four hours, but somehow he paid that bill. Actually, I'll never know *who* paid that bill.

Inevitably we would go weeks without getting paid. Once we didn't get paid for an entire month—I mean *nobody* got a check. But we hung in there, as dedicated to the classical music as he was. The miracle being that he was able, for years, to scrape up the money to keep us on the air and finally pay us all we were owed. He'd find investors, people who believed in his vision. My friend John Henning even joined the madness there for a few years.

■ ■ ■

In 1961, I was promoted to program director, a position I held until 1968. Meanwhile, our stiffest competition was WCRB, which also ran full-time commercial classical radio. During the fifties and early sixties there was enough cultural interest to support these two stations, but WCRB was really running away with it.

Meanwhile, Harvard Square was jumping with Vietnam War protests, demonstrations, even the occasional riot complete with tear gas. These scruffy kids would come in off the street and visit the station, fresh off the picket line and reeking of pot. They'd flop on the couch and beg us to play The Kinks, The Doors, Janis Joplin, Chicago. Mitch would show up an hour later, take a sniff at the studio, and say, "Now that's a mighty interesting odor we have here. Have our little friends been by again?"

"Yeah, and they brought us some LPs..." I said, staring at a pile of Jefferson Airplane, Sly and the Family Stone, the Beatles.

"Well, isn't that nice."

But Mitch couldn't avoid the writing on the wall. He told us it was time to ask for money—up, down, and sideways—in whatever ways we could think of; at the same time he began to give in to the notion of a mixed format. There was a time when we'd segue from Bach fugues in the evening to Cream blasting in at midnight.

The station began its transition to an underground progressive rock station format on the night of March 15, 1968. WBCN's first rock DJ, "Mississippi Harold Wilson" (Joe Rogers), was the first to use the station's new slogan, "The American Revolution." At first the new format was only heard during the midnight hours, but in May 1968 they went full time. In early June, the station's air staff: Peter Wolf, Tommy Hadges, Jim Parry, Al Perry, and Sam Kopper, who later became Program Director, were joined by Steven "The Seagull" Segal. In December, Peter Wolf left to take the J. Geils Band on the road, and Charles Laquidara was hired to take over the 10:00 PM to 2:00 AM air shift. He later hosted *The Big Mattress*, which became one the most popular radio shows in Boston radio history. The station became a social and political force from the moment it hit the air, both defining and promoting popular culture and politics in Boston for the sixties' boomer generation in a way that nothing had before.

Meanwhile, thank God, I had been working part time at WGBH, getting my feet wet there. Mitch wasn't the only one tripped up by the rock invasion; I mean, here I was, weaned on the American Songbook, Broadway, film, jazz, opera. These guys were playing Vanilla Fudge. The whole scene soon morphed into this raw, cutting edge rock station, from Prokofiev to the Stones, in what felt like a matter of weeks.

In the end though, T. Mitchell Hastings was kept on as a figurehead at the American Revolution. He very much wanted to keep me on the ship, even though I think we both knew my days there were numbered.

"Well, Ronnie, how would you like to be Public Service Director?"

"I'm sorry, I think I'll have to be moving on."

"Well, we're going to miss you." He got a misty look in his eye as he stared out his office overlooking Newbury Street. "Atlantis is really out there, you know, we just have to find it. These things happen. With today's technology and my know-how, it's a matter of time before this magical place is discovered and brought to light..."

Though Mitch never did discover Atlantis (as far as I know), he did sell the station in 1968 for a couple million dollars to Infinity Broadcasting. Rude, irreverent, and wild, it became one of the most listened to and profitable rock stations in American history.

■ ■ ■

I entered a new phase of my life when I joined WGBH on a full-time basis in 1969. I think I'll be forever grateful for the opportunity to be surrounded by the kind of talent and innovation that especially marked my earlier years at the station. The explosion of creativity going on in the studios, then located at 125 Western Avenue in Allston, was remarkable. Full operas were performed and broadcast from the studio. Leonard Bernstein himself conducted his orchestra for live broadcast. Gunther Schuller, Pulitzer Prize–winning composer, would visit and perform regularly. *The Boston Pops, Evening at Pops, Boston Symphony Live, This Old House* (still on today) were new in public television and really set us apart.

Though I started off hosting *Morning Pro Musica*, over time I cycled through an eclectic mix of shows. I became the television booth announcer not only for Channel 2, but part time at Channels 4 and 7 as well. Though now, of course, everything is taped and automated, in those days there was always a live announcer at the station. Every single station break: live. There was no spacing out or missing a cue.

I am also indebted to the good people at WGBH—the best—who had my back every time I was slow to round the technological learning curve. During all my decades at the station, advancements seemed to come fast and furious. To think we used to edit reel-to-reel tape by actually cutting it with a razor and taping it together. Over the years we progressed from vinyl to CD, analog to digital, reel-to-reel to cassettes, and finally to digital audiotapes or DAT. Accessing my playlist from a computer versus literally a pile of tapes still feels like a revelation at times.

During those early years I felt myself growing into my own skin—filling in the person I had sketched out as a bad-at-baseball thirteen-year-old broadcasting into a cardboard microphone in my bedroom. I could feel myself blossoming professionally, like my brain was expanding. I had such a sense of being in the right place at the right time, with the right people, doing the right thing with my life.

Isolated in the studio, I became more intimate with sound than ever before. Bands and the musicians in them, the orchestras, all became the voices of friends. I no longer had to read the notes to know who was in the room with me; there's Count Basie's band, that has to be Renata Tebaldi as Desdemona, that's George Shearing on piano, there's Illinois Jacquet's "Flying Home." Even the BSO had its own signature sound.

I also learned the absolute necessity of being able to turn it on and off. By that I mean: no matter how I was feeling: upset, sad, angry—when that second hand swept past go-time—I was BING!—on the air. In radio as on Broadway: the show must go on.

But if I wanted a few role models for broadcasting, I didn't have to look far; legends surrounded me, both figuratively and literally. The always elegant William Pierce, the original voice of the Boston Symphony Orchestra, had an office a few doors down. I'll always be grateful for his one-on-one lessons on articulation and pronunciation, especially for German, French, and other classical music names.

William Pierce, my predecessor in the broadcast booth at Symphony Hall.

Photo courtesy of BSO archives.

Bill Cavness was another terrific voice to learn from. An actor, musician, and scholar, Bill knew more about literature than anybody I had ever met. His series "Reading Aloud" brilliantly presaged talking books, bringing Pasternak's *Dr. Zhivago* alive—including voices and dialects of all the characters—in 1958, when the book was not yet widely available. In his thirty-plus years on the air, he made over a thousand recordings for the series. When asked why he devoted his life to radio, as opposed to television or other media, he responded, "Radio, with its appeal to a single sense, forces me to keep my imagination working, while television somehow blocks much of its use. When I listen to a play on the air, I design the sets, costumes and the lighting—even the faces and the characters' movements."[6]

Robert J. Lurtsema hosted *Morning Pro Musica* for close to thirty years with a sonorous voice that was a cross between Orson Welles and Arthur Godfrey. He was known for his long, languorous pauses between phrases, which sometimes stretched out over a minute, an eon in radio time. Audiences either tolerated it or hated the habit, but most people loved the way the show began: birds chirping for a few minutes at seven in the morning...much, much longer if he was running late. On one occasion he was running at least twenty minutes behind because of a blizzard. He called to tell me two things: "start the birds," and to instruct me in no uncertain terms to stay off the air. He said if I went on, people would think something had happened to him. I'll never forget the sight of him standing in the doorway looking like the abominable snowman.

Each morning began with a different theme, as he systematically explored a composer's work such as the Beethoven string quartets or Dvorak symphonies, at times sampling more obscure music, confessing that he learned as much as his audience through his explorations. Respighi's *Ancient Airs and Dances Suite* and Giovanni Gabrieli's triple brass quintets were among his opening themes.

As a compatriot, Robert J. was a bit of an enigma. Here was a man who, on April Fool's Day, made fun of his own pomposity by chirping out the birdsongs himself (surprisingly few people noticed!) and who did a great Gabby Hayes—all off microphone. He was obviously a beloved character: when the station threatened to end his news broadcasts, there was such an uproar that his role was immediately reinstated. People loved his style. On the other hand, there were some unfortunate experiments including the pure, unmitigated strangeness of R. J. Lurtsema wandering around the Museum of Fine Arts, rambling on about paintings and sculptures, quoting ponderous references and dates at great length. Brevity is the soul of wit, especially in radio.

Many of us learned where Robert's sense of humor about himself began and ended. Nat Johnson, a great talent with the triple roles of producer, announcer, and audio engineer, preceded Robert J.'s role as host of *Morning Pro Musica*. When Robert had Nat back as a guest on his show to discuss Nat's program about the organ, "The King of Instruments," Nat made the mistake of calling him "Bob." Lurtsema snapped off the mic the moment the show concluded. "Never, *never* call me Bob on the air...."

Louis Lyons was a great character on Channel 2, a crusty veteran newsman for *The Globe* and the *Christian Science Monitor*, as well as curator of the Nieman Foundation. Blessed with a quick delivery, he was not a man to mince words. One evening, a crew member was signaling him to conclude his broadcast. He said, right on the air, "Young man, I'll get off when I want to. Don't signal me like that. The news director told me I can have as much time as I want." And he went right back to the news. In a neighboring studio, Boston's leading drama critic, Elliot Norton, might be interviewing Richard Burton, Carol Channing, Rogers and Hammerstein, or Anthony Hopkins on *Elliot Norton Reviews*. In our studio kitchen, Julia Child was revolutionizing the world of cooking in her uniquely charming way on *The French Chef*. Any time I had the chance I would watch her do her show. One episode stays with me: while preparing suckling pig she took out the cooked one to showcase the finished product. With her little finger she tucked the tail of the pig right inside, commenting, "And you know, there's always a convenient place to put this little tail."

Speaking of candid moments, nothing keeps you on your toes quite like doing live radio or TV. I was a bit intimidated by WGBH in the early years because the place had such a vaulted reputation. I was so excruciatingly conscious of every word I uttered on the air and its implications that it was only a matter of time before

I royally screwed up and stepped in a big pile of it. But the thing is, you have to keep going. You cannot go back, and more than that, I've learned it's best to pretend that whatever dud has fallen out of your mouth, it's best to feign complete ignorance. Not unlike a belch at a state dinner: let it pass. *It never happened.* Yes, I will try some of that merlot, thank you so much...

It was a beautiful fall day, and I had just finished with *Morning Pro Musica.* I took a few seconds to look over a simple public service announcement: a reminder about Daylight Savings Time.

I said, "Daylight Savings Time is right around the corner. This coming Saturday night, in fact. So don't forget to set your cocks back before you go to sleep. And that's it for our show today..." I don't remember anything else. It's possible I blacked out.

Yes, it went out over the airwaves to thousands of Boston listeners. No, I was not reprimanded. I think the powers that be knew I needed no such beating, that I would be replaying, red-faced, that particular quote in my brain for the rest of my natural life.

Another good rule of thumb in broadcasting is to never assume the mic is off. In fact, it's best to assume it's on while you're in the studio, the hallway, the cafeteria, the men's room, even all the way out to your car where it might be okay to open up the pipes and scream, curse, or whatever you need to do. I know this because once I didn't follow that rule. One morning in the TV broadcast booth, after being assured my mic was off, I went on a rant about the program director and, lo and behold, the mic was on, and *we were live.* I wrapped up with something like, "Well, at least that sonofabitch isn't listening," when in fact, the sonofabitch *was* listening. The only reason I think I wasn't maimed was because there was enough music playing over my comments that the object of my scorn really didn't hear what I said. What did listeners hear? I'll never know.

I do know I went directly to mass after work that day.

On one beautiful spring morning, perhaps inspired by Robert J., I decided to do a little piece on the swallows of Capistrano that return every year after a fifteen-thousand-mile journey—almost a complete flight around the world—to the Mission San Juan Capistrano in California on March 19th. A compelling phenomenon of nature, and one certainly worthy of a few minutes of radio time. After much shlepping around, I found a tape of swallows chirping and cheeping, and I cued it up to play after the Capistrano story.

"So that's the story, folks," I said. "No one knows why, but every year on this very day, thousands of swallows flock back to this beautiful mission by the bay, their cheerful chirping sounds a welcome sign of spring..." cue the engineer to play the bird tape: "Cheep, cheep, chirpy-chirp..." then some guy comes on and says, "...and those are the sounds of swallows from Hudson Bay, New York."

I hadn't listened to the whole tape.

A hundred corrective measures flew through my brain (like sparrows on the wing) but I realized, no: just let it go.

I'm telling you, between that and my advice about setting your cocks back in the fall, it's a good thing I had a sense of humor and forgiving bosses.

I had my rough days in front of the camera too. Occasionally I did the news for Channel 2 on Sunday nights, when the entire crew numbered just three: the announcer (me), the engineer, and the technician in the video room who jockeyed the tapes.

Picture this: I'm sitting at a desk, the one camera locked on me, monitor off to one side. We're live. I'm reading the news and I'm reading the news and I'm reading the news when I hear this little voice in my headset say, "You better slow down, you're reading too fast." I notice that, sure enough, seven minutes remain in the hour while in fact only a half page of news remains to be read.

I slow down, but how slow can you read, anyway? I drew out the weather report as much as humanly possible. "Will it rain tomorrow? Well, you know, we have a forty percent chance of precipitation, but you never really know, do you, especially in Boston! Of course there's a higher chance of rain on the Cape and islands because of the effect of oceans on the weather..."

"Keep going, keep going..." came the engineer's voice through the headset.

"...which can tend to really pack a wallop, especially if a hurricane is expected, which of course, we certainly don't anticipate today..."

"...go on, Ron, go on..."

"...and so why don't we have a look at those headlines again, in case any of you missed anything..." and I reread the headlines, which brought us up to the hour, at which point I said, "And that's the news."

The camera stared at me and I stared back, watching myself watch myself in the monitor.

Nothing happened.

"Keep going, keep reading, we can't find the tape." Panic now in the voice.

"Thank you, and that's the news..."

"Anything, Ron, *just talk*..." the engineer pleaded.

I flipped the AP sheets over, desperate for any other news that might be lying around.

Blank paper.

I actually opened the drawer praying for anything—old news, a flyer, a coupon, a shopping list, something to fill the time.

"And don't forget to stay tuned for the David Suskind show, a favorite here and across the country for ten years now, and we've got a great show lined up for you tonight..."

"Go...go...one more minute!"

I think it's then I realized the engineer's cues were being broadcast as well. I don't know how I maintained bowel control. I imagined tapes flying in the video room as the technician tore through stacks of them looking for the next show.

"And don't forget, we've got Julia Child coming up for you too. Yes, *The French Chef* with Julia Child herself waiting in the wings, so don't touch that dial. That woman can do things with a suckling pig that would blow your mind..."

"Don't stop!"

"...and let me tell you, no one goes home hungry here at the station after one of her shows. So stay tuned, and we'll have that wonderful new show for you coming right up. All kinds of great stuff coming up for you..."

I stood up.

"No, Ron, don't leave—one more minute, come on..."

"Thank you very much, and that's the news."

And I walked off as the camera stayed, broadcasting an empty chair behind a desk for four endless minutes before we found the tape.

■ ■ ■

Though I had begun to grow steadier on my "air legs," I had a ways to go with my personal life at the time. I had married a wonderful woman named Jackie; however by 1970 things were not only extremely shaky between us, but Jackie became pregnant.

Around the same time, my dad suffered a stroke which impacted his ability to do the thing he enjoyed the most: paint. It also meant that my mother had to take on the role of caretaker for him. Within two years, my dad had passed away.

Though we tried counseling, in the end Jackie moved to Phoenix with our almost two-year-old son, Aldo, and I was left in a lonely suburban house staring at an empty crib, wondering how everything could have gone so completely wrong. Working at one radio station and two TV stations and frankly being less available than a husband and father should be had finally taken its toll.

What was important in life? I began trying to figure that out, in big ways and small, and everything in between. By this point, I knew two things: the marriage had ended, and that I must nurture a relationship with my son. Though my schedule was challenging, I had to devise ways of going to Phoenix to spend time with him, as well as bring him here to Boston to do the same.

I had him for the summers, and we squeezed every moment of joy we could out of every day. He loved animals, so I took him to the Trailside Museum in the Blue Hills where we roamed around the woods for hours. Or we'd hit the go-carts (he was obsessed with them!) at amusement parks in the South Shore, or slip off to Faxon Park in Quincy to see the ducks. I took him swimming at Nantasket Beach, where I first learned to swim, and he spent time with my mother who I'm so grateful he got the chance to know.

Every other Christmas was a desert Christmas, when I visited Aldo in Phoenix under the hot summer sun. We'd do the same things out there as in Boston: zoos, go-carts, collect bottle caps for prizes; whatever rocked a five-year-old's world, I wanted to do.

I thanked God for music, and my wonderful, life-affirming job. I was beginning to understand that this is life, now, every minute we're here, that it's not some practice run, and that everything I said or did mattered and had consequences. I also learned to understand that though I certainly had my faults, I was not to blame for everything.

Pain breaks you open in good ways sometimes. I started to think about what I really wanted out of life, both for Aldo and myself. Never mind building a foxhole; having a kid makes you an adult—changing diapers, staring at the face of a human you helped create. Now *that's* frightening. Not to mention all the love I felt, and it was a new kind of love I hadn't experienced before and didn't know existed. I remember listening to a lot of love songs at that time, or songs of love and loss, which is I guess one definition of the music of the Great American Songbook. Tony Bennett, Rosemary Clooney, Bobby Short, Ella Fitzgerald, Nancy Wilson, anything by Gershwin. I would listen and think about what I did right, what I did wrong, what I had hopes of doing right the next time around. In short, I returned to my original therapy: music. Filtered through the newly beat-up lens of my life, each song took on new meaning and richness, and carried me, note for note, through those dark and troubled times.

CHAPTER 5

A World of Joyce

IN JANUARY OF 1977, I BEGAN HAVING CONVERSATIONS WITH THEN-station manager John Beck, who'd been turning over a few ideas about my hosting a new show. At the time, WGBH featured a mixed format in the afternoon, and we both agreed the lack of consistency was thinning down and scattering our audience. When I suggested the concept of a show on American music beginning around the turn of the century, he surprised me by jumping on the idea. I asked him why he wanted to take a chance with something so new and untested, and he said, "Ron...*anything's* better than what we have on the air right now!" I still have a good laugh every time I think about that remark. Together we came up with the name *MusicAmerica* as a fitting title for this pilot.

If someone asked you to describe *MusicAmerica* in a word, I doubt you could do it. Imagine visits in your living room with Dizzy Gillespie, Benny Carter, Illinois Jacquet, David Raksin, John Williams, Gunther Schuller, Fred Astaire, Eileen Farrell, and countless others. From noon to five every weekday for what turned into eighteen years, I hosted what I would describe as a variety entertainment show that had at its core the Great American Songbook, showcasing the innovators of American music.

As the years went by, the show became a mix of live interviews with current recording artists, as well as selections from genres such as Broadway, jazz (America's classical music), film, and swing. The show was an opportunity for me to debut something never before attempted in the Boston radio market. Certain stations aired segmented shows such as all folk, all jazz, all blues, all classical, but *MusicAmerica* was a novel concept. Even though I'd been involved in radio for over twenty-five years (thirty if you count my debut at age ten!), I never dreamed I'd see the day when I'd be able to express myself on the air the way I could with this show. I was quite simply a kid in a candy store.

What a privilege for me to develop this program! If someone had asked ten-year-old Ron what he'd like to do as a broadcaster when he grew up, the answer would have been: *MusicAmerica*. At my fingertips were literally thousands of pieces, decades of wonderful music from which I could create a unique show each day. The opportunity to overlap that collection with the work of current artists and modern interpretations of the standards only added to the richness of what I could offer.

■ ■ ■

In the beginning, the show focused on American classical music composed from 1900 to 1960: works by George and Ira Gershwin, Aaron Copland, Ferde Grofe, Walter Piston, and Charles Ives, with a lively, soulful mix of selections by Cole Porter, Irving Berlin, and so many other greats of that era.

On the very first show, which broadcast on September 1, 1977, I wanted to ease into things slowly with classics I felt most people loved and would recognize, though of course the plan was to grow the program organically through listener feedback and my own musical intuition. I opened with the "Three Preludes" by George Gershwin, followed by his *Concerto in F.* From there I played Ellington's "A Drum Is a Woman," then Leonard Sillman's "New Faces of 1952," dropping in favorites by Cleo Laine and jazz violinist Joe Venuti.

As time went on, I became more comfortable introducing changes here and there. Feedback from listeners helped shape the show; in fact, an ongoing, eighteen-year conversation with my audience led to the rich variety that followed. The pure synergy of the thing inspired me every day of the week. Talk about jumping out of bed excited to go to work in the morning! I believe I was creating that show at some level of consciousness twenty-four hours a day and loving every minute of it.

For me, the best thing about *MusicAmerica* was its spontaneity. I could play whatever I wanted and put together shows based on what was happening at the moment. Listeners never knew who would drop by for "delightful conversations," wrote *Boston Herald* columnist Joe Fitzgerald, concluding: "...Dizzy Gillespie, Dave McKenna, Joe Williams, Margaret Whiting, maybe the Four Freshmen, (listeners) just knew (they) were going to love it."[7]

If a musical was in town such as *Ain't Misbehavin'*, I'd invite the entire cast on the show. If Tony Bennett, or Bobby Short, or Rosemary Clooney, or Mel Tormé happened to be in Boston, they wouldn't get back on the plane before stopping by. I might get a call tipping me that Hoagy Carmichael, Jr. was in town, and we'd book him for the following day. And they wouldn't just pop in and chat for a few minutes, they'd stay for half an hour, an hour, sometimes even longer. Most interviews took on a life of their own, but I found the best format was to splice in generous tracks of the artist's classic recordings between frank discussions about their lives, their musical philosophies, and their creative process.

As much as I enjoyed snaring out-of-town talent as they were passing through, I felt just as passionate about inviting local artists on the show, especially those who might be at the beginning of their careers: Rebecca Parris, Scott Hamilton, Deborah Henson-Conant, Gray Sargent, Steve Marvin, and Donna

Byrne became regulars in the studio. As the show gathered steam, *MusicAmerica* became a magnet for this new talent. Artists like Harry Connick Jr., Diana Krall, Wynton Marsalis, and Michael Feinstein also came on the show when they were first starting out and touring through Boston. I loved being in the position to provide another place (besides Scullers or the Regattabar) for budding or local musicians to showcase their talent.

One of the best aspects of the show was the freedom to do impromptu tributes to musical giants who had passed away, or those who had a birthday. Many times, after learning in the morning that an artist had died, I was able to play a wide selection of their work that very afternoon, or certainly the next day. With a library of recordings at my disposal, I could create a tribute that put an artist's entire career in perspective. When Fred Astaire died in 1987, I realized I had one of his only interviews: the tape from the day we called him on his eightieth birthday; so I was able to put together a five-hour show on his career. I did similar tributes for Sarah Vaughan, Ella Fitzgerald, Dizzy Gillespie, Stan Getz, and Mel Tormé after they passed. Though sad to see these giants go—many of whom had become dear personal friends—I felt privileged to have interviewed them.

Half the fun was advancing my own musical education as I put the show together from day to day. As much as I knew about music, I'd inevitably learn something new. Let's say I was playing a whole afternoon of Duke Ellington. I'd put on "Take the 'A' Train" and maybe the soloist was Ray Nance, inspiring me to dig out and play something by Ray. Or perhaps the alto sax player was Johnny Hodges, leading to something by Johnny that might turn me on to other aspects of Ellingtonia. On an artist's birthday, such as Cole Porter, I grabbed the chance to play his lesser known works, most of which I had never heard before. Listeners would call and tell me about musicians I never knew existed and send me their recordings. I branched out even further, interviewing authors with a connection to the musical world such as Neal Gabler who wrote *Winchell: Gossip, Power and the Culture of Celebrity* about Walter Winchell, a journalist immersed in the lives of Broadway celebrities in the twenties and thirties. Putting the show together was like opening a series of musical doors that led to daily discoveries of obscure musicians, composers, and others whose voices I felt should be heard.

To me, there was an everlasting quality about this music. The feeling that, yes, all things must pass, but these songs would forever be deeply appreciated and enjoyed by the American public. I realize now that timeless quality was a huge draw for the show. The peerless music of the 1920s, '30s, '40s, and '50s will never be duplicated. There is only one Leonard Bernstein and *West Side Story*, just one Rodgers and Hammerstein and *Oklahoma!*, one George Gershwin and "Rhapsody in Blue." The songwriters and lyricists—Cole Porter, Harold Arlen, Hoagy Carmichael, Harry Warren, Johnny Mercer—were the innovators of their time, while the musicians—Louis Armstrong, Lester Young, Coleman Hawkins,

Mabel Mercer, Ethel Waters, Lena Horne, Anita O'Day, Sarah Vaughan, and Ella Fitzgerald—all added their unique interpretations to original scores. Just as one never tires of discovering elemental truths in great literature or entering the landscape of a Winslow Homer or John Singer Sargent painting, in my mind it is just as impossible to be untouched by the experience of listening to Gershwin, who drew classic musical portraits with notes on the page.

Perhaps the lead editorial in the August 31, 1995, edition of the *Boston Globe*, which lamented the decision to cancel the show, expressed it best: "We are not talking nostalgia here. Many songs carry memories to some listeners—they are a vital part of the nation's cultural fabric. But this goes beyond history. The songs continue to be sung, to be revived, and reinterpreted, because they are literate and swinging in a way that makes them a monument for the ages."[8]

■ ■ ■

As the years passed, *MusicAmerica* became an integral part of the Boston jazz scene and exploding music culture. Over sixty thousand listeners tuned in to hear who was in town, what I'd seen that week, and what was coming up. And it worked both ways: well known musicians told me the show had no equivalent in other cities they played, and thus sent the talent my way. Musicians have their own network, of course, so word about *MusicAmerica* spread from coast to coast. Eventually, my phone rang off the hook with club owners and promotion managers hoping to snare their clients some air time.

I always thought the show had a New York feel to it. I was very influenced by New York radio hosts such as William B. Williams at WNEW. William B.'s format was also a mixture of big band, swing, jazz, and the American songbook. As host of the William B. William's show, he had the chance to interview top talent such as Lena Horne and Nat King Cole, even befriending Frank Sinatra, Jr. when he recorded an early broadcast at the station. Williams mused that if Benny Goodwin was the "King of Swing" and Duke Ellington was a duke, then surely Sinatra was "Chairman of the Board," a moniker Frankie ended up embracing completely.

I also listened closely to Al Jazzbo Collins' show, broadcast from his studio which he called "The Purple Grotto," referencing not only the purple paint job but the stalactite-like sound-absorbing cylinders suspended from the ceiling that completed the feel of a funky cave. Or, it could have been the weed. In any case, "JazzBeaux" (as he renamed himself) was one of the coolest voices in radio for fifty odd years, a professional hipster who did everything from twisted readings of *Grimm's Fairy Tales:* "78's from Hell: Grimm's Fairy Tales for Hip Kids," to a brief stint in 1957 hosting NBC's *Tonight Show* (then called *Tonight! America After Dark*), to his own TV show in the early sixties where he hosted personal favorites such as Moe Howard from *The Three Stooges*.

Jean Shepherd—the great American iconoclast—kept me laughing and in awe of his prodigious talent. A master of stream of consciousness monologue, writer, narrator, and radio host, Shepherd told hilarious, off-the-cuff tales on his radio show about growing up, working in steel mills, being in the army, pretty much anything that came to mind. We carried his show, taped in New York at WOR, on delayed broadcast and commercial-free.

Edward Grossman in a January 1966 *Harper's Magazine* piece caught his spirit:

> *Quite as often, (his) stories are informed by a mass of details that ring true. Shepherd has total recall of the name, rank, and shape of everyone in his barracks; of who played first base for the Chicago White Sox in 1939 (Zeke "Banana-nose" Bonura); of how the* Little Orphan Annie *theme song used to go. He remembers sounds, too, and mimics them convincingly. His Heat Lightning over Camp Crowder is distant and ominous; the Gurgling Sink over which his mother struggled forever "in her chenille bathrobe" is enough to give a hardened plumber pause. Together with this realism Shepherd throws in a stiff dose of hyperbole. When his squad is on an overnight hike, for example, it covers "ninety-seven miles," and the mercury during the day hovers at "a hundred and forty," while at night it plunges to "eighteen below zero."[9]*

His satiric narrative style was considered a precursor to the work of Garrison Keillor, Spalding Gray, and especially Jerry Seinfeld who said in the "Seinfeld Season 6" DVD set, "he formed my entire comedic sensibility—I learned how to do comedy from Jean Shepherd." Seinfeld even named his third child "Shepherd."

I especially admired "Shep" for his uncanny ability to convey the feeling that he was speaking to every listener personally, one on one, through the radio. He inspired me to reach out in my own way to my audience every chance I got. I'd toss out a movie or jazz trivia question or play a piece of music, giving people a chance to win tickets or CDs. What band first recorded "Sing Sing Sing"? What was Tony Bennett's real name? It always amazed me what a knowledgeable audience I had out there; they were so hip I could never stump them. No matter how obscure the question, there was always someone out there who knew the answer.

I also enjoyed programming according to mood. If it was a dark, dreary day, I'd play upbeat music. As *Boston Herald* columnist Joe Fitzgerald recalled in his 1996 piece on *MusicAmerica*, "On the muggiest day of the summer, (listeners) were apt to hear Tony Bennett's 'Winter Wonderland,' or Ella Fitzgerald's 'Santa Claus is Coming to Town,' or maybe Billy Eckstine teaming with Sarah Vaughan on 'I've Got My Love to Keep Me Warm.'"[10]

But at times I did feel like shaking it up behind the mic to make sure people were paying attention. One day I decided to conduct the show as usual, but with one exception: I'd substitute names of Italian dishes for the real last names of the singers or musicians. "And that was Joey Tetrazzini on drums, Rico Manicotti on tenor sax, and Bobby Gnocchi on the horn...next up, Freddie Ravioli and his band with, 'One O'Clock Jump...'" Finally, *finally*, at the end of the day, someone picked up the phone and called to ask, "Hey...are those real names?"

■ ■ ■

Being on the radio is incredibly personal. There is this beautiful intimacy to it. You're in the studio by yourself, yet you're everywhere. Because of the quality of what I programmed for *MusicAmerica*, listeners often told me they felt they should be dressed up while tuning me in. But in reality, people did and of course do very intimate things when they listen to radio. As the voice of the program, I was in their car, their workplace, or their bedroom, the voice they listened to as they danced with their loved ones in their living room. In fact, I often wondered what percentage of the population of Boston was conceived during the hours of twelve to five on weekdays. The guests I brought in—Rosie Clooney, Mel Tormé, Tony Bennett—spoke so frankly and vividly about their careers and even their personal lives. I'd play their music, the kind that many people fell in love to and grew up with, or raised their children with the show in the background. People wrote telling me they planned their day around the show, or that they didn't get out of the car until a piece of music or an interview had ended. I even heard from one of the world's leading orthopedic surgeons, Dr. Michael Goldberg, who told me he scheduled his days in the operating room around *MusicAmerica's* opera programming.

In essence, I never knew who was listening or how what I played would affect them. I felt that, for one gentleman in particular, the show helped provide a validation for a life that revolved around a record collection. Through Larry Katz, I had access to one of the greatest assemblies of recordings I've ever encountered. An avid devotee of big band releases and radio shows, Larry was an endearing sort of eccentric who I first met at a benefit I was doing for a hospital in Lynn. Clutching a stack of LPs, he stepped right up to me and asked for my autograph, then offered to share his entire collection with me. He began to bring his records to the station until finally we had to create a special section of the library just to house his massive donation. I was blown away by what he'd gotten his hands on over the years! This incredible resource made it possible for me to play rare performances of artists no one else had access to, such as Streisand's very first recording, shows from the Golden Age of Radio including those starring Jack Benny, Burns and Allen; big band broadcasts by Benny Goodman, Duke Ellington, Stan Kenton; and so many others. Larry was my secret weapon for programming the show if I was looking for some obscure piece of music. A lot of collectors don't like to share their material, but Larry was bighearted and just the opposite.

If a broadcaster is lucky, there's at least one time he feels humbled by the understanding that his show has made a unique contribution to someone's life. One day I picked up the phone and heard loud wheezing, followed by the voice of a young man who told me his name was John Hersey. He said, "That woman you're playing now, when did she start singing?"

"That's Billie Holiday. In the thirties."

"Why was she called Lady Day? Who gave her that name?"

"Lester Young. But I'm not sure why..."

The next week he'd call and ask me to play anything by Louis Armstrong, peppering me with questions about his life. About the evolution of jazz. Or why Dizzy's horn was bent up that way. Week after week he called, entranced with George Gershwin's "Rhapsody in Blue" and begging for more, or enthralled with Coleman Hawkins' classic recording of "Body and Soul."

Finally, one week his father called and explained what I think I knew intuitively: his son had polio and was in an iron lung. He asked me if I would visit his son someday, speaking so softly I had to ask him to repeat the question. I realized later he never thought I would say yes. Ed Henderson, then president of the Boston Jazz Society, joined me on my trip to meet this young man and his family.

My visit to John Hersey changed me forever. I'll never forget this handsome young man, his head the only thing free of the enormous cylindrical machine that was keeping him alive. His face was full of life, vibrant, lit with excitement about music, thrilled that we were there to answer his questions in person. He'd been in that machine since he was five years old.

I could barely collect myself to do the show that afternoon.

After a few months his calls tapered off, then stopped completely. His father called to tell me that his son was at peace, and that for the first time he was able to lay him down on the couch in the living room, something John had always wanted to do. I told him how grateful I was to have had the chance to spend some time with his son.

One day I got a call from a man whose wife was dying of cancer. He wanted to thank me for playing the music they had fallen in love to. His wife's favorite song was Sinatra singing "Time After Time," which, knowing these were her final days, I played as often as I could. In a couple of weeks he called to tell me that it was the last song she heard.

Everybody felt they knew me, which was usually fine, but there were those who thought they knew me a bit too well, and I had to draw the line. In a scene straight out of *Play Misty For Me*, a woman kept calling and talking to me as if we'd been out together and knew each other well, each call becoming more suggestive as time went on. She'd ask me if I was feeling all right that day; tell me I didn't sound as upbeat as usual. Very creepy. Then the photos started coming: her in bed in a nightie holding a cocktail...anyway, I stopped taking her calls, the mail tapered off and hopefully she's moved on to someone a bit more receptive by now.

■ ■ ■

Just as there were great experiences with listeners as well as not so great, the same held true for interviews, though I have to say most of the time they went extremely well. I certainly did my best to make guests feel at ease, learning as much as I could about them and playing their music as they were on their way to the studio. I was keenly aware of their often grueling schedules: many times musicians arrived jetlagged and exhausted or hungry, or who knows, they could have just come off another interview where the host barely knew who the hell they were. I would watch them physically relax the minute they understood that I knew them and their work. And if things were going well, it was fun to keep things rolling, perhaps ask them to stay longer, mixing in chat about music history, or relevant composers and lyricists.

Though most interviews were a delight, two stand out as particularly difficult. Besides the chronically troubled Anita O'Day, who simply got up and left in the middle of an interview, my all-time worst was with Eartha Kitt.

I certainly knew that the woman was volatile. It was common knowledge that she'd driven Lady Bird Johnson to tears at a 1968 luncheon at the White House when she remarked, "You send the best of this country off to be shot and maimed. No wonder the kids rebel and take pot."[11] But I wasn't quite prepared for the storm that blew into my studio that day. She showed up with her agent who sat scowling as Ms. Kitt arranged herself, wordlessly, in the studio. It was clear she was in a nasty, foul mood. I thought I had my trump card, however, because I'd tracked down a rare recording of one of my favorites of hers, "Lilac Wine," to start the show.

I opened the mic and said, "We are delighted to have the wonderful dancer, actor, and recording star Eartha Kitt with us in the studio today—"

"Why did you play that? That's the worst record I ever made."

"Well, I've always liked that one, and I'm sure our listeners enjoyed—"

"Out of everything I've recorded you had to choose *that*?"

A touch of dead air here as I regrouped... "I just saw you in *Timbuktu*, and I thought you were terrific. The dancing, the singing...I'm so impressed with the diversity of what you can do—"

"You don't know what you're talking about, do you?"

I cut her mic and spliced in a song in record time.

Eartha took a sip of coffee and made a lemon-sour face. "You actually *serve this to guests*? It tastes like it's been sitting around for days. It's weak, it's cold..." Her agent jumped up to remove the offending brew. I told her it was all we had, but she went on attacking me. It was a complete disaster. I let her rant and rave and stuck to music till the show was over, and she stormed out and proceeded to destroy *Say, Brother*, a TV show being recorded next door, where she was scheduled next.

All I knew was I didn't deserve what she was dishing out, and somehow I wanted another crack at her. In fact, when I met her again, twenty years later at a benefit I was hosting, I was mentally locked and loaded to return fire if I caught any. She couldn't have been more delightful and charming; it's possible she remembered nothing of meeting me or our interview.

On that particular day, however, it took me a while to collect myself and finish the show with my dignity intact. I was still processing things at the end of the day even as I was packing up to leave, wondering what sort of response I could expect from listeners, management, and so on. In short, I had a little black cloud over my head.

Just as I was closing the studio door, the phone rang. I stepped back in and picked it up.

"Ron Della Chiesa."

This soft-as-cotton voice said, "Hi Ron, I want to thank you so much for playing my music."

"Who's this?"

"Peggy Lee."

"Peggy Lee..." I nearly dropped the phone. "*The* Peggy Lee?"

"Yes."

"Peggy—Ms. Lee—I'm such an admirer of yours!"

"Well, that's one reason I'm calling, Ron. I heard about you out here on Bellagio Road in Hollywood. The musicians on my records—they say you play my music all the time."

"Every chance I get."

"And you know, I'm so glad you're playing my newest CD. A comeback is never easy, but I'm in my sixties now, so it's even harder. I so appreciate all you're doing."

"It's an honor to play your music, Ms. Lee."

"Please call me Peggy."

And so Peggy Lee and I became friends even as I watched from my studio window as Eartha Kitt's limo took a long, slow left turn out of the lot toward Boston. But that's the way it was at WGBH: challenges every day followed by moments of magic.

■ ■ ■

Though *MusicAmerica* was rolling along, gathering momentum and evolving every day, I was doing my best to have a personal life and not doing too well. After my marriage ended, I'd entered another long term relationship that looked headed toward a real commitment, but in the end it didn't work out.

And though I was a man about town, which sounds fun and rather romantic; unless you're with someone you have an affinity with, it can make for a lonely life. Or at least it did for me. I began to look for other ways of challenging myself.

While my dreams of becoming a great baseball pitcher were on the wane, I still felt the need to do something athletic. Preferably something that didn't involve too much coordination or the letting down of team members. Something like—running! For years I'd thought about running as I watched joggers trotting along the Charles River; finally one day I stopped thinking about it, bought some decent running shoes, and hit the pavement.

On the first day I ran a mile. I thought I was going to die. It was wrong to be that sore. But after babying myself for a few days, I took to the road again and made sure that no matter what, I ran two miles a day. My blisters had blisters and my hamstrings screamed afterwards but no matter how tired I was or how bad the weather, I did my miles.

I can't remember exactly when two miles started to feel like nothing, as natural as breathing, or when I felt I could have kept on running another two miles with ease. But I do remember one gorgeous fall day, the air tasting like apples and smoke, and I never felt so alive. I was forty-three years old, and except for those times lifting weights as a teenager, I'd never before felt this sense of grace and integration with my own physicality.

Running saved me. Problems with women, my worries about my son Aldo, issues with the show—everything fell into perspective as I racked up mile after mile. The rhythm of running was like music to me; I ran listening to Lester Young, Sousa marches, Count Basie, even Wagner. Sometimes I was so lost in the running and music I had a sensation of floating. I began to run the four miles to the studio and back from my South End condo, keeping a change of clothes at the station.

One day I blew into the building after a brisk run from home and made my way to the men's dressing room to shower. Standing in his underwear, shaving, was Vincent Price. It took me a few seconds to reconcile the star of the *The Fly*, and *The Pit and the Pendulum* and at the time the voice of *Mystery Theater* at PBS with the tall man I saw before me, who calmly kept on shaving as I stood there staring.

"I'm sorry, Mr. Price, I can come back..."

"No, no, come in, young man. I'm just finishing up here."

I introduced myself, tossed my bag down, and threw some water on my face. "You have such a wonderful voice, I've enjoyed listening to it all my life."

"My voice is nothing. You want to know who had the most beautiful voice in the world? Mario Lanza. We'll never hear anything like that again on earth, my boy," he said, rinsing his razor.

"Weren't you in that movie with him, *Serenade?*"

"Indeed I was."

"Such a shame he died so young," I said. "At least we have another great tenor today, Pavorotti!"

"You're right. Thank God for Luciano."

We talked for at least fifteen more minutes about his art collection, acting career, cookbooks he'd written, everything under the sun until he was clean shaven and dressed. Later I learned he'd offered to lend his best *House of Wax* voice on outgoing messages for several WGBH employees. He was a real gentleman, as elegant as you might imagine him. I, on the other hand, did my show in sweaty jogging clothes because I had completely forgotten to take a shower.

■ ■ ■

If you had told me back in 1978 that I'd soon meet a woman who would change my definition of what a relationship could be, I'd have laughed in your face, laced up my Nikes, and taken off for a really, really long run.

But that's exactly what happened. And I'll be forever grateful it did.

At the time I'd rescued myself from the suburbs—I am *not* a suburban guy, I learned—and settled into a small rental in Somerville. I started hanging out with my dear friend, jazz pianist Dave McKenna. Whitney Balliett, critic for the *New Yorker*, called him "Super Chops" and "the hardest swinging jazz pianist of all time."[12] Dave had an unending repertoire at the keyboard and a magical left hand that made a bass player seem unnecessary. For a decade he was pianist-in-residence at the Copley Plaza Hotel where everyone came to hear him play, including Tony Bennett, Stan Getz, Zoot Sims, Rosie Clooney, and Joe Venuti. But beyond his brilliant playing, he was a gas to hang out with, always up for fun, and ready to hit the town for a good meal.

Inman Square was our stomping ground. We had our choice of the Inman Square Men's Bar, Ryles, Joe's Place, and the original Legal Sea Food, although mostly we'd hit the Chinese restaurant around the corner for the General Tso's Chicken.

It was around this time that I started hearing about Joyce.

Marty Elkins, a singer friend of Dave's, told me Joyce ran this place called the Turtle Café with her business partner, Nancy Madden. Every time Marty saw me she said the same thing: you have to meet my friend Joyce; you'd like her, I just know it. And every time Dave and I went out, we'd walk right past the Turtle, with its glowing purple neon turtle in the window. I never stopped in at first; I'm not sure why. Later I learned Joyce had spotted me a number of times passing her restaurant on my way to eat Chinese next door. Finally Dave said, "Look, I'm playing at the Turtle next Friday. You're coming with me."

A world of Joyce: Joyce Scardina Della Chiesa.

Author's collection, photo by David Wade.

You know how sometimes you know things even before you know them? That's what that Friday night was like for me. I put a bit more thought into what I wore; I heard Marty's words, "You have to meet this woman" over and over in my brain, and my heart beat a little faster as I walked past the Chinese place, ignoring that moo goo gai pan smell, and opened the heavy mahogany door of the Turtle Café for the very first time.

And, oh dear God, there she was. This woman mixing cocktails behind the bar with supernatural grace. A ringer for Jennifer Jones. I was officially knocked out.

And then she *smiled at me.*

I guess I must have frozen in place because Dave gave me a shove and I snapped out of my stupor.

"Joyce," Dave said, "This is Ron Della Chiesa."

"Oh yes," she said, with a brief glance, "I listen to you sometimes."

And that pretty much wrapped that up. In contrast to my needing life support, she didn't seem particularly blown away.

Then again it was Friday night, and the place was booming. A bar full of boisterous patrons, a jam-packed dining room, and Dave already off and getting set up to play his set. A cutting edge restaurant (which became the East Coast Grill), the Turtle featured contemporary regional cuisine, changing its menu every three or four days not only for variety but to continually showcase whatever was in season, a relatively new concept for its time. On weekends they'd feature jazz greats: Teddy Wilson, Scott Hamilton, Sammy Price, and Gray Sargent, a guitarist who these days works with Tony Bennett. I quickly learned it was a great place to hang out and meet these legends, since they'd usually come in to eat before their gig. I had to admit, it was certainly cooler than the Chinese place.

The next morning I got Marty on the phone and asked her a thousand Joyce-related questions.

"I think she might still be involved with someone, I'm not sure," Marty said. "But I get the feeling that's wrapping up."

"I'm in the same boat. Sort of in, sort of out, but mostly out. You know, the gray area."

Marty laughed. "I hear you. But Joyce is an amazing woman, you know. Did you know that Gordon Hammersley started out at the Turtle as Joyce's protégé? The woman cooks like a dream."

"No kidding," I said, staring at the lonely can of King Oscar Sardines and stale bread on my counter.

"Oh yeah, and she's not so crazy about Chinese food."

By the end of the day I couldn't take it any more. I looked up Joyce's number, picked up the phone, and dialed.

She answered. She sounded a little sleepy.

"Hi, Joyce? It's Ron Della Chiesa. We met last night at your restaurant. I really enjoyed meeting you."

"Oh yes...hi Ron. It was fun to finally meet you; I mean I listen to you all the time."

"Wow, that's great. We should get together sometime."

"I don't know about that..."

"Well, when's your night off?"

"Tonight, actually."

"Do you want to go out tonight, then?"

"I can't...."

"Why not?"

"Well, I'm ironing. I have this big pile of ironing to finish up."

"OK, then maybe some other time."

And we said goodbye. I stared at my dingy bachelor pad a few minutes, threw on my jogging clothes, and went out for a six mile run in the pouring rain.

A few weeks later I was sitting at the bar at Ryles nursing a drink when I caught sight of her sitting at a table with Nancy and Nancy's fiancé, Bill. Though I began to sweat, I decided this was my turn to play it cool. Well known Boston radio personality sipping a martini at the bar; what could be more alluring than that? So I sipped and gazed thoughtfully at the middle distance.

But I couldn't help stealing glances at her. Finally she noticed me, and all she did, all she moved in fact, was one eyebrow. Just lifted it a tiny bit.

I put down my drink and sprinted over to her, leaping over a rail and knocking over several chairs in the process. Once everyone stopped laughing, I was finally able to talk to the woman I'd been dreaming about for weeks.

People have asked me what first attracted me to my wife, and of course, that was her beauty and her smile. I have to say, however, that she was and is my soul mate. How many women would sit through the Wagner's entire Ring Cycle with me, crying at the same moments, or finding the same things hilarious or moving? I remember both of us nearly losing it when, while watching *Tosca* one day at the Met, the heroine jumped off the balcony of the Castel Sant'Angelo screaming, "We'll meet in hell!" and bounced right back up from the mattress beneath the stage.

One of our slogans at WGBH at the time was, "A World of Choice." My personal slogan quickly evolved into "A World of Joyce." In short, I don't think I've ever had so much fun with anyone in my life. Her sense of humor; a similar passion for opera, jazz, the symphony; her love of travel; her fabulous cooking; all there, of course, but mostly it is her heart, that intangible essence of humanity and kindness that defines her that allowed us to bond. Moreover, she embraced my son, Aldo, as if he were her own. She even put him to work at the Turtle Café when he was ten or eleven, trusting him to do the work, which instilled in him some real pride.

Though our courtship mostly took place all around Inman Square, we loved going to Nantucket on weekends. She was living on Beacon Hill with a gay couple when we met, George Ormiston and Vince Scardino; but over time, she moved into my condo, and we became a part of each other's families.

I also appreciated that we not only had our own passionate interests, but that there was a mutual respect about their pursuit. By that I mean, in particular, that she put up with my growing marathon addiction. I'd been training with my old friend Paul Antonelli, now a distance runner who convinced me to jump in the pack (unofficially as a "bandit") at the Boston Marathon, where to my amazement I not only completed the race, but crossed the finish line at just over four hours.

After running two more Boston marathons illegally, I ran the New York Marathon three times with a number, Joyce cheering me on all the way. I think she understood how important this was to me. The third race was especially grueling; a cold rain beat down for most of it, and I almost quit. At the very beginning of the race on the Verrazano Bridge I saw a woman running roped to a blind man, and I thought, my God, if they can do it, I can drag my sorry butt through this. Twenty-two miles later in Harlem, cramping badly in both legs, I had serious doubts about crossing the finish line; then, like a vision, I saw a man under a wide black umbrella who looked like Fats Waller handing me a cup of something. It was Sammy Price, a jazz piano player known as the "King of Boogie Woogie"

Finish line, New York Marathon, 1983.

Author's collection.

and a guest on *MusicAmerica*. He'd actually shown up to support me, as he said he would! He handed me the cup of water saying, "It's gin, buddy. Go, paesan, go!" He was like an angel guiding me through those last excruciating steps. In the end I made my best time of 3:43, not bad for a forty-eight-year-old, and close to my goal of 3:30. The best part was seeing Joyce's smiling face at the finish line and hearing Sinatra's "New York, New York" blaring over the loudspeakers, then celebrating with her family in Brooklyn.

We were married on June 10, 1986, Joyce's birthday. To this day she reminds me that she rates two presents on that day: anniversary and birthday, but hey, it's fewer dates for me to remember. The Turtle Café also closed the same year, and it was an honor to host that event with old friend John Henning and feature Dave McKenna, who on that final night burned up the piano like I'd never seen before or since.

I Miss You in the Afternoon

BECOMING THE VOICE OF THE BOSTON SYMPHONY ORCHESTRA on October 4, 1991, has to be one of the highlights of my life in broadcasting. Henry Becton Jr., President of WGBH at the time, was a major force in developing PBS in America. Under his guidance, WGBH launched some of television and radio's best known shows—a full one-third of PBS's prime-time lineup—including *Nova*, *Masterpiece Theater*, *Mystery!*, *The American Experience*, and *Frontline*; groundbreaking children's shows *Arthur*, *Curious George*, and *Zoom*; and radio series including *The World*, *La Plaza*, *Basic Black*, *Classics in the Morning*, *Jazz With Eric in the Evening*, and a *Celtic Sojourn*.

Henry was so excited about our new presence at the BSO that he arranged for our first broadcast to be videotaped, not only to capture the inner workings of what we did in the booth, but to mark the beginning of a new era. Twenty years later we're still bringing the Boston Symphony Orchestra to thousands of listeners from that very same booth.

By that point in my career, I was rarely nervous on the radio, but being the voice of the BSO took some getting used to. Keenly aware of whose shoes I was filling—the venerable William Pierce with his thirty-eight years and three thousand BSO broadcasts—I at first took a more conservative path than usual with my delivery. In fact, early broadcasts probably came off a bit stilted before I relaxed a bit. I believe that by now we have our own signature sound and identity: a more conversational, casual style; however, I've never lost sight of the huge responsibility I carry in this role.

Being the voice of the symphony both at Symphony Hall in Boston, and in Tanglewood, week after week, year after year, is a profound honor. I feel as if I've come full circle: from being a young boy enthralled by Milton Cross, the voice of the Metropolitan Opera, to actually sitting down in the broadcast booth and lending my own voice to the BSO. The challenge is to properly represent this wealth of talent: the musicians, conductors, and singers who've spent a lifetime preparing for the chance to appear at the hall. I can't help but picture not only the countless hours of practice, but the grueling auditions, in fact, everything it must take to be able to walk across that stage to your seat with your instrument, whether you're Joshua Bell with his violin or a debuting soloist with a magnificent voice. I try not only to present these performers in the best possible light, but also to provide an all-around exciting, challenging, and vibrant listening experience.

Symphony Hall itself carries its own *gravitas*. It is considered to be one of the three most perfect halls in the world: a hallowed, sacred place. I'll never forget one winter evening when Tony Bennett had just wrapped up a rehearsal and sound check. Everyone had left the hall—the technicians, musicians, and a few spectators—leaving only myself, Joyce, and Tony. He walked across the stage and said he wanted to try something out; did we have time to stay? We said of course, and moved to sit closer to the stage. He sang, *a cappella*, just a few measures of Jerome Kerns' "All the Things You Are." It was one of the most beautiful things I've ever heard, just the natural sound of his voice, all alone in that place. It was as if the hall took his sound, caressed it, and gently handed it back to us. Afterwards he leaned down, touched the stage, and said, "It's in the wood, all this music, for all these years."

I love the fact that the show is live, and I never know exactly what's going to happen. Is there chemistry between the conductor and the orchestra, or not? When there is a disconnect the audience picks up on it, just as when they know they're witnessing a spectacular musical synergy between conductor and orchestra. Regardless, nothing is more exciting than watching a conductor tame an orchestra, which feels to me at times like it has some sort of wild energy all its own: as if it could kill you with sound during a Schoenberg crescendo or just as easily curl up in your arms during a Brahms melody.

I often get goosebumps as I sit listening in the booth when I realize this symphony or opera will never be played or sung the same way twice. Beethoven's Fifth, conducted by ten different conductors, will result in ten unique performances. In fact, there are times when the performance is so hair-raisingly brilliant that I want to bolt out of the broadcast booth, sprint right into Huntington Avenue traffic, and shake passersby who are calmly going about their lives and say, "Don't you know what's going on inside this building? You're crazy to be missing this!" and drag them in to listen...

■ ■ ■

When I say you never know what's going to happen in live radio, I mean just that. Many years ago, during the Boston Jazz Festival, (then held at Symphony Hall), we were planning to broadcast Benny Goodman and his orchestra. The problem was, he didn't show up on time. Thank God I had another broadcaster with me, my friend Tony Cennamo. We winged it with no script—nothing, ad-libbing about the history of jazz, the weather, more history of jazz, the history of the hall, until thirty-five minutes later Benny showed up, leaning against the piano and probably half in the bag. Regardless, he put on a great show, definitely worth the wait.

From any vantage point—either in the audience or from the stage—the tiny broadcast booth where I sit, and its equally tiny window, is not easily pointed out. I have to see what's going on while at the same time remain inconspicuous. Unlike my cohorts, producer Brian Bell and audio engineer Jim Donahue who watch the action onstage via TV monitors, I enjoy a perfect bird's eye view of everything that happens on that stage through that small window. And it can get pretty jammed down there, especially with an opera cast, or the Tanglewood Festival Chorus (the BSO's in-house chorus), where as many as eight soloists might take the stage. Just watching the changes unfolding below can be like witnessing a miracle of coordination: getting everyone on and off and on again with the proper music, music stands, and instruments; moving the piano on or off; assembling the risers for the chorus. Every last detail must be planned with precision. Stage manager John Demick and his crew have been doing a masterful job for decades.

Meanwhile, up in the booth, we're on our own tight production schedule. I might arrive at six for a seven o'clock broadcast start; but Jim, one of the best audio engineers in the business, has been in his booth since rehearsal that afternoon, making sure the sound is balanced, bringing the brass down if it's too booming, bringing up the timpani if that's needed. Brian Bell and I sit down with his lead-in script to do the final edit, drop in whatever sound clips are needed, and time it out. This first script, which we call the pre-game show, usually includes a historic BSO recording and precedes the live broadcast. At intermission, Brian might air previews of upcoming performances, present an analysis of that evening's symphony, or interview the soloist or guest conductor. With his vast knowledge of music and music history, as well as an intuitive sense of what the audience is curious about, Brian's contribution to the program is incalculable. After the live broadcast, I tie it all together with a bit of *ad lib* over the applause, acknowledging the conductor and soloist. Lastly, we fill in with another BSO recording until we leave the air at eleven in the evening.

We didn't always have Brian to create fascinating musical commentary or lively interviews to fill the down time during intermission. Twenty years previous, in William Pierce's day and when the BSO program was produced by Jordan Whitelaw, nothing was broadcast during the eighteen- to twenty-minute intermissions except ambience. That is, the sounds of people as they got up from their seats, distant conversations, the rustle of programs, a cough here and there, basically nothing. The feeling back then was that going to the symphony was akin to attending church: everything about it should be treated with a kind of reverence. Nothing should infringe on the audience's experience of being at the symphony, even if in fact they were *not* at the symphony. They were, of course, driving their car, or at work, or at home, ironing, wondering what the hell was wrong with their radio.

During those early years, every week without fail, I'd get a call from some elderly lady. (It actually could have been the same lady every week, who knows?)

"Hello, is this the symphony?"

"Yes, it is. This is Ron Della Chiesa with WGBH radio."

"Well, where did everybody go? Is it over?"

"No, ma'am, it's intermission."

"Is my radio broken?"

"I don't think so. You're hearing sounds from the hall. Your radio's fine."

"I heard someone coughing."

"Yes, you did. The orchestra will be back in about twenty minutes."

"Are you sure you're still on the air? I thought that fund drive would never end. I know it's not much, but I've sent in my check every year for forty years now."

"And we so appreciate that, ma'am."

"And you'd think after forty years I wouldn't have to listen to coughing."

"The orchestra will be back soon, ma'am."

"But I like you, Ron, you're a nice man."

And so on.

One day during some downtime in the broadcast booth we tallied it up. Twenty years of twenty-minute intermissions broadcasting "ambience" totaled over SIX MONTHS of dead air.

■ ■ ■

"I miss you in the afternoon..."

It's amazing how often I heard that comment from friends, from strangers, and even from people walking down the street who recognized me that fall of 1995, after *MusicAmerica* was cancelled. Even today, over sixteen years later, I still hear the same lament. That simple sentiment revealed more to me about the impact of radio on people's lives than five decades of working in the business.

As much as *MusicAmerica* was my creation and my passion, I never would have predicted the impact its cancellation would have on my life, as well as the lives of countless listeners. It's possible I'd been having such a good time those eighteen years—interviewing some of the greatest songwriters, musicians, and composers on earth—that I didn't realize how successful I'd been in conveying my enthusiasm for the American Songbook. I don't think any realization has given me such joy on one hand, and such melancholy on the other.

On August 31, 1995, the *Boston Globe* featured the following editorial:

"The Day the Music Dies?"

> Would the Museum of Fine Arts stuff its John Singer Sargents in the base-
> ment? Could the Wang Center forget the great American musicals? What if the
> Symphony did without Copland or Ives? Or the Pops without Sousa?
>
> Impossible? WGBH is doing it.
>
> Today's edition of MusicAmerica on WGBH-FM is scheduled to be the last,
> ending 18 years in which the program has been an ornament to the city.
>
> Over those years, Ron Della Chiesa has won the loyal affection of many
> thousands of listeners—a fact that apparently tone-deaf potentates at the sta-
> tion may be beginning to realize—for hanging the ornament with such style and
> verve.
>
> But the ornament itself, as Della Chiesa is the first to say, is the music.
> Leading with Gershwin and Ellington and tumbling through decades of fabu-
> lous writers and performers, MusicAmerica has given soaring voice to what is
> unquestionably the golden age of American music.
>
> Like the powerful music that sustained black South Africans through bond-
> age to freedom, America's great songbook will survive.[13]

Of course I knew my audience was out there, but I had never pictured the thousands of people who were listening to me. Instead, alone in my tiny studio, I'd conjure up a loved one or a friend, a fellow music lover sitting in front of me who was as excited about what I was playing as I was.

At the time the program was cancelled, *Boston Herald* columnist Joe Fitzgerald wrote: "Soon the music of Johnny Mercer, George Gershwin and Jerome Kern is going to be a little harder to find in a world that needs to hear it more than ever, and the worst part of it all is that it didn't have to be this way."[14]

No one was more surprised by the cancellation than I; however, when I think back on it, the whole thing wrapped up with very little fanfare. On a hot, humid July day in 1995, I was called into the Program Director's office and told that *MusicAmerica's* last broadcast day would be on the thirty-first of August.

One part of my brain was listening to the "why" behind the cancellation: strategic planning goals dictated programming consistency, in this case, classical music throughout the day. As things stood, the afternoon was a mixed, unpredictable blend of features, music, and interviews...nothing that fit into their "strategic plan." Another part of me was busy piecing together clues from the past months, all pointing to the show's demise. In its early years, the show aired from noon to five, but over time became pre-empted for other programs both at the beginning of the show, pushing the start time to one or two o'clock, or eroding it at the other end, thereby shutting me down at four o'clock or earlier. Still, I left the office in a state of shock.

■ ■ ■

Until we'd made these program changes, I had no idea of the true size of our audience. Numerous articles popped up in the local print media including the *Boston Herald* and the *Boston Globe*, the *Regional Review*, the *Current*, the *Patriot Ledger*, the *Brockton Enterprise*, and so many others.

A letter by Frank Haigh printed in the *Brockton Enterprise* best summarized the feelings of a lot of listeners as they grappled with the loss:

> *Who will be there to present live performances from Studio One and preview the new CDs by local talent like Dick Johnson, Rebecca Parris, Kenney Hadley, Steve Marvin and Donna Byrne? Who will interview Herb Pomeroy, Dave McKenna and play recorded interviews with legends such as Sammy Cahn and Arturo Sandoval? Who will announce daily the increasing number of local venues featuring live entertainment? Where will stars like Cleo Lane, Tony Bennett and Mel Tormé go when they're in town, just to chat and give us some insights into the personality behind the talent? Who will celebrate the birthdays of Artie Shaw, Frank Sinatra and Nancy Wilson with tribute programs? Who will educate, promote, enlighten and keep alive the music that has distinguished America culturally? Others may try, but no one will do it with the class and style of Boston's mayor of music, Mr. Ron Della Chiesa. It may be crossed off your broadcast schedule, but replace MusicAmerica? It can't be done.*

The real impact of the cancellation was on the listener who felt the loss of a close and intimate companion in the afternoon. Through letters and calls, I learned I wasn't the only one who took the sudden loss of the sort of joy and comfort this music provided very hard. People wrote or called telling me they first learned about Frank Sinatra, Jr. from my show, or about Louis Armstrong, Luciano Pavarotti, or Ella Fitzgerald.

I was also surprised by the age range of my audience. Ten-year-olds who regularly had come home from school and listened to the broadcast contacted me to tell me goodbye; nursing home residents called me in utter disbelief and dismay; office workers, students, lab technicians, doctors, mothers at home all reached out to me. Grieving listeners called to tell me that the music I played was music they'd heard in their homes growing up, when they first got a radio, and that the music sustained them in difficult times. Things were made a bit worse by the timing: many were still away at the end of August and didn't hear about the cancellation till weeks later, sending a second shock wave through the listening community.

■ ■ ■

What had snowballed into a cause célèbre finally marshaled itself into the "Save MusicAmerica Committee," an organization that included media and business leaders from throughout the city and beyond. An initial trio, Steve Lowe, John Brady, and Carp Ferrari, were instrumental in giving the group real structure and goals. They demanded a meeting with station management. Entertainers and club managers were also disappointed and saddened by the loss of the show. *MusicAmerica* had given Scullers and the Regatta Bar as well as other venues generous, commercial-free radio time to promote whoever was in town. Carol Sloane, one of the country's great jazz singers as well as a substitute host for me whenever I was away, also lent her strength by becoming a member of the committee. Even the legendary Tony Bennett voiced his support for the cause during a Boston concert, calling WGBH's cancellation of the show a "music emergency." Tony added that he made it a practice to never speak out on issues from the stage, but this was important enough for him to break that rule.

Money donated to the cause of reinstating *MusicAmerica* was placed in the Save MusicAmerica Trust. Even though funds ballooned to over sixty thousand dollars, negotiations with management proved fruitless. The station was as adamant in their decision to drop the show as listeners were who dug in their heels to save it.

That's when the sleepless nights started. I had to walk a narrow line between my management and my audience. *MusicAmerica* was the peak of everything I'd done in radio. That eighteen-year body of work represented not only the biggest part of my career, but also the time during which I had the most impact on people's lives: it was the ultimate experience in sharing the music I loved and believed in. The issue became, for me, that a refusal to budge, to wholeheartedly join my supporters, likely would result in my being let go completely. Eighteen years of tenure could be gone in a flash.

As funds continued to grow in the Save MusicAmerica Trust, pressure mounted to determine just how to use it. Justifiably, people wanted the money either to be used in some way to bring *MusicAmerica* back, or to have the money returned to them. More sleepless nights for me as I tried to negotiate an ever tighter space between that rock and this hard place. I wanted nothing more than to be true to those who were sacrificing so much for me, at the same time I had no wish to sacrifice myself. I understood the evanescent nature of entertainment, with radio being no exception. Even I was surprised at times at how long I'd been able to stay in the game, and I had no wish to throw in my chips. I thought of that old joke:

"Get me Ron Della Chiesa!"

"Who's Ron Della Chiesa?"

That's how quickly one can be erased in the entertainment world.

Over time a halfway measure was reached. The Trustees of Save MusicAmerica decided to use the money to sponsor a series of concerts, beginning with an "Ellington Evening" with Carol Sloane and Herb Pomeroy. The idea was to create an even deeper and wider support base to further pressure WGBH to renege on the cancellation. I knew that eventually the station would come to me with some sort of compromise. I just wasn't sure I wanted to hear what it was.

■ ■ ■

Though the *MusicAmerica* circus had turned me on my head, I knew I had to save some of myself for my family and their needs. My mother had turned ninety-five that year and had begun to require some live-in help. Like a gift from the gods, a wonderful woman named Jerri Walsh, in her seventies and in better health than my mom, volunteered to live with her. A registered nurse who (like my mother) said the rosary daily, Jerri was someone I couldn't have conjured in my wildest dreams to step in and be a companion for my mom, but there she was. For four years they did everything together: shopped, read, ate meals, watched television, even met and visited each other's children and their spouses. I really believe this wonderful woman extended my mother's life for years.

Over time, my mother met and got to know Jerri's daughter and her boyfriend, who was illiterate. Even though she'd begun to lose her vision through macular degeneration, Florence took on an amazing project. She was determined to teach this young man how to read. A schoolteacher until age seventy, my mother had a profound understanding of the learning process, as well as how different people approached and assimilated knowledge. She displayed such sensitivity with this man, helping him overcome shyness and embarrassment to finally reach the point, as the light faded from her own eyes, when he could read her the *Patriot Ledger*.

Meanwhile, I'd begun my own project with my mother. Deep in the recesses of mom's basement were boxes and boxes of my father's letters, which he'd written to her while in the war: nearly five years of letters from the very first one he wrote after being called to active duty to the time he was discharged in 1946. She asked me to read them to her one last time, now that she was legally blind. Most of these letters I'd never laid eyes on before.

Every week we'd sit down in the sunny kitchen in the home I grew up in to go through a dozen or so letters or post cards. The letters dealt with all he had gone through in the war; passages could be harrowing or simply tell stories of just how hot it could get in Virginia in the summer. As I read, I occasionally came across some very personal thoughts from my dad, and I'd ask her if she was sure she wanted me to read them. With no hesitation in her voice, she insisted I go on. One of the letters revealed I would have had a brother or sister, had things been different. I had to stop for a moment to take that in, but again, she insisted I continue reading. My father also included clever little cartoons he drew or wonderful sketches of animals he saw in Virginia: cows, pigs, horses, chickens. I did my best to describe them to her. I'm not sure who enjoyed the process more: me as I got to know my dad through his words, or my mother, whose face was a constantly changing map of emotion: delight, joy, sadness, even laughter as she relived those years with me.

I would leave her at these times feeling such a mix of joy and melancholy: joy in sharing these letters with her with such frankness, melancholy because I couldn't truthfully answer all her questions, often about my own son. Without fail she would ask about Aldo, and I would say he was fine, doing well with his life but just too busy with work to visit.

In reality, even I hadn't been able to deal with my son. His teenage years had been marked by the typical rebellion, but he hadn't grown out of it as quickly and neatly as we had all hoped; in fact, I divided my time between worrying about him and worrying about my radio career. Joyce was remarkable during this period: never giving up on Aldo, always reaching out to talk to him, taking care of me as I stumbled in my own attempts to try to fix everything, often revisiting guilt from the divorce so many years ago. Countless times I had to remind myself of what was and was not in my power, a philosophy that on one hand can be depressing, while on the other, freeing. But the fact was, my son was drifting away from me, and I will never forget that feeling of helplessness.

■ ■ ■

At WGBH the pressure mounted. I continued to find myself between the conflicting obligations of supporting the Save MusicAmerica committee and maintaining my longstanding career. After months of meetings and discussions, the station finally issued a press release stating I would be hosting a new program called *Classics in the Morning* along with *The American Songbook* for two hours on Friday nights. I'm sure they saw it as the best of both worlds: appeasing my audience by keeping me there in some fashion, as well as providing the station with classical music all day, the programming consistency they needed to satisfy their so-called "strategic planning."

In the end, I had no problem hosting a classical music show; after all, that's the way I started my career at the station in 1969, so it was almost like going back to my roots in radio. The disappointment was that the show would be pre-taped, thereby lacking the spontaneity of *MusicAmerica*. I missed not only conducting interviews but creating a show that felt timely and alive. I found myself grateful on one hand to still have a presence on WGBH, while on the other I was still hurting from the loss of what had become so much a part of me.

A promotional piece the station created for the show a few years previous really captured the meaning the show had for me:

Some of its hardcore listeners will try to nail it down as a jazz show. And there is jazz, lots of it. Jazz that goes way back, and jazz musicians who are just blowing through town and thought they'd drop by the show to talk and play for their friend, Ron Della Chiesa. But the heart of Ron's show beats with more than jazz. It rushes with the pulse of the big bands; Glenn Miller, Benny Goodman, Harry James. It taps along to the elegant touch of Astaire and Rogers. It delights in the lyrics of Cole Porter and the style of Sinatra. It lingers on the musical sidestreets of America, listening to forgotten songs. It celebrates Ellington, Bernstein, Gershwin and Copland. It plays Broadway. It runs like a happy kid across an endless playground of 20th century music.

■ ■ ■

In a pattern perhaps common to all humanity, loss seemed to come in clusters during those years. My mother, a depression baby who never owned a credit card but who made a storybook home and loving life for my father and me, passed away on a cold February night at the New England Medical Center.

Around this time, however, all sorts of positive things started happening in Aldo's life. I sometimes wonder if she was controlling the whole thing from above—if all that praying and saying the rosary was finally kicking in. I still imagine how happy she would be, knowing Aldo as the fine young man he eventually became.

He was terrifically gifted with his hands (probably something he got from my dad), not only great at building things and woodworking, but he could also take apart and put together any car you could think of. When some well deserved work came his way, he found himself able to stabilize financially and to take justifiable pride in that accomplishment.

I'll never forget the day we visited my mother's grave at Mount Wollaston cemetery. It was a brutally cold day, a deep freeze locking the ground under sheets of unbroken whiteness. Hands jammed in the pockets of his too-light coat, Aldo asked if I could give him some time alone. For a good fifteen minutes he kneeled at her grave, crying his eyes out.

Before that moment I'd never realized what she meant to him. Perhaps that was the first time he'd understood that as well. From the cemetery we paid a final visit to her home, to say goodbye to the place he'd spent so much time, including entire summers, as a very young boy. He kept asking on the way over what we'd kept and what we'd given away or thrown out. In every room we walked through he shared a memory of her I had no idea he possessed or even experienced. When we reached the living room he stopped short and gasped.

"You didn't get rid of the chair, did you?" he asked.

"What chair?"

"The green one in the corner, you know, that old beat up recliner."

"That's at Goodwill, probably long gone."

"I wanted that chair. I sat in her lap in that chair while she read me Christmas stories. Out of everything in this house that's the only thing I cared about keeping. I wish you'd have let me know..."

I looked at Aldo like I'd never met him before in my life. Who was this sensitive, sentimental young man with all these warm memories of his grandma? In the coming years he'd talk about things we did together thirty years previous with utter clarity: his first opera, meeting Buddy Rich, the great jazz drummer, or John Williams, the composer. He even remembered things that endeared my mother to me as well: her wonderful muffins, fruitcakes, and pies, the way she made cookies and stored them in old cans so they stayed chewy. He recalled the saxophone I got him as a teenager, which he eventually replaced with a banjo that he still plays, and all the classical music we shared together, the jazz concerts, the bumper cars, everything I'd concluded didn't register with him during the time he had stopped communicating with me.

All this was a revelation. That my son, no matter how much evidence there was to the contrary, had been listening to me, and to Joyce, and to everyone else who loved him the entire time. I realized that you never know how what you say will be tapped for strength by the listener. Children will remember a kindness, remember love, and revisit those odd, sweet gestures or words in their hearts when they need nourishment or strength, most likely long past the time you were trying to reach them. So I guess the lesson is: you must never give up. I feel blessed to have a son who loves his kids and who wants to be a part of their lives.

CHAPTER 7

Fly Me to the Moon

OVER A YEAR AFTER THE CANCELLATION OF *MUSICAMERICA*, A DEAL was struck between WGBH station manager Marita Rivero and Alan Anderson, then manager of WPLM in Plymouth. This new arrangement was unconventional as well as unprecedented in Boston radio history: a sharing of one radio personality between two stations. Via the WGBH frequency I would be able to continue hosting *Classics in the Morning*, Friday evening's *Jazz Songbook*, the BSO broadcasts, *and* go to WPLM and do something called the *Strictly Sinatra* show as well as Sunday night's pre-taped, shortened version of *MusicAmerica*.

Paul Kelly of Kelly Communications, a true *MusicAmerica* addict and a force in sports communications, was the one who put me in touch with Alan and in the end helped broker the deal with WPLM. Paul knew all about the local broadcast industry and where the different formats were than anybody else. At first Paul played a big part in the Save MusicAmerica committee, but as he got to know me and the situation better, he decided the best thing for me would be to not only maintain my present audience but to seek out other horizons as well.

There was a big difference between seeking other horizons and pacifying management at WGBH; however, Paul went to Alan Anderson at WPLM and convinced him I had enough of an audience and enough of a draw to make it all worthwhile. I don't think anyone has a good count on how many meetings it took to bring everything about, but I am forever in Alan and Paul's debt for the patience and tact they brought to bear on not only helping maintain my presence at WGBH, but in reinventing me in a certain way with the new shows.

There even came a time when I had to take a firm stand with the Save MusicAmerica committee and tell them we were pretty much done; to put down their arms and leave the battlefield. It's not that I didn't appreciate everyone's efforts and their passionate commitment to the show (what better compliment could there be?), but it was time to move on. Sometimes I think if I had not been adamant about my decision, they'd still be rallying. They also wanted back all the money they had raised—understandably—but I believe to this day, well over a decade later, it's still tied up in escrow.

So in the end, with some wonderful people behind me, I was able to turn the cancellation of *MusicAmerica* into a positive thing. There was even a small scholarship set up in my name for musically gifted, college-bound students from Quincy High School. Though I missed the ability to do interviews as well as the spontaneity of *MusicAmerica*, the fact was that WPLM's version of the show kept the music alive. In fact, over the years I've developed a whole new audience for the American Songbook show on Sundays and for *Strictly Sinatra* on Saturdays through the WPLM frequency at EASY 99.1, as well as via their website, EASY911. com, where the show streams online.

In all honesty, I was a bit apprehensive about the Sinatra show at first. Five hours of programming is no easy feat, especially when you're showcasing just one artist, week after week. Even though "Old Blue Eyes" is a worldwide favorite, I had to ask myself if any entertainer could sustain all that airtime. I just had to put my best efforts in the show and see what came of it. After programming a few of them, I came to realize once again what a giant and an innovator Sinatra was, what massive influence he had over the American Songbook. One way of looking at the Songbook, in fact, was pre- and post-Sinatra: his interpretations expanded the meaning of every song he touched. Enigmatic, brilliant, tempestuous— I wanted to present the man, warts and all.

Before Frank there was Bing Crosby, who sang things relatively straight, as they were written. Then Sinatra arrived taking great liberties with both the music and the lyrics, particularly when he teamed up with Nelson Riddle, Gordon Jenkins, and Billy May in the fifties. Frank knew instinctively not only where to pause but how to get the most out of a pause. He knew how to shape a line, so that in many cases, a song sung by Sinatra was an adventure in swing. On the other hand, he could get inside a poignant ballad like no one else.

In the end, a lot of people started spending Saturday night with me and Frank, even, to my shock, kids under the age of ten. After a benefit I did one evening, a six-year-old boy came up to me with his grandfather in tow. He grabbed my arm and pulled me down so I could hear him.

"I love that Sinatra show!"

I asked him, "What do you like about Frank?"

He thought for several seconds, taking the question very seriously. "He's a classy guy. I guess that's it."

"What's your favorite Sinatra recording?"

"'Mr. Success.'"

Now *that's* timeless.

■ ■ ■

In 1999, Joyce and I packed up and moved from our small, South End penthouse condo to a ten-room 1880 Victorian on the Dorchester/South Boston line. I was sixty-one, the time in many people's lives when they think about downsizing, but after twenty years in the condo, we both missed the feeling of living in a one-family home.

Living in the South End was terrific, don't get me wrong. We could literally reach out and touch the John Hancock building, and we were within shouting distance of the Cyclorama, the Boston Ballet, and a burgeoning jazz and restaurant scene. But I was tired of keeping so much of my music collection and memorabilia stored in boxes because of space limitations, and Joyce was craving not only a kitchen of her own design but to live closer to the water. I also thought it was high time to create a studio in my home. We were both losing patience with the condo restrictions via the South End Historical Society. At one point, Joyce painted the steps two shades lighter than "allowed" and was subsequently summoned to a hearing. I think our decision to move was sealed when we learned the committee would grant us six months to repaint the steps in their officially approved color. Ironically, the gentleman who conducted the hearing knew me and told me he was a big fan of mine, but that rules were rules and those steps had to be repainted. Long story short, we couldn't wait till we could build a fence and not cower in fear as the neighborhood committee swooped in to make sure it was regulation height.

It was only the second house we looked at, but we were in love with it. Even though it was just two miles from the condo and the bustle of the city, we felt like we'd moved to New Hampshire. To have a driveway and a yard, however small, was a balm for the soul. Still, I could walk straight up Massachusetts Avenue to Symphony Hall in about an hour.

The location couldn't have been better: minutes from the red line and a short distance to Carson Beach and Castle Island. Walking along the promenade where the sunset meets the skyline is an experience second to none on the Eastern seaboard. We both felt great to be back in a real neighborhood again; for Brooklyn-born Joyce it was an especially strong sense of returning to her roots. Even my music sounded better playing in that house, as if we had all finally come home.

Still, the house needed work, and Joyce did a bang-up job during her seven-month stint as general contractor. Her brother Ritchie, a contractor, and his wife Rosie flew in from Los Angeles to help supervise the renovations. Without them I don't how we would have done it. We're also forever indebted to dear friend Carolina Tress-Balsbaugh, one of America's best interior designers, who took the time to really look at the home, room by room, space by space, and offer priceless advice about paint color, wallpaper, even placement of our furniture, but always with our needs and personalities in mind. Freshly painted in beige and putty with dark-green trim and rich in period detail, the house seemed to exude a wonderful warmth and sense of history. We've been so happy over the years adding our own history: visits not only from our children and grandchildren, but wonderful meals

Joyce has prepared for long evenings of great conversation with dear friends. Renovations to the second floor included the transformation of four small bedrooms to a master suite and guest room, while the third floor turned from an attic to a cozy reading room. I cherish especially the winter nights sitting there under the skylight, reading to my grandchildren or listening to old LPs with our cat Giacomo on my lap, snowflakes swirling outside the window.

The foyer, otherwise known as the "Opera Hall of Fame," is hung not only with rare, autographed prints of opera singers and composers, but with another collecting passion of mine: Disney animation cels. These are transparent sheets on which objects were drawn or painted in traditional animation. Stills from *Fantasia*, *What's Opera, Doc?*, *Lady and the Tramp*, and *Jungle Book* line the walls.

But a descent into the basement is like a journey into my heart, soul, and an over sixty-year romance with music. We renovated it to include a sitting area, a soundproof recording studio, and, of course, the music: floor to ceiling shelves of vinyl, cassettes, and CDs including my very first 78 rpm: "Rusty in Orchestraville" sitting next to the Pinocchio album, both Christmas gifts from my parents. Plaques, favorite photographs and awards, vintage "Nippers" (the RCA Victor dog), antique radios, and microphones line the shelves, along with a fair number of Tom Mix glow-in-the-dark-spurs and Disney toys. My collection of vintage magazines including *Life*, *Playboy*, *Mad*, and *Opera News* fills the rest of the space. Joyce even created a subterranean wine cellar, formally a half bathroom. Removing heating pipes resulted in the perfect 62-degree environment.

Above the reel-to-reel recorder that I used to do some of my very first interviews are photos of Bill Marlowe and Milton Cross, a signed photo of Arthur Fiedler, a drawing of Dizzy Gillespie by "Benedetto," the name with which Tony Bennett signs his artwork, and even a photo of the old Boston Opera House that once stood on Huntington Avenue and Opera Place, today the site of a Northeastern University building. Sometimes as I look around at the magnitude of what has come and gone, I can't help but feel melancholy; but that feeling soon passes, and I become energized by the joy of listening to the music again and again.

Even though the Turtle restaurant is gone, the neon sign still hangs in our dining room over the mantel. The pale yellow walls here make a striking backdrop for a collection of black and white illustrations my father did for a series of "noir" mysteries published in the thirties and forties. In the adjoining living room, an exhibit of his work continues with watercolor seascapes, primitive landscapes, and charcoal portraits, which to me recall the style of John Singer Sargent.

I'd always wanted some way of commemorating my dad's art work, and in the spring of 2000, at the Adams Academy Building, home of the Quincy Historical Society, Joyce and I were finally able to make that a reality. A 1926 graduate of what is now the Massachusetts College of Art, my father studied with the famed sculptor Cyrus E. Dallin, known for his sculpture "Appeal to the Great Spirit," which graces the entrance to Boston's Museum of Fine Arts; and with Ernest Major, a pupil of John Singer Sargent himself. My dad taught art in Waterville, Maine, and Lynn, Massachusetts, before returning to the South Shore, where he became director of the art department at Braintree High School. In his native South Quincy, he directed the Quincy Adams Drawing School, giving art lessons to local children.

It was Joyce who had the vision of rescuing my father's paintings from my mother's basement and having them cleaned, re-matted, and re-framed. The result was the first complete retrospective of Aldo Della Chiesa's art work, from his early student days in the 1920s to his last paintings in the 1960s. I often think how wonderful it would have been if he could have attended this event himself; he was never honored in such a way while he was alive. Quite possibly he would have delighted us all by bursting into song with his gorgeous tenor voice. I do know that the sharing of his love of music and the arts was his greatest gift to me.

Tony Bennett and me at exhibition of Aldo Della Chiesa's paintings in Quincy, June 2000.

Photo courtesy of Joyce Scardina Della Chiesa.

■ ■ ■

Paul Schlosberg, my manager, entered my life in 1990. Here is a guy who doesn't stop moving until all the guests are seated, drinking, and happy. He's got the kind of energy and chutzpah and gutsy promotional instinct one simply doesn't find very often. My producer and partner for both *Strictly Sinatra* and *MusicAmerica* on WPLM, Paul has been instrumental in changing my viewpoint about myself and what I could offer beyond the scope of public radio.

Paul had represented Bill Marlowe, which impressed me no end. He kept drilling it into my head that I had an audience, and that they would follow me, and that I could also reach out for a whole different demographic. In other words, why not start selling myself? No one but me owned my identity, after all. The whole idea at least gave me a sense of control and optimism.

I decided it wasn't the end of the world to work at a commercial station; after all, that's where I'd begun my career. I had to look at it as a new bend in the road, one that had the habit of paying the bills just as well as public radio, often even a little bit better. It was a kick to learn that there were people out there who wanted to jump on board as sponsors, such as David Colella, a big Sinatra fan and the manager of the Colonnade Hotel. David was also responsible for one of the city's most successful restaurants, Brasserie Joe, and he's been one of my loyal sponsors from the beginning. Raphael's restaurant, then in Nantasket and now in the South Shore Country Club in Hingham, and Tony Floramo's restaurant in Chelsea signed on as sponsors. Chuck Sozio, who'd been one of Bill Marlowe's sponsors, turned the second floor of his Neponset appliance store into a Sinatra room, completely fitted out with hip fifties furniture, jukeboxes, as well as my Sinatra show piped in to all his stores. I still return the favor by appearing at home shows with him whenever possible.

But still, flipping my brain over to commercial radio took some getting used to! Here I came from this very insulated and dignified public radio station:

"Good afternoon, and welcome to *MusicAmerica*. Thanks so much for joining us today during our fundraiser. We certainly need your pledges to keep bringing you the best of the American Songbook..."

...to...

"Tony Floramo's in Chelsea is the *place to go*! I'm telling you right now, you've *haven't lived* until you've tasted these succulent baby back ribs! The meat falls *right off the bone*!"

There were days I might interview Yo-Yo Ma in the morning at WGBH, race to WPLM in the afternoon to pitch surf 'n' turf, then in the evening, host an event such as a "Strictly Sinatra Dance Party" at Raphael's on Nantasket Beach, where women would swoon over Dean Martin and Frank Sinatra, Jr. impersonators. Hell, they even swooned over me now and then, coming up to meet me, hug me, touch my hair. At events like this, which continue to this day, I get the chance to ham it up and improvise a bit, indulge my actor-ly side. Here was a Vegas crowd with a bone-deep enjoyment of the American Songbook, unafraid to get up on the dance floor and show their love. It's been so refreshing to get out there and meet the people who've listened to me and the music we all cherish.

Paul created our website, www.musicnotnoise.com, arranging sponsors, handling all ticket sales and promotion. Streaming our music 24/7 has inspired joyous listener responses from Los Angeles to Rome, as well as a phone call from Dan and June Weiner at Galaxsea Travel. They convinced me I had enough listeners to do a cruise. Our first was in 2006, and it was a huge success; we've been doing them ever since. These adventures draw people of all age groups, from young couples celebrating their honeymoon to people in their seventies and eighties who love to dance. The unifying factor is a love for this kind of music. So often by the time we pull into port, lifelong friendships have been forged as well as indelible memories. Our February 2010 "Tribute to Frank Sinatra and Dean Martin Cruise" (featuring Michael Dutra as Frank and Steven Palumbo as Dean) sailed to the Eastern Caribbean on the *Atlantica*.

■ ■ ■

Branching out certainly widened horizons for me, but every now and then I would get in a little over my head. Pulitzer Prize winning composer Gunther Schuller, a friend for over thirty years, once asked me to act as narrator for a performance of his composition, "Journey Into Jazz." This twenty-three-minute piece explores a young trumpet player's discovery of jazz, the complexities of which confound him initially. First, he looks for answers through the music of other jazz musicians but soon realizes the real "journey" to jazz is to follow his own instincts and be himself.

Gunther Schuller began his career playing principal French horn with the Metropolitan Opera Orchestra under the baton of legendary conductors such as Fritz Reiner. Later, he collaborated with Miles Davis on the historic "Birth of the Cool" jazz sessions, developing into a prolific composer of classical and jazz music, ultimately inventing the term "Third Stream," which combines the two techniques. He's the author of two major books on jazz, winner of the Pulitzer, MacArthur Genius grant, and several Grammy awards, as well as the recipient of ten honorary degrees. His full resume would require another nine or ten more pages. Being with this man is like being in the same room with Gershwin or Schoenberg, just an extraordinary experience. He really has done it all, and so when he asked me to be the narrator for this piece, I have to say I was thrilled as well as terrified.

At the same time here was a guy who'd been over to our home for dinner many times, and he was no stick in the mud. We knew just how he liked his steak and his gin martinis, and he was great company. After all, I'd interviewed him a number of times, and he never put on airs. Here's what he said when asked about his teen years: "When I was eighteen, my parents told me you have to sleep eight hours every night. I said, 'God, you know, if I sleep eight hours every night, I'm going to piss away one-third of my life just by sleeping. And life is too short.'"

"Journey Into Jazz" is a complex piece for any musician, but because he liked how I sounded as host of the BSO, Gunther entrusted me to narrate it for a performance at the Sanders Theater in Cambridge. I guess he respected my knowledge of jazz, but when I reminded him I didn't read music all that well and that I wasn't a musician he said, "That's okay, you hear with your heart."

Hopeful words from a good friend; how could I let him down? I squirreled myself away with Leonard Bernstein's narration of the piece. I must have listened to it a hundred times, and eventually I thought I had it down.

We had only one rehearsal at the Sanders Theater. It's there I discovered I did *not* have it down. Improvisation mixed with the notes on the page threw me off, I think. Long story short, I was off by a few measures, which is of course a crime when you have an entire orchestra counting on you, and you are performing the conductor's own work. During a break in rehearsal, Gunther took me aside. He was looking awfully pale.

"Man, you can't read music, can you?"

"I told you back at the house, I played trumpet in the army. It got me out of KP—"

He looked grim. "I don't know what we're going to do."

I pictured our friendship evaporating no matter what I did. "What would you like me to do?"

"I don't know, but I don't have time to work with you. This plays next weekend. I'm going to have to bail you out somehow."

The following week I was sitting onstage with my score in front of 1,300 people and a full orchestra. To say I was sweating doesn't do justice to my poor tuxedo. Gunther's solution was to hire a flutist to sit directly in front of me and cue my every move. At first I thought I was pretty much in the groove, that I might actually live through this.

Then, during the performance, Gunther shouted out over the orchestra something like, "Number fifteen!" and after that it seemed like my cues were all over the place. I was a basket case. Later I learned I was off a couple of beats. My performance still is a blur to me.

I'm still not sure what actually happened up there, but people in the audience told me it was fine. Everything sounded "intentional," which is something I'm still trying to figure out. All I know is, Gunther still takes my calls, and that's what matters.

■ ■ ■

I'm often asked how it felt to finally retire, but in fact, I never really have. I'm busier than ever. After thirty-five years with WGBH, I accepted the buyout package with the provision that I could continue my relationship with the station, hosting the Boston Symphony and conducting Learning Tours. I also serve on a number of boards of arts organizations as well as host a number of events around Boston. The AARP has had me all over the country at conventions drawing sometimes upwards of thirty thousand people. It's been an honor sharing program spots with everyone from Bill Clinton to Queen Latifa and Bo Derek, giving talks on the history of jazz, opera, or the Boston culinary scene. In fact, this past decade has been one of the richest of my life, perhaps because everything feels so integrated now both personally and professionally.

Best of all has been the opportunity for Joyce and me to host the WGBH Learning Tours all over the world, including tours in Santa Fe (known for its opera company's fantastic outdoor stage), Los Angeles, Italy, and Tanglewood, as well as a jazz tour in the Caribbean with Oscar Peterson and Dave McKenna. But I think going to Italy both to conduct several Learning Tours and to enjoy subsequent trips on our own has moved us most of all.

Finally going to the country I'd read about and imagined for six decades was like a dream come true for me. It was everything I imagined and more. Just seeing the countryside, driving through picturesque villages, and sampling unparalleled cuisine with Joyce are among the richest experiences of my life. After attending hundreds of operas, listening to thousands more, interviewing opera singers, and studying opera for as long as I have, it was a revelation to finally set eyes on the countryside, meet the people, and visit the places where opera was born.

We visited Roncole, the birthplace of Giuseppe Verdi, and walked from the farmhouse where he was born to the church where he played the organ as a boy; then visited the Verdi Theatre in the town of Busetto, where he grew up. We stayed at "Il Due Foscari," which is the name of a hotel as well as one of Verdi's operas. Owned by the great tenor Carlo Bergonzi, the hotel also houses an opera school that draws young singers from all over the world to study with him.

We stopped at Puccini's home in Lucca, followed by the Puccini museum. What an experience it was to listen to his music while poring over his final letters to his wife, Elvira. A chronic cigar and cigarette smoker, he died of throat cancer in 1924. Even in bronze as a statue in front of the museum, he holds a cigarette in one hand. We also visited his summer villa, Torre Del Lago, where the Puccini Opera Festival is held every summer. It was there we met his granddaughter, Simonetta Puccini, who I had the opportunity to interview (years earlier) for WGBH. We saw the piano he composed on and visited the small chapel inside the lower level of his home where he's buried next to his wife and son, Antonio.

Parma is, of course, known for its Parmesan cheese and prosciutto di parma, but it's also the birthplace of Toscanini, the maestro who first ignited my passion to learn about classical music. Joyce and I delighted in the beautiful opera house, Teatre Regio di Parma, where only the most discerning opera lovers sit at the top of the gallery. If you don't get it right in Parma, they'll make you sing it over and over until you do. The spirit of the place is interactive, to say the least. On one occasion, an American baritone was having an off-night, and the audience booed him. He cursed at them and called them "cretini." By the time the opera had come to a close, he needed a police escort to leave the building.

One evening, a tenor who'd also had a less than stellar performance the previous night took a cab to the airport. The singer paid the cabbie, then waited for some help getting his bags out of the trunk.

The cabbie squinted at him in the rear view. "Were you singing last night?"

The tenor gulped. "Yes."

Glaring at him, the cabbie popped the trunk. "Carry them yourself."

We visited La Scala opera house in Milan where Maria Callas sang, as well as the Teatro Massimo opera house in Palermo, Sicily, where a good deal of *Godfather III* was filmed.

The culinary and wine tours we did in the chianti region and visits to Tuscany were truly life changing. I used to plan on traveling to places all over the world and I still hope to, but as I get older I want to be more thoughtful about where I spend my time, perhaps confine myself to places that hold deeper meaning for us. I think Italy—for both of us—is a place where we simply can't spend too much time. As I've said many times, it's hard to leave Italy.

Being with Joyce has deepened my understanding of a true partnership, and ours is one I cherish and for which I am so grateful. We're a team, even though I'm not always easy to live with. I listen to over forty hours of music a week, and when we're driving, one hand is on the wheel and the other is constantly cruising the dial. There are weeks we're out on the town five nights a week: for a movie preview, a benefit, an opening, the symphony; and every night feels like an adventure. Last year alone we saw twenty-six operas together.

Traveling with Joyce has deepened our relationship in so many ways. I think that's when you truly get to know someone—when you're jetlagged, lost, or stumbling upon wonders new to both of you. Once or twice a year we escape to Cape Santa Maria Bay on Long Island in the Bahamas where Joyce's mother was born. No TV, no phones, just pristine white beaches stretching out for close to a hundred miles. In fact it was Joyce's Bahamian mother, a natural born chef, who first taught her how to cook.

Our travels also included a cruise on the *Queen Elizabeth II,* an ocean crossing from Boston to London where Joyce was a guest chef and I lectured on jazz; a very long trip to Buenos Aires; and several jaunts to Hollywood. Being movie junkies, we visited the cemeteries: the graves of Mario Lanza, Marilyn Monroe, Cecil B. Demille, Bella Lugosi (who's buried in his Dracula costume), Bing Crosby, Tyrone Power, and Sharon Tate. Al Jolson being the winner in the ostentatious category: High up on a hill near Los Angeles International Airport next to a magnificent white marble fountain is a bronze statue of him on one knee, arms out-stretched in his famous "Mammy" pose.

Thanks to our dear friend Dale Pollock, who was a producer at the A&M Studios and who used to manage the Orson Welles Theater in Cambridge, we were able to visit some off-limit sets at Warner Brothers, 20th Century Fox, and Paramount. We explored the original studio lot where *Casablanca* was filmed, the Paramount lot where Marilyn Monroe had her cottage, Culver City where the original MGM studios were located, and the original soundstage for the *Wizard of Oz.* We also looked up another old friend: Bob Genest, who worked with me at WGBH, but who had transitioned from public radio to CEO of Frederick's of Hollywood, which included a Bra Museum among other attractions.

None of these adventures would have happened, however, if I hadn't gotten over my fear of flying. I had it all—the sweaty palms, the racing heart, the sudden deepening of my Catholic faith every time we hit turbulence. One day Joyce said, "Okay, we're going to take care of this." This was a few years ago when we were traveling more than ever before, and I was probably driving her crazy.

I believe the cure came during that brutal, ten-hour flight to Buenos Aires. We're flying, the plane is bouncing, I'm sweating and flipping out, and she pops an Atavan in my mouth. In a few minutes my whole body melted into the seat and I'm sitting there smiling, then I leaned over and French kissed her. She said, "I think your fear of flying is officially over." But we still carry the Atavan, or at least she does, if she wants to get French kissed.

Still, I've got to have a window seat. I just have to see what's going on, even if it's the ground shooting up to meet me; and I still pray when I step on a plane. But I have to say, going first class helps a lot. I finally got what people were talking about the first time we ditched the coach seats.

FLIGHT ATTENDANT: "What can I bring you?"

ME (RECLINING ALL THE WAY): "What do you have?"

FLIGHT ATTENDANT: "Everything."

ME: "I'll start with a Bloody Mary."

FLIGHT ATTENDANT: "How would you like your filet mignon done, Mr. Della Chiesa?"

ME: "Medium, thank you very much."

AN HOUR LATER:

FLIGHT ATTENDANT: "Can I get you an ice cream sundae? Profiteroles? Tiramisu?"

ME: "Yes, thanks, and also a pillow and blankets and earbuds and a martini and...."

And then I wake up over Rome to the smell of bacon and eggs.

■ ■ ■

Though no one would accuse me of being a curmudgeon, even I sometimes forget that this world is a charmed place. Sometimes it took a little magic to remind me, such as the sight of my eight-year-old granddaughter, Tia, walking off the plane and into Logan airport some years ago. My heart skipped a beat as she emerged from the crowd. She had been a toddler the last time I'd seen her, but here she was dressed to the nines in a pink dress and shoes, carrying a Barbie Doll suitcase. She was just so beautiful. Her face lit up when she saw us, and she broke out in a run and jumped into my arms.

A good friend said to me once, and I concur: "When you get to be our age, it's all about the grandchildren." I don't know who benefits more from our relationship, my five grandchildren or me. My intention is to hopefully instill in them a love for beautiful things: the arts, music, theater, painting, as well as a love for the outdoors, nature, traveling, seeing and appreciating different cultures. While there are the less tangible lessons about how to confront the constant obstacles in life with a positive attitude, things that they will no doubt learn through experience, as a grandparent I somehow wish I could shield them from any sort of pain.

While there are all these things I want to teach them, I find myself delighted by everything they have to teach me. I'm fascinated by their wildly different personalities and interests: Gabby who smiles all the time like a little butterfly and most resembles my mother, Florence; Nico, who is a dynamo of a boy, an athletic kid who fights with his sister Gabby like an old married couple. Dominick reminds me of a young Fred Astaire, and young Donovan, who resembles Mary's father Gabe, looks like he could grow up to be a linebacker for the NFL. Tia, the angel I'll always remember running to us in the airport, is now a lovely young woman who I tend to worry about the most. It seems there's no natural, gentle transition to womanhood these days; instead, the pressures and influences of the media throw so many young girls into the fast lane before they're ready to be there. I'm happy to report, however, that she's turned into a level-headed, sophisticated, but fun-loving young woman, and is headed for her freshman year at Arizona State University.

We don't see them enough because they live in Boise and Phoenix and we're in Boston, but we love sharing the joys of New England with them when they're here. I love reading to them, watching movies with them, just observing them relate to each other. As they're playing around me, laughing or fighting over a toy or generally destroying a room, I suddenly feel as if I'm no longer an only child; that I truly have become, finally, part of a large, extended family, a new and wonderful sensation for me.

■ ■ ■

Many times I'll look back and wonder what would have happened if I'd made different choices. The good news is that every time I do, I see why I made the choices I did. I had a chance to go to Los Angeles and program a classical show there, but in the end I'm glad I stayed here and worked to establish my career in Boston. Most of the time I felt like I was having my dream cake and eating it too, so why leave? Besides, where else could I interview James McCracken, one of opera's greatest who sang a few measures from *Otello* for me in my studio?

I could never envision myself doing angry, mean-spirited talk radio. In fact I can't help remembering what Jerry Williams, one of America's most popular talk show hosts, said to a woman who approached him on a cruise he was hosting. She expressed to him how glad she was to be on the ship with him. His response was something to the effect of, "Ma'am, I'm glad you're on this cruise, but that does not mean I have to talk to you." I'm afraid there are a number of DJs who want to get away from their audience at the end of the day, whereas I seek out opportunities to spend time with mine; I want to be with the people who go to the opera, to the BSO, to Scullers, and everywhere else where wonderful music is being played.

That said, I still had a bit of an actor bug in me, so it was fun to dabble in that. For a year I hosted a show called *Cooking Around Town* at WGBH TV. I'd been approached by a young producer named Laurie Donnelly who has since gone on to become a major PBS television producer. Don't get me wrong: I'm a dunce in the kitchen, but I like knowing how things are done—how to *theoretically* cook a chicken, for example. We'd showcase a different restaurant each episode, interview the chef, then sit down for a memorable meal with chefs such as Gordon Hamersly or Jodie Adams of Rialto.

Amuse Bouche: A Chef's Tale—named after the chef's complimentary appetizer—is a documentary film about Barbara Lynch, a remarkable young woman who came out of the projects in South Boston to make a name for herself as an award-winning chef. Cat Silirie, a dear friend and one of the leading sommeliers in the world, introduced us to Barbara when she was an up and coming chef at Rocco's restaurant in Park Square. Through Barbara and Maryanne Galvin, a prolific filmmaker as well as a practicing forensic psychologist, I was given the chance to narrate the film.

One of seven children in a hard-scrabble Irish Catholic family, Barbara lost her father when she was quite young and was raised by her mother during one of South Boston's most troubled periods. Through sheer determination as well as generosity of spirit, this young woman overcame the poverty, depression, and violence that marked her childhood and rose through the ranks of the culinary world to establish herself in a male-dominated business with a 60 percent failure rate. She won the James Beard award, began Number 9 Park on Beacon Hill, and has since become a nationally recognized chef. By 2010 she had opened Drink, B&G Oysters, The Butcher Shop, and Sportello, and published a terrific cookbook called *Stir*. A real life tale of true grit, *Amuse Bouche* compiled family photographs, archival and animated footage, and exclusive interviews with some of the top names in Boston's culinary world including Lydia Shire, Todd English, and Jodie Adams, as well as a few clips of Mayor Menino, and running legend Bill Rodgers as he served food alongside Lynch at a fundraising race in South Boston.

What an honor that Barbara sought me out to narrate such an intimate, inspiring story.

■ ■ ■

Another friendship, this time with tenor sax innovator Illinois Jacquet, led me to be a part of his story in the (1992) film *Texas Tenor*. The first time I laid eyes on him was at Symphony Hall: I was sixteen years old and his playing knocked me out. One morning, more than thirty years later, Illinois drove all the way from the Sandy's Jazz Revival in Beverly to pay me a visit during an early morning jazz show I was hosting on WGBH. While I was playing one of his recordings, he stepped into the studio with his entourage.

"What's your name, man?"

"Ron Della Chiesa."

"Della Chiesa? Well, I can't remember that. Sounds like it should be Ron Delicatessen. Mind if I call you that?"

How could I say no?

Over the years, we became very close, so close in fact that during my marathon running years he wrote a tune for me called "Running With Ron." One day I got a call from his manager, Carol Scherick, announcing that a film crew would be joining Illinois during our interview on *MusicAmerica*. That segment became a part of Illinois' film, *Texas Tenor*—no connection to the Lone Star state: Jean Batiste Illinois Jacquet was born in Louisiana. "Texas Tenor" refers to a certain style of playing the sax which brings out its greatest sound and volume—an excellent technique for rooms that at the time were rarely miked. The film followed his life and music starting at age nineteen when Lionel Hampton had him change from alto to tenor sax and gave him the opportunity to record his groundbreaking solo "Flying Home."

It was so gratifying to be a part of Arthur Elgort's documentary, which I felt really captured not only Illinois' music, but life and spirit. The camera follows him everywhere from the cramped backstage of the Blue Note jazz club in Manhattan, all the way through Europe on the band's debut tour. Shot in grainy black and white, we eavesdrop as Jacquet reminisces with some fellow jazz musicians aboard a floating junket, visits a saxophone factory, and gives an impromptu performance at Rayburn Music, a well-known instrument repair shop in Boston run by Emilio Lyons. Interviews with world class musicians Dizzy Gillespie, Sonny Rollins, and Les Paul, among others, shed new light on the man, Gillespie making note that Jacquet used to make more money gambling on the tour bus than playing his horn. Low key offstage, Illinois came to life with his instrument, inventing a rompin' stompin' sound that has become a feature of great R&B ever since. I think Jacquet became, finally, aware of his stature as a legend, but only commented, "I just want to be part of something that will last."

■ ■ ■

Every now and then I used to just get in my car and drive, without any destination in mind. Actually, that's a lie. I may have taken the scenic route, stopping for this or that along the way, but my heart knew where I was headed if my brain didn't.

I would sit in my car, eyes closed, and it was if I'd turned the clock back half a century...

Something about Nantasket Beach in Hull always drew me back. I guess the curse of a great childhood is that you wouldn't mind reliving it; in fact you seek it. There is a photograph I have of my mother and me at the beach. In it, I'm only six months old. Perhaps it's a little movie my mind has constructed from staring at the photograph all these years, but I swear I remember the moment I was dipped in the vast Atlantic, screeching as the frothy waves licked at my toes. Afterwards, my mother put me down on the sand. I crawled a few yards away, turned, but didn't see her. Pure panic! But I looked again and there she was, next to our bright yellow and orange umbrella under blue skies, laughing and waving at me, and all was well.

In the background, behind my mother and me on the sand, Paragon Park's roller coaster snaked up and down, riders screeching with delight at each stomach-dropping twist or hairpin turn. Dusk was always the best time at the park; the heat of the day had lifted while the ocean's cool breezes finally turned toward land. The funhouse seemed more fun, the houses of horrors a little more scary. The smells of hot dogs and salt water taffy wafted through the air; boys chased squealing girls around the carousel with horses that rose and fell, rose and fell. There was the Congo cruise, kid's fantasyland, the Schlitz Beergarten. Up in the hills, classic wooden hotels dotted every corner: Nantasket, Rockland, the Atlantic House.

Even as a teenager, there was nothing like a day at Nantasket. There were even magical ways of getting there: A train used to make stops at the beach; boats would drop you off from Boston Harbor. For my old friends and me, it was the endless summer. Paul Antonelli, Bob Buccini, and I used to hang out in a section called Little Weymouth and chase girls. When that wasn't happening, we'd just go on ride after ride till we made ourselves sick.

Heaven!

■ ■ ■

One bitterly cold winter day a few years ago, I was walking along the main drag of Nantasket, when I saw a sign in a window: "Condo For Sale," with a phone number. Next to it was a picture of a pyramid-like building on top of Atlantic Hill, the site of the original Atlantic Hotel. My heart skipped a beat. Caruso had sung there; and I knew that Sarah Bernhardt and Gloria Swanson had both stayed there.

I called Joyce.

Time for fantasy to intersect reality, if at all possible. Joyce had, after all, been asking me to bring her along on one of these nostalgic journeys, and that moment had come. Problem was, she was from Bayridge; would this place that held such sentimental value for me strike the same chord of yearning in her?

We walked around; I talked a lot. I told her that back in the 1880s and '90s this was considered one of the major resorts on the Eastern seaboard. Sure, the roller coasters were gone, Paragon Park razed, but the carousel remained... I told her to close her eyes and imagine a Coney Island of the mind...only in Massachusetts...

I plied her with drinks and dinner at Raffael's, which used to be the Surf Ballroom, another old haunt. All the great bands had played there in the fifties and sixties: Stan Kenton's, Count Basie, Duke Ellington; even Arnie Woo-Woo Ginsberg used to do his record hops there.

We took a look at the unit for sale. The style was Frank Lloyd Wright, each unit unique, angular, with walls of glass where it faced the sea. In fact the building leaned out and over the rocks, so the ocean actually reached beneath a few of the lower units. I gasped when I looked out the windows: I could see

Nantasket Rat Pack: Tony Del Greco, Kathy "Red Sox" Darling, me, J. L. Sullivan, and Joe Giampaolo.

the very spot my mother dipped me in the surf so many years ago. Because Nantasket is on a peninsula, we could see north to Gloucester and Rockport, to Graves Light and Boston's skyline, and to the west where the sun was setting in streaks of orange and purple. We were only four stories up, but we felt like we were at the bow of some giant cruise ship just setting out to sea. Joyce smiled and took my hand, and I finally relaxed. I knew this wasn't the last sunset we'd watch from these windows.

Little did I know that moving to Nantasket would lead me to a community of like-minded souls. Thomas Wolfe said you can't go home again, but in a way I have. I've been lucky enough to find a group of guys who share my history; in fact we've dubbed ourselves the Nantasket Rat Pack. During long, hot summer days we hang out together and tell tales about days gone by. We've even got official titles: Tony Del Greco is the president; Charlie Lopresti, VP; John L. Sullivan, treasurer. Wearing our official orange jackets (Frank Sinatra's favorite color, of course), soaking up the sun, and leaning on the rail in front of Barefoot Bob's, we bring it all back: the big bands, old movies, old radio shows, old flames. It's a beautiful thing to be able to share these memories of the golden age of Nantasket Beach with such dear friends.

■ ■ ■

I think it was Picasso who once said, "At sixty, you know everything, but it's too late to do anything about it." I agree in a way: It may be too late to do some things, such as join the circus or train for the Olympic pole vault; but the way I see it, the world is as rich in beauty and delights as it has always been. I'm not saying time isn't a cooker: There is radio time which couldn't be more black and white: a commercial is 59 seconds long, not a breath more; your live show starts at seven in the morning; there is no such thing as: I was stuck in traffic...being late is not an option in radio. But time is slippery too: I'll remember a trip Joyce and I took and I'll say to her, Wasn't that trip to Normandy last year fantastic? When we visited the beaches there in honor of my father and the sixtieth anniversary of D-Day? And she'll say, Ron that was five years ago...and we'll get into a discussion: Can you believe we've lived in this house ten years now? Or that my first grandchild, Tia, turns seventeen this year?

As time goes by, I am ever more respectful of it. How can I best use it? Listening to an opera is four hours, five and a half, sometimes six. It's certainly not something done quickly, in a soundbite, like so many other things in life these days. For those few hours, it owns you; so I say, give in, let it envelop you, sweep you off to parts unknown. A symphony takes an hour or two. An afternoon to visit a museum. But it took Wagner thirty years to create the Ring Cycle, Caravaggio countless hours to master chiaroscuro, while Puccini didn't even live to complete *Turandot*—don't I owe these people a few hours of my time to witness their work? And then it comes down to choosing even further: I admit a strong bias here, but I've often spoken of how I never really explored the world of rock music. My reasoning is: If I only have limited time, I choose Beethoven, or Verdi, or Handel. I also believe it takes time for people to develop a sense of appreciation, and just as often it takes a guide of sorts to help them get there. Part of the mission of my life is to encourage people to take the time to listen to not only "beautiful" music but challenging music as well.

Besides, for me there's a spirituality in music, almost a mystical quality; it's a constant source of sustenance. And seriously, if you're listening to Debussy's "Afternoon of a Faun" or "La Mer," it's impossible to experience road rage.

And what about friendship? Of the hundreds of people one meets in a lifetime, it eventually becomes clear that true connections are rare and wonderful, and worth the time to explore. My friendship with Tony Bennett has been life-changing for me. Of course I'd been a life-long admirer of his incredible singing, but I never dreamed we would have so much in common both musically and aesthetically. We even reacted the same way when we first saw the Sistine Chapel: we were both so moved we broke into tears.

In so many ways he reminds me of my father: he's a true Renaissance man. He not only paints on canvas, he creates masterful song pictures with his voice. When he sings the lyrics, you feel he's not only singing directly to you, but that he's lived every word. There's a tear in his voice, a genuine melancholy. And yet the man can swing! When he's upbeat, the euphoria is palpable. He's over eighty years old and his voice is in incredible shape, hitting the top notes like a much younger man.

But beyond the talent, Tony is a human being who cares deeply about people, and I think that's what has really kept our friendship alive. He's always asked about my family, while over the years Joyce and I have become a sort of surrogate aunt and uncle to Antonia, his youngest child, especially during the years she studied voice at Berklee and delighted us with her visits. Here's an icon, known worldwide, who's the warmest human being I know. He'll walk in the room with his wide smile and light it up and it's not an act, it's just Tony.

So it all comes back to time: time flies; time is precious, decades pass more quickly than years; so at seventy-three, timing is everything. I didn't think about sixty, though fifty gave me pause. In another seven years, I'll be eighty. Now *that's* interesting; I may actually put that in my date book: "Think about this one." But as long as everything goes as well as it has for me, I'm just a zen guy, hosting the BSO on Saturdays, walking Nantasket Beach with Joyce, and drinking my Diet Yahoo. I feel blessed and lucky to be healthy, even as I mourn dear friends who have passed. But they say eighty is the new seventy, which makes seventy-three the new sixty-three...which sounds swinging to me!

After all, many have said our essence doesn't change over time; we only become more intensely who we are. Joyce Curel watched me at work one day and then observed in a 1992 *Post-Gazette* article: "In his small studio, Della Chiesa is the orchestra's conductor—one hand flipping the records, the other answering the phone, one eye on the clock, the other on the promo sheet, a quick smile to the visitor, feet tapping 1-2-3 the beat, thoughts focused on the upcoming 2:01 PM network news tie-in. He is a boy at play. 'Isn't this fun?' he chuckles."[15]

A boy at play—she got that right.

As Louis Armstrong sang, "What a wonderful world!"

PROFILES

I. THE WORLD OF OPERA

1. LUCIANO PAVAROTTI
King of the High C's

Luciano Pavarotti

Photo: The Metropolitan Opera Archives.

It was over thirty years ago, driving to work and listening to the Metropolitan Opera broadcast of *L'elisir d'amore*, when I first heard Pavarotti sing. I was so thunderstruck by the power and beauty of his voice that I had to pull off the road. He stopped the show, literally: the ovation after his aria, "Una furtiva lagrima," went on for close to three minutes. His voice swept me right back to those of the classic tenors I'd grown up listening to, huddled around the radio so many years ago.

Each spring the Metropolitan Opera toured and performed several operas in Boston at the Hynes Auditorium, a rather soulless building in my opinion; however, it was the only venue large enough to accommodate an audience of four thousand as well as the company's lavish sets. Unfortunately, our own beautiful Boston Opera House met the fate of the wrecking ball in the 1950s.

In the early 1970s I was hosting a weekly opera program on WGBH radio in which I interviewed many of the singers on the tour. Needless to say, there was a great deal of excitement for the scheduled appearance of this new young tenor who was the talk of the opera world.

He had been scheduled to appear in Boston to sing in Donizetti's *The Daughter of the Regiment*, an opera he had already performed at the Metropolitan in New York. This opera is the ultimate test for any tenor; it contains an aria with nine high C's. Pavarotti had just recorded an LP entitled *King of the High C's*, already a best seller.

My friend Francis Robinson, assistant manager of the Met, was kind enough to set up an interview via telephone with Luciano at his home in New York City. He told me the tenor's English wasn't that good, but I assured him I'd manage with my libretto Italian. The next day I placed the call and the tenor answered sweetly, "Pronto!"

Our conversation touched on many subjects, including his early days growing up in the city of Modena, where he was born in 1935. His father was a baker who also had a lovely voice and sang in the local church choir. Luciano began to listen to some of his father's favorite opera recordings that included the voices of Caruso, Gigli, and Bjoerling.

When the legendary tenor Beniamino Gigli came to sing in Modena, Luciano had the opportunity to meet him after one of his rehearsals. Young Luciano told him he wanted to be a tenor when he grew up. Gigli patted him on the head and said, "Bravo! Ragazzino, but you must work very hard!" Luciano told me that was the best advice anyone ever gave him, since from that day he'd never stopped studying. The meeting with Gigli was pivotal, because it was then, at the age of twelve, that Luciano made the decision to become a singer.

When I brought up the subject of the great Caruso he said: "As for Caruso, there are no comparisons. To me he is the tenor against whom all the rest of us are measured. To try and imitate his voice, you will destroy yours!"

One of the most charming moments in our interview was when we talked about his childhood days with his hometown friend, soprano Mirella Freni. In later years they were to sing all over the world together. Luciano said, "Mirella and I did everything together except sleep together…we studied voice, attended the opera, partied with friends who shared the same interests, and most important of all, we were 'milk babies' together; we shared the same 'wet nurse'! There must have been something very special in that milk!"

We discussed some of his favorite roles, and without hesitation he chose Rodolfo in Puccini's *La Boheme*. He made his debut in that role in April of 1961 in Italy, and it also served as his debut at the Met in 1968. In many of those performances, his Mimi was his dear friend Mirella Freni.

Some twenty years after our interview, I met Luciano again. He was making a movie, *Yes, Giorgio* in Boston and was scheduled to give a concert on the Esplanade on the Charles River, which was to be used in the movie. Thousands of people packed the grounds. Following the concert, he kindly signed his book, *Pavarotti, My Own Story,* for me. At this point in his career, he was the undisputed reigning tenor of the day.

Walter Pierce, at that time the director of the Boston Celebrity Series, was the gentleman largely responsible for bringing Luciano back to Boston's Symphony Hall for recitals on numerous occasions. These events became almost yearly and were always sold out. One evening Walter scheduled a post-concert dinner at the Wang Center with the great tenor. I'll never forget the sight of Pavarotti eating pasta with one hand and signing autographs with the other!

When Luciano died in 2007, Italy and the world mourned for months. The outpouring of love and affection at his funeral was overwhelming. I received dozens of calls from listeners all over the country asking to hear his music. National Public Radio aired a tribute in which they included my 1972 interview with him, one of his first on radio. A PBS special on his life raised more money for the station than any in history.

He was an exuberant, larger-than-life man who succeeded in bringing opera to the masses, not only through "The Three Tenors" phenomenon, which won him millions of fans, but through his appearances on *Johnny Carson* and *Saturday Night Live*, as well as performances with everyone from Barry White to Celine Dion and Vanessa Williams.

SUGGESTED RECORDINGS

Pavarotti's Greatest Hits: The Ultimate Collection

This two-CD collection is a must for Pavarotti lovers. He sings most of the famous tenor arias known the world over including "Nessun dorma," which became his signature showpiece during his period of "The Three Tenors."
London/Decca 2LH2458000

Tutto Pavarotti

Another two-CD set devoted primarily to Italian song by Tosti, Leoncavallo, Lucio Dalla, and others. The great Caruso made many of these songs famous during the early days of recording.
Decca 425681

Volare with Henry Mancini and His Orchestra

This unique collection presents Pavarotti in a collaboration with Henry Mancini who did the arrangements of popular favorites such as the title song made famous by Dean Martin. It gives us a chance to hear Luciano in a lighthearted mood, and he charms us all!
Decca

The Incomparable

Placido Domingo

Photo: The Metropolitan Opera Archives.

My first encounter with Placido Domingo was in the mid-1960s when I was working for radio station WBCN, which at that time stood for Boston Concert Network. During those years the station was devoted 24/7 to classical music and opera. The studios were located at 171 Newbury Street in a cozy attic jammed with LPs, a newswire, and a small recording suite. Directly across the street was the headquarters of the Opera Company of Boston and its legendary music director, Sarah Caldwell.

My colleague Nat Johnson and I were given the responsibility of recording all of Sarah's operas for her own personal archives. One of those operas happened to be Puccini's *La Boheme*, which featured the great Renata Tebaldi and the young tenor Placido Domingo. At that time, Domingo had already performed numerous roles with the New York City Opera and was well on his way to becoming an established name in the opera world.

It turned out to be a magnificent performance. I invited the young tenor to join me in our modest studios for an interview. He graciously consented, and we talked about his early days as a singer. Born in Madrid in 1941, he told me both his parents were well known performers of a special kind of operetta known as "Zarzeula," a Spanish lyric-dramatic genre that alternates between spoken and sung scenes. The family later settled in Mexico where they formed their own company. It was there the young tenor started to seriously study voice. He had his major breakthrough in the New York City Opera with his debut as Pinkerton in *Madama Butterfly*. From that moment his career took off, and he began to perform in the world's major opera houses.

At the end of our interview, I congratulated him and thanked him for his time. He said, "I enjoyed it...tell me, do you have a piano somewhere?"

I replied, "Unfortunately no; this is a low budget operation."

"Too bad...I would be happy to record some arias for your show."

To this day I regret that I was unable to record Domingo. What a tape that would have been!

My next meeting with him followed his debut at the Metropolitan Opera. The Met had come to Boston for the annual Spring Tour in 1972, and I attended a performance of *Andrea Chenier* at the cavernous Hynes Auditorium. The title role was being sung by the great tenor Franco Corelli; and the baritone, Anselmo Colzani, was having vocal difficulties. An announcement was made during intermission that despite his indisposition, he would continue with his performance. While in the lobby, I spotted Domingo and reintroduced myself. He remembered our interview and remarked that he was covering for Corelli. I asked if this was one of his favorite roles and without hesitation he replied, "Oh yes...I've sung it several times along with the baritone role, and I can conduct it also!"

From those days to today, Domingo reigns supreme, singing well over a hundred and fifteen roles in Italian, French, German, Russian, Spanish, and English; everything from works by Tchaikovsky to Wagner's *Parsifal*, to even more obscure roles such as Alfano in *Cyrano de Bergerac*. He is also an established conductor, Artistic Director at both the Los Angeles Opera and Washington National Opera, teacher, and a great champion of young singers. As the late Beverly Sills mentioned in the preface to the book *Domingo, My Operatic Roles*, "he has the charisma of a rock star, the charm of a movie star, the voice of a god, and superstar is written all over him."[16]

Another critic once said, "If Pavarotti is the King of the High C's, then Domingo is undoubtedly the King of Opera."[17] I recently heard him sing a performance of *Otello*. Although in his mid-sixties at the time, his voice rang out as clear and strong as if he were still the young tenor I heard in Boston all those many years ago.

Suggested Recordings

Bravo Domingo

A two-CD collection of arias and songs by Puccini, Rossini, Verdi, Donizetti, Mascagni, Weber, and Bizet.

DG 459352

Domingo Songbook

Selections include:

> "Maria"
> "Siboney"
> "Besame Mucho"
> "Autumn Leaves"
> "Time After Time"
> "Annie's Song"
> "Moon River"

Sony MDK 48299

Domingo: Scenes from Wagner's Ring

This collection features highlights from *Siegfried* and *Gotterdammerung*.

EMI 557242-2

Placido Domingo Sings Caruso

Domingo in a program of arias made famous by the great tenor.

RCA 09026613562

Viva Verdi!

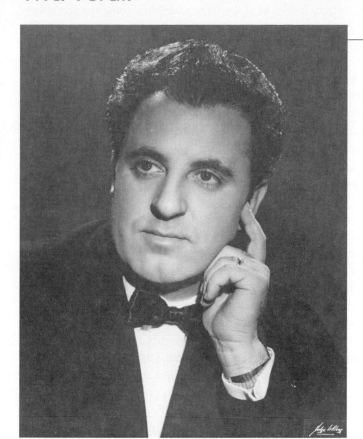
Carlo Bergonzi

Photo: The Metropolitan Opera Archives.

In the fall of 1988, I was invited by Phyllis Curtin, the head of the Boston University opera department (herself a renowned singer), to observe a master class given by Carlo Bergonzi. With the aid of good friend and translator Gino Gemmato, I was also given the opportunity to interview the maestro directly following the class.

Born in 1924, Carlo Bergonzi is a tenor who is mostly associated with the operas of Giuseppe Verdi, including many lesser-known works which he helped revive. Known for his superb diction and elegant phrasing, he is also acclaimed for his attention to style required in Verdi's operas.

The master class itself proved a transforming event to witness. Carlo was coaching a young soprano, and as an exercise had her sing an aria from *La Boheme*. He prompted her to sing the aria measure by measure, and after she vocalized each phrase, he sang it back to her. We all sat mesmerized as we witnessed a kind of metamorphosis. Carlo examined everything—the phrasing, interpretation, meaning, tempo—conducting her as if she were an orchestra unto herself. He stopped her phrase by phrase, word by word, even syllable by syllable to make her think about what exactly she was singing and ultimately delivering to her audience. It was as if we were watching someone learn how to hear, then vocalize, in a way that united meaning, emotion, and sound. I've never witnessed anything like it before or since. By the time she'd sung it the second or third time, she'd created a whole new interpretation of the aria. It was like watching a musical butterfly emerge from a cocoon, the way Carlo drew fresh notes out of her, transforming her and the piece entirely.

Carlo granted us just a few minutes of his time after the master class, but we were still able to glean some wonderful insights into his world before he was off to his next engagement.

On Busseto, Verdi's hometown, Carlo said: "There is something in the air that has produced great voices. The town is steeped in music! From the time they are children, everyone is encouraged to sing, both in church and at home. The spirit of Giuseppe Verdi is everywhere you look: there are posters of him in stores, portraits of him in the town hall, and of course at the Verdi library. Every year, young singers gather to study, to train in Busseto at the school I founded, the Academia du Bussettiana.* For two months a year, we host between eighteen and twenty students chosen from all over the world, and every June there's a contest among the students where only the best of those are chosen to perform."

On vocal longevity: "Never forget the phrasing of the diaphragm. If you don't study technique, you will not sing properly. There is no such thing as a closed sound or an open sound, only a covered sound. What is a covered sound? To place the breath on the diaphragm and turn the sound in the mask, abolishing the closed and open sound. These are the best medicines for longevity.

"You must remember that the life of a singer is a life of great sacrifice. Every single morning of the forty years of my career—summer, winter, during vacations, no matter what my schedule—I never neglected my exercises. I vocalize for forty minutes and do breathing exercises for half an hour. This is the way to preserve the voice."

On the use of modern day settings for operas: "Earlier you mentioned *Rigoletto* set in little Italy. This phenomenon doesn't even exist for me. I am a traditionalist. I believe operas should be performed the way composers intended at the time they were written; however, I do believe greater emphasis should be placed on strong acting ability, rather than the singer just standing there singing. But again, I believe it would be ridiculous to see Rigoletto dressed in contemporary clothes; the opera was written in 1850! Please don't misinterpret me—I'm not against young directors, I know directors who are great talents; but the system should remain the same, the traditions must remain the same. I admire Zeffirelli and Ponnelle because somehow they're successful in keeping the basic spirit of

*Now known as the Academia Verdiana

the composer while bringing them into contemporary times. I loved, for example, singing with Renata Tebaldi for the soundtrack of *Moonstruck*."

On classic Verdi phrasing: "What is lacking today is the ability to sing the true Verdi phrasing, which is one of the reasons these students came to Busetto. There are some very fine voices around, but they don't know the Verdi phrasing."

On his legacy: "I've had the great fortune of singing in the golden age of opera. God has given me the longevity to sing with Renata Tebaldi, Leontyne Price, Joan Sutherland, Birgit Nilsson, Carlo Tagliabue, and Robert Merrill, and to work with conductors such as Bruno Walter, Tullio Serafin, Georg Solti, and Fausto Cleva."

On his connection with Gigli: "I am one of his greatest fans and have had the wonderful fortune of singing baritone to Gigli's tenor: as Marcello in *La Boheme*, Belcore in *L'elisir d'amore*, and Germont in *La Traviata*. He was like a father to me. I'll never forget his generosity, especially with his advice to young people. What good luck I had to know him as an artist and a human being. I'm looking forward to paying tribute to him on the hundredth anniversary of his birth, which is in 1990. I want to celebrate the man who has not only inspired my own life's work but to also help young singers as he has helped me."

Now retired, Bergonzi spends most of his time at I due Foscari, a beautiful hotel in Busseto, which Joyce and I have visited many times.

SUGGESTED RECORDINGS

Carlo Bergonzi — The Sublime Voice

Opera aria and scenes by Puccini, Verdi, Mascagni, Leoncavallo, Cilea, and
  Ponchielli.

Decca 467-023-2

Esultate!

James McCracken

From the Howard Gotlieb Archival Research Center at Boston University.

A contemporary of Placido Domingo, James McCracken began his career singing comprimario roles, or minor roles such as pages. He made his debut at the Met in 1953 as the toy vendor in *La Boheme*, but left in 1957 because Rudolph Bing refused to offer him any major roles. James quickly realized he wasn't getting anywhere with these secondary parts and took to heart that he had more potential as a singer than these roles offered, ultimately deciding to take himself to Europe to build up his repertoire.

Upon his return, James found that Bing had changed his tune. McCracken had come back so strong from overseas, evolving into such a talent that he simply could no longer be ignored. Critics flipped over him. He had built up valuable experience singing big roles including Otello repeatedly in Bonn, then in Zurich, gradually coming to the attention of the larger European houses. He specialized in the biggest Italian parts: Calaf in *Turandot*, the tragic clown, Canio, in *Pagliacci*, and the Verdian heroes of *Aida*, *Il Trovatore*, and *La forza del destino*.

The high point in his career came in the early 1970s when he starred in new productions in five consecutive seasons at the Met: *Otello*, *Carmen*, *Aida*, *Le Prophete*, and *Tannhauser*, his first Wagnerian part, which he accepted after declining many earlier offers to sing Wagner.

In Norfolk, Virginia, in 1954, he sang in a concert performance of *Samson et Dalilah* with mezzo-soprano Sandra Warfield, and the two were married soon after that. In short order, Warfield had a Met contract as well—slightly better than the tenor's, but still modest. They had four roles between them by 1955: they sang Nathanael and the Voice of Antonia's Mother in the matinee of *Les Contes D'Hoffmann*, then the Judge and Ulrica in *Un Ballo in Maschera*.

McCracken was a true dramatic tenor, a larger-than-life character possessed of a dark voice with tremendous power. Yet in person, he was the kind of guy you felt like having a couple of beers with. A big, burly presence with a great white mane of hair, he exuded the gruff aura of a man who might work in a steel mill. As an actor onstage he was completely involved in the role.

I'll never forget his performance of Otello in Providence in May of 1985 when he shook the rafters. I visited him backstage afterward, and found him sitting in his dressing room, his daughter blow-drying his hair off his face to cool him down. I told him it was one of the most powerful performances of Otello I'd ever witnessed and he said, "Thanks, but I think I could have done better," in his oddly high speaking voice.

During our 1983 *MusicAmerica* interview, he asked if he could vocalize along with himself as Otello in the death scene. What an unforgettable show: listening to McCracken on record along with the real live McCracken in the studio.

He also commented on the vagaries of critics: "Twenty-five hundred people could have enjoyed a performance, but then twenty-five hundred more could read a bad review and decide not to come." And on his own battles with stage fright: "I have my own profound inner turmoil going on before each and every performance. Let me tell you, you earn your money before the opera even begins. But then, after your first at bat, you just settle."

Here was a man who had an incredibly charismatic presence even before opening his mouth to sing, yet he sang like there was no tomorrow. His face reddened with concentration each time he vocalized from what sounded like the bottom of his feet. He used that voice to fill enormous auditoriums, and in the end, his technique proved equal to the challenge of sustaining a thirty-year-plus career, most of it at the top of his profession.

SUGGESTED RECORDINGS

McCracken Onstage with the Vienna Opera Orchestra

Arias from *Il Travatore, Faust, La forza del destino, Die Meistersinger, Tannhauser,* and *Otello.* James McCracken was at the peak of his vocal powers when he recorded this collection in 1965.
Decca CD 475 6233

"Gurrelieder" by Arnold Schoenberg

James McCracken teams up with soprano Jessye Norman, the Boston Symphony Orchestra, and the Tanglewood Festival Chorus, conducted by Seija Ozawa in this 1979 Gramophone award-winning recording.
Philips—CD 475-7782

Hip Heldentenor

Ben Heppner

Author's collection.

Ben Heppner is one of today's leading tenors. Born in Canada, he was a finalist at the 1988 Met Opera auditions and won top honors when he received the first Birgit Nilsson prize in the same year. He has enjoyed singing in the world's great opera houses and concert halls and has recorded with some of the foremost singers and orchestras of our time.

His vast repertoire encompasses such diverse roles as Calaf in *Turandot,* the title roles in *Lohengrin, Tristan and Isolde, Peter Grimes, Otello, Andrea Chenier, Samson et Dalila,* and Florestan in *Fidelio,* to name just a few.

No other tenor today combines the lyric beauty of the voice of Jussi Bjoerling with the stamina and power of Lawrence Melchior. Along with his intelligent musicianship and sparkling dramatic sense, Ben has set new standards in one of the most demanding repertoires in all opera.

He has been honored on numerous occasions for his recordings and performances including being named a member of the prestigious "Order of Canada" in 1999. Ben even has a street named after him in Dawson Creek, British Columbia.

During our first interview in 1999, we spent a good hour discussing his career and his fascination with jazz and the popular songs he heard on the radio as a youngster. He told me that much of his early education was simply listening to the voices of Nelson Eddy, Vera Lynn, Jeanette MacDonald, and his mother's favorite, Mario Lanza. Some of his fondest memories from childhood were of those days surrounded by music at home and in church.

At the time we talked, Ben had just released his first "non operatic" CD entitled *My Secret Heart: Songs of the Parlour, Stage and Silver Screen.* He shared with me that these songs were chosen with his mother (who was born in 1910) in mind: they're all in English and all love songs. These are the songs he imagined she would have heard on the radio growing up, from the first one: "Roses of Picardy," to the last: "Be My Love."

During the course of our interview, we played almost the entire collection from *My Secret Heart.* The phone began ringing off the hook with listeners clamoring to find out where to get this CD. To this day, this collection remains his favorite of his many recordings.

The evening of our interview, my wife Joyce and I attended his recital in Jordan Hall at New England Conservatory. Ben had mentioned that it was one of his favorite halls to sing in. Known for both its stellar acoustics and intimacy, Jordan Hall remains the perfect venue for many of the world's greatest artists.

Among the many attending the sold-out recital that evening was another friend, the great Irish actor Shay Duffin. It turned out that Shay was a big fan of Ben's and was in town performing his one-man show: *Confessions of an Irish Rebel,* based on the life of Brendan Behan.

The recital was a tour de force and included arias, lieder, as well as songs from the new CD, *My Secret Heart.* When Ben sang "Roses of Picardy," I watched as tears streamed down Shay's cheeks. Heppner received a standing ovation. The night was an unquestionable triumph, both critically and emotionally.

Ben has been back in Boston numerous times since, appearing not only at Jordan Hall, but with the Boston Symphony Orchestra and the Berlin Philharmonic in Mahler's *Das Lied Von Der Erde,* singing with the great bass baritone Thomas Quastoff. He continues to add roles to his already vast repertoire including Siegfried, the ultimate test of any Heldentenor.

Some of the qualities that endear Heppner to his many fans all over the world are his unpretentious personality, humor, and good nature. During a performance of *Parsifal* at the Met, Ben (singing the title role in the final scene) raises the chalice high to give communion to the knights of the holy grail. In this pivotal scene, the chalice is supposed to glow bright red in a totally darkened theater, while Wagner's music surges passionately, creating a fantastically dramatic effect. In this instance, the chalice remained completely dark.

Afterwards, Joyce and I went to see him backstage. I said, "Ben, you were so godly as Parsifal, I hope you'll hear my confession."

"But the light in the chalice didn't go on; did you notice that?"

"Yeah, but you pulled it off anyway."

In the end, he had the good humor to laugh it off, and we all went out for a beer.

In a 2004 interview, Ben had some fascinating things to say about James Levine, then Music Director of the Boston Symphony Orchestra.

Regarding the rehearsal process, Ben said: "James Levine is the only one who gets to know you instead of giving pedantic notes such as: faster, you're flat, more crisp, etc.—those are given, but by musical assistants. He looks at the big picture—your personality. He understands you as a person first, *then* leads you through the performance. He always phones before a performance and during intermission, and if things aren't going that well—he may say I can see you're struggling, but he'll say I'm with you all the way. He provides a level of support that's unique in a *way* that's unique.

"James is very concerned about the connective tissue between notes—it's always an issue for him to follow the Italian tradition in this way—and after a while all I would need to do was follow minute movements of his hands to make these vocal transitions. During the final two weeks of rehearsal for *Otello* I requested a few hours of coaching with him and it's funny, we didn't play it, we just talked it through, and it was enormously helpful. He just has this special way of dealing with people."

In the spring of 2010, in Dallas, Texas, Joyce and I had the privilege of hearing Ben in a magnificent performance of an opera based on Melville's *Moby Dick* by Jake Heggie and Gene Scheer.

SUGGESTED RECORDINGS

Ben Heppner: Great Tenor Arias

Selections include some of the most popular and best loved arias from *Aida*,
    Carmen, Turandot, Manon Lescaut, Andrea Chenier, and other operas.
RCA 090126-62504-2

Ben Heppner Sings Ricard Strauss with the Toronto Symphony Orchestra

Conducted by Andrew Davis

A magnificently sung collection of arias from *Daphne, Guntram, Intermezzo,*
    Die Frau ohne Schatten, Der Rosenkavalier, and other Strauss operas.
CBC SMCD5142

Ideale: Ben Heppner: Songs of Paolo Tosti

A must for any lover of Italian song by the so-called "Prince of Melody."
Selections include:

    "Ideale"
    "A vucchella"
    "Entra"

"Vorrei morire"
"Seconda mattinata"
"Chitarrata abruzzese"

DGB 0001850-02

My Secret Heart: Songs of the Parlour, Stage and Silver Screen

Ben's personal favorite and mine, too.
Selections include:

"Roses of Picardy"
"I'll See You Again"
"Serenade"
"The Desert Song"
"Be My Love"
"I'll Follow My Secret Heart"

RCA 09026-63508-2

6. MARCELLO GIORDANI

La Dolce Vita

Marcello Giordani

Photo: The Metropolitan Opera Archives.

I had the great pleasure of interviewing tenor Marcello Giordani for the WGBH Forum in January of 2009. Born in 1963 in the small Sicilian town of Augusta, Marcello showed talent at an early age, taking private lessons in his church choir. He finally left a job in a bank and moved to Milan to study voice with Nino Carta.

As he tells it: "My father was a big opera fan. He always wanted one of his children to sing, or at least to love opera. I'm the youngest of four, and the other brothers couldn't care less about it. I was twelve years old when my father played my first opera for me; I heard Jussi Bjoerling and Giuseppi Di Stefano and fell immediately in love. I used to sing along with the recordings—probably a little too loudly, but my father encouraged me. My love for singing grew more powerful every day.

"I moved to Catania when I was eighteen and studied with Maria Gentile, but I won my first competitions in Spoleto in 1996, eventually coming to New York to study technique. Twenty-five years later I'm still here, now with my wife and two sons; and now I consider the Met my second home, and America my second land, or country. The truth is—when I was in my twenties, Europe wasn't interested in me. I'm lucky to be here where the opera community feels more forgiving, more supportive of young singers, indulgent of mistakes developing singers might make. I'm very thankful."

On keeping the voice in shape: "There are four thousand seats at the Met and no mics, so you need to fill that house with your voice. The very last person in the very last row has to hear you, even if you are singing pianissimo.

"Some say it's like sports. We are vocal athletes responsible for training the muscles of the voice. I vocalize every single day, try to be healthy, be careful what I eat, not drink too much, not smoke, of course, or ever be in an environment with smoke. It's kind of a boring life. I'm also mindful of not talking when I don't need to.

"I was always very conscious of choosing my repertoire because it affects my voice. My feeling is that I have a gift and I need to take care of it not just for myself, but for those who come to hear me. There are so many different shades of tenor, but now, after thirty years of singing, at age forty-six I know I'm a lirico spinto. I never pushed myself to be this; perhaps people believe I could have been singing a heavier repertoire, but this is how my voice has developed naturally."

On learning a role: "My approach certainly has evolved over the years. At first I would just learn my part, that's it; then I learned that didn't work! Hey, I was young...of course now I know I need to understand the context—the whole story. Now I have a routine: first, I learn the real history surrounding the story, read everything I can about the composer's own process, the concepts or thinking behind a piece of work, then I go over the libretto. My second step is to look at the orchestral score, if I have it. See which instrument is playing at certain points in the score...sometimes it all makes sense and sometimes not as much, so I ask the conductor: why this instrument at this moment and not another one? It's an interesting, beautiful process. My next step is to study with my vocal coach and my pianist, and after that I listen to whatever other versions of the role I can get my hands on."

On recalling roles, often years later: "It's amazing how the brain retains what it's been exposed to. The music will bring you to the words. Maybe I haven't sung a role for five years, if I hear a certain phrase of music, it comes to me like I sang it yesterday. In fact, if I made a mistake somewhere in the score five years ago, or had vocal trouble of some kind, five years later the music will cue me to make the same mistake. It's maddening, because when I was younger I made so many mistakes with so many operas, used the wrong rhythm or vocal position. I'll catch myself making the same mistakes I made twenty years ago! It takes so much work to retrain the brain and the muscles, it's unbelievable."

The affect of high definition TV on opera: "It's made a big difference in so many ways. Instead of reaching four thousand in one night we can hopefully reach millions. People who would never otherwise know my name approach me now. And it makes *us* more aware of what we're doing. It's a challenge, because now the camera is on us and we can't break our concentration. It's a great way to critique myself as well."

On keys to success: "Even though I have roles I'm comfortable in, I choose to be versatile. I don't want to be thought of as only being able to sing Italian opera. I'm lucky because I'm able to switch roles, vary my repertoire. I'm in a privileged position; at this point I'm able to really choose what I want to sing. This is the best job on earth, and I do it with great joy."

Any opportunity you have to hear this remarkable singer is not to be missed. Giordani is the real thing, a true Italian tenor in the great tradition of Gigli, Del Monaco, and Bergonzi.

SUGGESTED RECORDINGS

Marcello Giordani—tenor arias by Bellini, Donizetti, Mascagni, Rossini, Verdi, and Bizet
NAXOS 8557269

"Knew Them All!"

Norman Kelley with me wearing Shuisky costume

Author's collection.

Born in Maine in 1911, Norman Kelley was one of the most unforgettable characters I've ever known. I was just leaving a Met opera audition in the early 1990s when he was pointed out to me as someone I should meet. Even though he was in his eighties at the time, I was struck by his fireplug energy and simply his joy in being Norman Kelley. That night we went out for dinner, and both Joyce and I fell in love with this charismatic dynamo of a man who prided himself on knowing everyone from Carmen Miranda to Jose Ferrer to Gigli, even a number of singers who opened the original 1883 Metropolitan Opera House!

He clearly hailed from a different era. Always elegant, always dramatic, from the way he tilted his chin just so, to the way he walked into a room—even the way he posed under the lights—Norman was a joy to be around. When asked about any opera singer alive he would spout, "I knew them all! Every single one!"

The fact is, he did know them all. His career went back to the 1930s where, as a young man, he performed at the Radio City Music Hall. From there he worked his way into opera. His first big break came at the Met when he sang Herod in *Salome.* He went on at the last minute, the third cover after two replacements became unavailable. When he finally walked out onstage, the woman singing the role of Salome had no idea who he was. After this performance he received a note from Rudolph Bing, of which he was quite proud, and which he would often quote: "From now on, all of the Herods will be sung by Mr. Kelley."

Norman also sang the role of Mime (an extremely challenging role) opposite Wolfgang Windgassen, a well-known tenor at the time, in an otherwise all-German cast of *The Ring.* Reviews singled Kelley out as one of the best in the cast—though at the time he didn't speak a word of German.

After thirty-five years in New York, Norman left the state and settled in Easton, Massachusetts, where he stored all of his costumes in a series of trunks in his new home. He worked a great deal with Sarah Caldwell and the Opera Company of Boston on projects including *Good Soldier Schweik* by Robert Kurka. He also learned Russian and French operas by rote since he didn't speak any Russian or French.

One such role was Prince Shuisky in *Boris Godunov*, which he sang in a production directed by Sarah Caldwell in the mid sixties. Singing the title role was Boris Christoff, one of the greatest interpreters of the Czar. During a rehearsal of the final scene in which the tormented Czar falls from his throne and dies, Norman calmly stepped over the prostrate Christoff and ascended the steps to take his seat on the throne. He told me that as he did so he could hear the enraged Christoff muttering, "How dare you upstage me you porco miseria (miserable pig); this is *my* music, Mr. Kelley!" To which Kelley replied, "My dear Mr. Christoff, please tell me where it says that in the score?"

Finally Norman did learn German; in fact, he is perhaps best known for his translation of *Hansel and Gretel* into English from the German, a translation used all over the world to this day. This work generated handsome residuals for him for many years to come. When the Met revived *Hansel and Gretel* in the nineties he proudly invited Joyce and me to the performance for which he rented box seats.

Some of the most memorable times with Norman have to include an Opera tour we took together in 1997, a two-week journey in the Mediterranean. I'll never forget walking around Istanbul with Norman as he instructed passersby who were smoking to quit this ugly habit: "Put that down! It's bad for you, bad, bad, bad! Don't you know it's bad for you?" When he wasn't saving people from themselves, he would be strutting all over the ship, getting to know everyone, inviting them to our table, especially if he suspected they were lonely, and never forgetting to fill them in on his career: "I sang over 600 performances of 'The Consul'! I knew them all—sang them all, every single one of them!"

Norman put on elaborate soirees at his home in Easton, where he'd open up his trunks full of costumes and let everyone wear whatever they wanted. He had an entire barn filled with opera memorabilia: letters, programs, props, costumes, wigs, backdrops. If it had to do with opera, he had it squirreled away in that barn.

These were wonderful evenings, full of laughter and singing. He loved supporting the careers of young singers and encouraged them to perform with him during these parties. I remember him saying, "Someday you'll get old and you'll know what it's like, but you've got to keep going, you've just got to do it! You've got to go forward." To this day I miss his outrageous *joie de vivre,* his flamboyant spirit, and his inspiring love for life and music.

Norman died at the ripe old age of ninety-six, and left over twelve hundred vocal scores and his recordings to the New England Conservatory of Music in Boston. He also donated a magnificent portrait of the American soprano Lillian Nordica (also born in Maine) to the Metropolitan Opera.

The Opera Couple

Photo: The Metropolitan Opera Archives.

Richard Cassilly

Photo: The Metropolitan Opera Archives.

Patricia Craig

Richard Cassilly trained in Baltimore, where he won the Arthur Godfrey Talent Scout Show in the early 1950s singing "Macushla," an Irish song made famous by John McCormick. He studied voice, married, started a family, and performed for several years at the New York City Opera Company before moving to Europe with his family to kickstart his career, a path similar to that of James McCracken. He landed in Hamburg, where he became a renowned heldentenor, a "heroic" tenor specializing in Wagner and other rigorous Germanic roles.

By the mid-1960s he had sung leading roles with almost every major opera house in Europe, including La Scala, the Opera National de Paris, the Vienna State Opera, and the Bavarian State Opera. Cassilly also forged a strong collaborative partnership with the Royal Opera in London, appearing in that house almost every year from 1968–1982. In 1978 he joined the roster of principal tenors at the Metropolitan in New York, where he spent the majority of his time until his retirement in 1990. His repertoire at the Met was incredibly wide, including Herod in *Salome*, as well as extremely demanding roles in operas by Berg, Schoenberg, Benjamin Britten, and Dalla Piccola. The *New York Times* described him as "a burly tenor with a bright ping on the top notes who had a supple lyric quality [to his voice]," and "was known to bring a musical intelligence and uncommonly clear diction to his work."[18] His portrayal in the title role in Benjamin Britten's opera *Peter Grimes* was praised by the composer as one of the finest he had ever seen.

Richard's life changed forever one evening when he played Don Jose opposite a very beautiful Micaela. Patricia Craig was a brown-eyed stunner, a soprano beloved for her Puccini and Verdi heroines, including *Madame Butterfly* and *La Boheme*. Very soon after their meeting, Richard's first marriage ended and he married Patricia. He had found his soul mate.

I'll never forget the evening Pat saved a performance of *The Queen of Spades* for Seiji Ozawa when the soprano Mirella Freni lost her voice. Ozawa was hours from canceling the performance when he enlisted Pat to take over the role for the evening. Everyone else who knew the role could sing it in Russian; Pat could sing the role, but only in Italian, which she did. Pat always sang with incredible passion; she reminded me and many others especially of Renata Tebaldi.

As their careers began to wind down, Richard and Pat moved to Brookline, Massachusetts, where they both became teachers: Richard taught at Boston University, while Pat taught at the New England Conservatory.

I first met Richard during a master class taught by Carlo Bergonzi at Boston University. It wasn't long before Richard, Pat, Joyce, and I bonded and began sharing good food, restaurants, and opera stories. They were like your average couple next door, except they just happened to sing roles like Peter Grimes, Mimi, Tannhauser, Otello, Billy Budd, and Tosca!

A big, burly Paul Bunyan type, Richard loved beer and oysters. For a time, he and I would haunt a restaurant in Brookline, where every Wednesday, oysters were a quarter each from five to seven in the evening. We showed up hungry week after week and kept on ordering dozens upon dozens of oysters until finally they canceled the special.

Richard also loved to cook, and he and Joyce were constantly sharing recipes. Every year he and Pat would have a "Crab Bash" at their home. Richard flew in boxes and boxes of crabs packed in ice, and we would sit around his kitchen table with mallets smashing open big fat Maryland crabs. Inevitably Norman Kelley would be with us, under good lighting, of course.

Toward the end of his career, Richard tried a variety of new roles, including a controversial production of *Tannhauser*, updated by the infamous Peter Sellers at the Chicago Lyric Opera. Instead of a minstrel knight, Peter Sellers made Tannhauser a Jimmy Swaggart bible belt hellion who steps off a 747 with a flask and ends up with a hooker in a hotel room.

I asked Richard how he felt about performing in this production and he admitted that his heart wasn't into it. In the end, he just wasn't one to be thrown into contemporary revisions of classic operas.

In January of 1998, Richard died of a cerebral hemorrhage at his home in Brookline. The world lost a great artist and we lost a dear friend.

Joyce and I feel fortunate to have seen him in his last performance, which was as Herod in *Salome*. Both Richard and Pat turned out great students, and Patricia continues to do so. Many are singing with major opera companies all over the world.

SUGGESTED RECORDINGS

Tannhauser by Richard Wagner

A DVD of a Metropolitan Opera performance from 1982 with Richard Casilly in one of his most famous portrayals of Tannhauser. The cast also includes Eva Marton, Tatiana Troyanos, and Bernard Weikl, conducted by James Levine.

Patricia Craig Live!

A double-CD collection of soprano arias from *Madama Butterfly*, *Tosca*, *Otello*, *La Rondine*, *Carmen*, *Pagliacci*, *Faust*, *La Traviata*, and many other operas. Available at Casamagda@aol.com.

The Singing Actor

Photo: The Metropolitan Opera Archives.

A Belgian bass-baritone born in 1940, Jose Van Dam entered the Royal Brussels Conservatory at the age of seventeen where he studied with Frederic Anspach. He graduated just a year later with diplomas and first prizes in voice and opera performance, debuting as the music teacher "Don Basilio" in Rossini's *Il Barbiere di Siviglia* at the Paris Opera. It is there that Van Dam sang his first major role, Escamillo in *Carmen*. He remained with the Paris Opera until 1965.

But as he shared with me in the studio in our *Classics in the Morning* interview, his career started much earlier than seventeen: "I was eleven years old when I started singing in a boys' choir. One day a friend of my parents heard me and took me to sing in his church where I became a soloist. When I was thirteen my voice broke, and I went to my teacher with a lot of questions about my future. But then it hit me, I knew I would be an opera singer, and nothing and no one could convince me otherwise. I just knew this would become my life, it was strange: it's as if I didn't choose it; it chose me."

On his work in film: "I loved working on *The Music Teacher*. It was a low budget film, but a very poetic one. There was this osmosis in that film that should be in every film: the music was wedded to the image, so that the connection became almost an unconscious one for the viewer."

On acting onstage: "When you are onstage and you play a role, the minute you're conscious of acting, it's simply too much. It must be natural. When I go onstage I become Mephisto, and I react as if I am the character onstage. I am no longer Jose Van Dam."

On playing the devil: "You must remember one thing: the devil in the street looks like you and me. I try to play it with lots of humor and irony. When I play Mephisto, I play it as if he knows the end of the story, because he does! He has this confidence, almost arrogance, because he has the power of knowing what's going to happen. The devil isn't stressed, he doesn't have to seem dangerous, he's the master of the situation. It's all a joke for him."

On preparing for a performance: "I don't do anything special, really. I'm like a battery. I feel myself charging up during the day, and by evening I'm ready to go—just very ready to enter into this personage, whoever it is, by the time the curtain rises. I can be myself one minute and the next minute I'm on stage and bang—I'm the devil! I'm Leporello, Mephistopheles, whoever I need to be. I have great concentration onstage. Perhaps I'm lucky that way. I'm not worried or nervous the day of a performance. It's funny—I don't need to be the devil all day to be the devil at night; I simply don't think about the role until I'm there, facing the audience."

On his favorite roles: "I've loved all my roles, so I have no favorites, really. I just sing and play every role I can. I've been singing for thirty-five years, yet there is such a legion of work to choose from, even though I have an insatiable musical curiosity. Think about it: Schubert alone wrote more than six hundred Lieder, and you have Schumann and you have Wolf; you have Strauss. In the French there's Faure, Chausson, Ravel, Debussy, Poulenc—it's endless!—and if I tried to sing all of this I would need fifty more years to begin to get through it all."

His advice to young singers: "It's simple. Sing, learn, listen. Remember, you are a singer but you are musician first. Your voice is your instrument, but don't just listen to opera, go take it all in: the world of music is your school, and the world is at your feet."

SUGGESTED RECORDINGS

The Very Best of Jose Van Dam

A program of arias and songs by Gounod, Offenbach, Hahn, Bizet, Delibes, Massenet, Berlioz, and Verdi.

EMI CD #2005

Star Spangled Baritone

Robert Merrill

Photo: The Metropolitan Opera Archives.

Born in Brooklyn on June 4, 1917, Robert Merrill became one of the most popular American singers of the twentieth century. As a youngster he wanted to become a baseball player, but blessed with a natural voice, he decided to study singing. His early days were spent as a crooner at weddings, at Borscht Belt venues in the Catskills, and on a local radio station. He also appeared as a straight man to comedians Danny Kaye and Red Skelton.

He won the Metropolitan Opera auditions in April of 1945, debuting on December 15 of that year as Germont in a performance of *La Traviata* that featured Licia Albanese and Richard Tucker. The great Toscanini chose him to sing this role in his historic broadcast with the NBC Symphony Orchestra.

On top of all his other talents, Robert had a killer sense of humor. As Germont in *La Traviata*, while Violetta lay dying, then perking up, then dying again…and dying a little bit more…he whispered to Richard Tucker (as Alfredo): "If this broad doesn't kick off in a few minutes, we're definitely going to miss the 6:20 to New Rochelle."

Richard Tucker and Merrill enjoyed playing tricks on each other. The tenor got his revenge when during a performance of *La forza del destino*, Robert Merrill as Carlo opened a locket that is supposed to contain a picture of his sister Leonora, pitting Carlo and Alvaro against each other. Instead, Tucker enjoyed watching his costar's face redden as he opened the locket, since Tucker had replaced the photo of Leonora with a rowdy photo of a couple making love.

On an episode of *Candid Camera*, Alan Funt placed Merrill, his face covered with a towel, in a barber chair, while an unsuspecting customer strolled in and sat down next to him for a shave. After a few quiet moments, Merrill burst into song with a fabulous rendition of "Largo al factotum," with its, "Figaro here, Figaro there, Figaro up, Figaro down." His face frothy with shaving cream, the customer jumped to his feet, exclaiming, "My God, what a voice! You should sing opera!"

But I think my most personal brush with his humor was standing next to him many years ago, in, of all places, the men's room at the Friar's Club. We'd been standing next to each other for, let's say, more than the usual amount of time, when he said, ever so casually, "How's the old prostate, kiddo?"

The first time I heard him sing was during a Met tour in Boston in the mid 1960s. The opera was *Rigoletto*, and Merrill's interpretation left an unforgettable impression on me. His sound was not only ringing and beautiful, but also big and powerful, recalling the great Italian baritone Titta Ruffo.

Later I got to hear him in many of his other signature roles: Amonasro in *Aida*, Escamillo in *Carmen*, Figaro in *The Barber of Seville*, Marcello in *La Boheme,* and Count de Luna in *Il Trovatore.* We shared many wonderful moments during our radio interviews talking about not only the world of opera, but also another of his favorite subjects: baseball. Bob, along with his wife Marion, were die-hard Yankee fans and even had the uniforms to prove it. No one ever sang the "National Anthem" at Yankee Stadium like Merrill. Being a member of the Red Sox Nation, I always delighted in discussing the greatest rivalry in sports with him.

I thought it fitting that when he passed away, he was watching the Red Sox in the first game of the 2004 World Series. Several years ago, along with my friend Nat Johnson, we produced a tribute to Merrill for Public Radio called: "Star Spangled Baritone." The show received favorable response from all over the country, and we shared many wonderful memories of interviewing him at the Friar's Club in New York.

Robert considered tenor Jussi Bjoerling to have one of the most beautiful voices of all time, and they shared a great friendship both on and off stage. The culmination of this relationship was on November 30, 1950, when they recorded what is considered to be the definitive version of the famous duet from the *Pearl Fishers* by Bizet. Beloved by so many, Robert was also a confidante of Frank Sinatra, who consulted with Merrill many times over the years whenever he had vocal problems.

The Robert Merrill Scholarship was instituted at the Julliard School of Music in New York City to assist young singers in their studies. Also, Bob's wife Marion informed me that the local post office in New Rochelle would be named after Robert Merrill. In Brooklyn where Bob lived, a street in his childhood neighborhood of Bensonhurst is also named after him. What a fitting tribute to one of the greatest singers of all time and a dear friend.

Suggested Recordings

Jussi Bjoerling and Robert Merrill: The Pearl Fishers Duet

A must for lovers of beautiful singing! Remastered by my good friend Nat Johnson, this collection not only includes the definitive version of the *Pearl Fishers* duet, it also includes duets from *Don Carlo*, *LaBoheme*, and *La forza del destino*. I can assure you this is a collection you'll return to again and again.

RCA7799-2 RG

Robert Merrill: America's Greatest Baritone: Live Performances 1944–1990

Produced by Ed Rosen and taken from live radio broadcasts of operas and recitals, this collection offers the opportunity to hear Merrill in some of his most exciting performances before an audience. Most of these performances have never been heard before and are real collectors' items.
Selections include:

"Figaro's Aria" from the *Barber of Seville* (1944)
"Di Provenza" from *La Traviata* (1950)
"Il Balen" from *Il Trovatore* (1969)
"The Prologue" from *Pagliacci* (1954)
"Some Enchanted Evening" (1953)
"Old Man River" from *Show Boat* (1988)

Biographies in Music BIM 710-1

***La Traviata* by Giuseppe Verdi: Complete Opera**

Recorded in 1969

This excellent cast includes Anna Moffa as Violetta, Richard Tucker as Alfredo, and Robert Merrill in perhaps his most famous role, Germont. He was never in better voice and turns in a career-defining performance. Fernando Previtali is the conductor in a performance recorded in Rome.

RCA 09026 68885-2

Devils and Demons

Jerome Hines

Photo: The Metropolitan Opera Archives.

Hines was born and raised in Hollywood, California, where his family was involved in the film industry. He studied mathematics and chemistry at the University of California while also taking vocal lessons. Imposing and regal at 6'6", Jerome Hines seemed born to be a basso—as he put it—"specializing in devils, demons, and despots."

As he tells it: "I started my career at eighteen on the West Coast tour of the Civic Light Opera, where I did *Pinafore* with John Charles Thomas. The year after, I debuted at the San Francisco Opera as Monterone in *Rigoletto* and Biterolf in *Tannhauser*, which is when I began singing with all the Met singers. At twenty I did my own concert in the Hollywood Bowl with the Los Angeles Philharmonic. About two years later I began singing Mephisto and Faust around the country. Then the war began slowing me up, so I went back to teaching chemistry and math. But the minute that time was over, I called the Met and they said come on over. My audition aria was the Boris monologue and Faust serenade. I was offered a contract right away. Did my first Mephisto at the Met just after my twenty-fourth birthday.

"The next season I sang eleven different operas, and little by little I just took over the repertoire; and that's when they let some of the older basses go because they had me. There were so many legends still around.

"In the end I did more Gurnemanzes than anyone in Met history, every bass role in the Wagner repertoire: Wotan, Fasolt, King Mark, King Henry, you name it! But like all American singers, I think, I didn't want to be known as a Wagnerian; we all wanted to do the Italian and French repertoire as well as the Russian."

On teaching and coaching: "I began the Opera Music Theatre Institute in 1987 and have really enjoyed coaching young singers. Mark Delavan—my pride and joy—when he came to me, he was so terrible my manager said, 'Look, don't bother, don't waste your time with the guy.' Mark sang for me and it was just awful—he sang right through his nose—and I yelled at him about it. When he sang back at me it was amazing; I mean it was as if he got it, right then and there. I asked him what clicked and he said, 'When Jerry Hines yells at me I yell right back at him.' Within a short time he had made it—he became just brilliant musically, and as an actor.

"We also had Franco Corelli at the school. If you ask me he was *the* tenor of the twenty-first century. Hell, even if you don't ask me, he just was. Franco taught for me at the school, and I think it really helped pull him out of his depression at the time: he was very broken hearted because he was losing his voice. We were great friends for the two and half years I knew him.

"Another great story: when I told one my students, actually one of my pet students with a gorgeous voice—Craig Hart—that I was going to be singing the role of King Phillip II of Spain in *Don Carlos* in Boston, he burst out with: 'I want to do the grand inquisitor with you!' I had to say to him, 'Craig, I'm warning you now, I'll be out there to blow you off the stage and I'll be expecting the same from you!' That's what it's all about, that scene. It's one of Verdi's greatest duets: the competition between church and state, and he pits two leading basses, I mean they are *fighting* each other, and of course, any two basses are going to want to wipe up the stage with the other. It was a thing of genius."

Hines spoke about his opera on the life of Jesus, *I Am the Way*: "I began fooling around with the idea for this opera in the early 1950s. I have to say it's through the writing of this work that I really became a Christian. I first produced it in 1956 with the Salvation Army in New York, where they have a beautiful auditorium. Nine of the disciples were not singing parts—they were just walk-ons—but we had trouble finding people, so we ended up using pan handlers from Skid Row; and it actually worked out great. Hey, what they lacked in talent they made up with enthusiasm! In 1963 the *Voice of Firestone* played a twelve-minute clip; and in 1966, we did it at the Lincoln Center with the help of the Lily Foundation. In 1968 we did a worldwide broadcast on the *Voice of America*, put it on at the Met, where it sold out two weeks in advance, and finally, [we] put it on in Moscow at the Bolshoi in 1993."

We were never fortunate enough to have *I Am the Way* come to Boston; however, Jerry continued performing virtually till the end of his life. In fact his last performance was as Philip II with Boston Bel Canto Opera at the age of seventy-nine. He also penned three books: a memoir called *This is My Story, This is My Song*, and two books on singing, *The Four Voices of Man* and *Great Singers on Great Singing*.

SUGGESTED RECORDINGS

Don Carlo by Verdi

A 1955 live Metropolitan Opera recording with Jerome Hines singing one of his
 greatest roles, Philip II of Spain.

Andromeda CD #5018

West Virginia Diva

Eleanor Steber

Photo: The Metropolitan Opera Archives.

I interviewed Eleanor Steber for *MusicAmerica* in September of 1988, starting off the show with a recording of "Pace, Pace, Mio Dio" from *La forza del destino.*

As the piece ended, she laughed and commented, "Fantastic that you chose that to play! That was the first aria I could remember in my ears, because my mother sang it; she studied with Rosa Ponselle and had such a lovely voice. She used to really go to town singing 'Pace,' and we kids—all three of us—used to learn it sliding down the banister."

At that, Eleanor sang the first few measures of "Pace," and it was easy to picture three kids swooping down a banister to that gorgeous decrescendo! Even at seventy-four, her voice remained supple and silvery.

Born in Wheeling, West Virginia, or "as we called it: 'west by God Virginia,'" Eleanor won the 1940 Met auditions, debuting in *Der Rosenkavalier.*

Eleanor spoke to me about opera in the 1940s: "A whole new school of opera opened up between 1940 and 1950, especially as a result of the Met Auditions of the Air. A new generation of singers became real contemporaries of mine: Richard Crooks, Lawrence Tibbett, Gladys Swarthout, and Robert Merrill. And we really had the best of it. Not only did we have the advantage of getting right on the stage, as opposed to cutting our teeth in Europe, but we were doing repertoire—there were a variety of roles we could do.

"We also had the best conductors and coaches at that time, though maybe not for the best reasons. They had to flee Europe because of Hitler. It was my great fortune to have been brought to the attention of Bruno Walter, who I called my godfather. He got me into Mozart because of the way I sang, a style developed wholly and completely via my years with William L. Whitney at the New England Conservatory of Music in Boston. It was that style Walter recognized—in fact when he was told I was American he didn't think it was possible; he said there is no American that can sing like that today. Together we all made a magnificent company, which carried through to the closing of the old Met.

"We also had great conductors like George Szell, and I was lucky enough to study all my German roles with Felix Wolfes, all my Italian roles with Renato Bellini, a direct descendant of Bellini himself, and my French with Jean Morel."

On the role of radio in opera: "The radio helped a great deal in developing a true listening audience for opera, which in turn helped with getting funding for the Met. *The Voice of Firestone* and the *Bell Telephone Hour* brought young singers to the attention of the American public, just fabulous exposure for us. That's when a whole new operatic style happened; they really pulled out all the stops with these glorious productions. We all came out of that period of the musicals starring people like Fred Astaire, Ginger Rogers, and Jeanette MacDonald, so of course we all felt we had to be glamorous and beautiful as well as great singers!"

On the operatic voice: "At that time there weren't a lot of 'big voices' per se; that is, you had to have projection, had to get to the back of the Met, yes, but that was not what defined the era. I think there's too much emphasis on having a big voice rather than having a beautiful voice and a well placed voice. It's more important to have a quality voice and sound."

On taking care of one's voice: "I'm asked about that a lot. Honestly, I was never conscious of being fanatical about taking care of my voice. I guess we *were* careful about yelling out at baseball games. The way I see it is: we lived, and as a result we performed, and we produced."

Eleanor continued, "It takes a special kind of person to be a great opera singer, just like it takes a special person to be a star baseball player. You have to have all the ingredients. You might have a beautiful voice, and you're missing the brains to go with it. You might have a beautiful voice, and an ungainly body. You might have charisma and not have a beautiful voice, but the charisma won't get you there. [At one time] you had to know how to be a prima donna. Today it's kind of iffy, the prima donna thing! The big hats, the big gestures, the big moments, there's still some of that left but not as much as in my time."

Eleanor was an operatic soprano star who, as she put it, could "not be slot-ted." Her art ranged from Berg to Puccinni, Mozart, Strauss, Barber, art songs, Lieder, and beyond. Her energy was boundless: in one year between concerts, radio, and opera, she did 233 performances. When she retired, she went on to teach voice at the Cleveland Institute of Music.

SUGGESTED RECORDINGS

Eleanor Steber: Her First Recordings (1940)

Arias and scenes from *Madama Butterfly*, *La Boheme*, *Faust*, and other operas.

VAI Audio #1023

The Feisty Soprano

Eileen Farrell

Photo: The Metropolitan Opera Archives.

My relationship with Eileen Farrell goes back to my student days at Boston University. While working at BU's student-run radio station WBUR, I was hosting an opera program and learned that Farrell would be appearing at Boston College singing in a performance of Poulenc's *Gloria*.

I scouted out where she was staying and called the hotel to inquire about a possible interview. The voice on the other end was unmistakably the lady herself. When I asked if she could join me on the show, she said, "Sure kid, come over after the performance."

I was taken aback by the casual and easy manner of this legendary diva. Later on, when we became good friends, I realized Eileen was like that with everyone: unpretentious, extremely funny, and always just herself. At our meeting I asked her about her relationship with the Met. "I really don't want to sing the roles they're offering me, so I can do without them." Maria Callas herself was said to have quipped: "Who needs the Met, anyway, they don't even have Farrell!"

Such was the admiration for a singer who started out performing with her family as a member of "The Singing O'Farrells" from Woonsocket, Rhode Island. While still a teenager, Eileen landed her own radio show in the early 1940s in New York City, where she belted out opera, musical comedy, and popular songs of the day. Her career as a concert and opera singer took off at age twenty-six when she sang with conductors Charles Munch, Leonard Bernstein, and Dimitri Mitropoulos. She performed everything from Wozzeck to Wagner and made her Met debut in 1960 singing the title role in Gluck's *Alceste*. From 1963–64 she sang forty-four performances in six roles. Other roles at the Met included Leonora in *La forza del destino* and the title role in Ponchielli's *La Gioconda*.

She shared a wonderful story of her performance in that opera. At the time, the great tenor Franco Corelli was singing opposite her as Chenier. In fact Farrell and Corelli were known for their fierce battles onstage. Eileen was in great voice singing Maddalena and brought the house down with her big aria "La Mamma Morta," taking the opportunity to nearly blow Corelli offstage with the power of her voice. Backstage between acts, Robert Merrill, her friend and colleague who was singing the part of Gerard, knocked on her dressing room door and said: "Eileen, keep it up, you've got Corelli sweating!"

She was, in fact, one salty lady who swore like a longshoreman and took no b.s. from *anyone*.

One well known story involved a rehearsal with Fritz Reiner, who was known as not only a great artist, but more infamously, one of the toughest, most tyrannical conductors around. So tough that some musicians were reputed to have taken their lives while under his direction.

No such thing happened with Eileen Farrell. She was rehearsing her part, when Reiner sputtered: "Miss Farrell, you are singing too loudly. Watch your markings! More pianissimo!"

She kept on singing, just as loudly as before.

"Miss Farrell. Your markings! Pay attention! You're too loud!"

She sang on.

He tapped his baton on the music stand. "Miss Farrell, this is unacceptable!"

She kept at it, singing the part as she felt it should be sung.

"Miss Farrell, can't you read? This is piano! Piano. Means *softly*."

She said, "If you want (expletive deleted) piano, get Dinah Shore." And she walked out.

During her later years, we kept in touch and enjoyed frequent lunches at "Arches," one of her favorite restaurants near her home in Fort Lee, New Jersey. The staff all knew and adored her and upon arrival always brought Eileen her favorite drink, a Manhattan with one rock. She spoke of her love for the great American standards and the album she made with Luther Henderson in 1959, called *I Gotta Right to Sing the Blues,* that proved she was indeed the very first "crossover diva." She loved hanging out in jazz clubs, joining her favorites such as Bobby Short. She had a ball belting out classics from the Great American Songbook, singing cabaret at the Algonquin in New York.

One of the highlights of her career came in 1979 when her friend Frank Sinatra asked her to record with him. Eileen always loved Frank, and their relationship dated to the early days when she appeared on his radio programs.

They got together on August 21 in New York City and made one of the great duo recordings of "For the Good Times" by Kris Kristofferson in a beautiful arrangement by Don Costa. It's included as part of the boxed set of the complete Reprise studio recordings of Frank Sinatra, consisting of twenty CDs.

Highly recommended is Eileen's biography by Brian Kellow, entitled *Can't Help Singing.* She said she had more fun and laughs telling her story to Brian than just about anything she did. It's a great read from beginning to end about the life of a woman who did it all, and as Sinatra would say, "her way"!

SUGGESTED RECORDINGS

The Eileen Farrell Album

This is one of the very first of the so-called crossover albums. Eileen shows she is equally at home swinging with the great American standards as she is singing Bach, Beethoven, Puccini, or Wagner. With wonderful arrangements by Luther Henderson, this collection recorded in 1959 has become a true classic. Eileen shows her great admiration for singers like Ella Fitzgerald, Mabel Mercer, and Sarah Vaughan in a style that is uniquely her own.

Selections include:

"Blues in the Night"
"Ten Cents a Dance"
"A Foggy Day"
"Old Devil Moon"
"The Man I Love"
"I'm Old Fashioned"
"The Second Time Around"
"My Funny Valentine"

Sony MDK 47255

Eileen Farrell: Opera Arias and Songs

This collection features the best of Farrell's opera arias and songs and proves that she was one of the great sopranos of our time. The power and beauty of her voice is showcased to perfection in this CD featuring arias from *La Gioconda, Ernani, Oberon,* and *Alceste* and a song recital featuring traditional favorites "Summertime," "Danny Boy," and "Though the Years."

Testament SBT 1073

Eileen Farrell: My Very Best

Between 1988 and 1991, Eileen recorded seven albums of great American popular songs that turned out to be some of the best recordings she made during her final years. Collaborating with arrangers Robert Farnon, Manny Albam, and Loonis McGlohon, often referred to as the "Super Soprano" who once said she loved to sing jazz as much as opera, Eileen proved that she is one of the most celebrated and versatile artists of the century. This collection features her own favorites from this period.

Selections include:

"Stormy Weather"
"My Foolish Heart"
"Little Girl Blue"
"Laura"
"Alone Together"
"Lush Life"
"Happiness is a Thing Called Joe"

Reference Recordings RR 60 CD

After the Golden Age

Aprile Millo

Photo: The Metropolitan Opera Archives.

After being welcomed into the Met's Young Artist Program at the age of twenty-two, Aprile quickly became one of the most celebrated sopranos of the late twentieth century, known for her spirited and nuanced interpretations of Verdi. On April 4, 1986, Donal Henahan wrote in the *New York Times* of Millo's performance in *Don Carlo*: "Miss Millo sounds more and more like the Verdi soprano we've been waiting for."[19]

While at the Met program she was mentored by such greats as Renata Tebaldi, Zinka Milanov, and Licia Albanese; before that time she had been trained solely by her parents, tenor Giovanni Millo and soprano Margherita Girosi.

I met Aprile for the first time when she came to Boston for her first recital at Symphony Hall in April of 1987. The event was billed as "Aprile in April." At that time she was the talk of the opera world; even Pavarotti praised her as one of his favorites. I was delighted to be asked to introduce her from the stage, as well as interview her the day before the recital.

She told me the following regarding her parents, also opera singers: "My parents were not a great commercial success; it's unfortunate life wasn't kinder to them. But they had the single greatest voices I've ever heard in my life, and I swear I'm saying this without bias! My father sang like a Gigli with Del Monaco's power. Sadly, he had heart problems and it sidelined him. My mother sounded like Muzio: she had this histrionic quality, on the stage you thought she would die before she would let loose of the moment because it meant that much to her. I have a long way to go before I can ever be that good.

"They presented those qualities to me, so I went elsewhere in search of other components: the Oliveros, Callas.... I wanted to adopt her qualities as a singing actress. Some people think of that style as melodramatic or not really true in some sense, but I like this quality; you don't want to go to Kabuki theater and see the men in sneakers, you know?

"There is a way of presenting an art form and keeping it true, and not selling out. When I'm out there singing Verdi I feel like I'm at the end of some long evolutionary line."

On growing up in Hollywood: "I'll never forget picking up the cover of Andrea Chenier's album with the young Mario Del Monaco dressed as a magnificent seventeenth-century French aristocrat with a walking stick! I was in awe. I thought: I must be—I have to be!—where people look this good. It was a wonderful inspiration.

"My parents and I were constantly flying around the world to opera houses. It was a vagabond existence; but when we did settle down, it was in Los Angeles and I went to Hollywood High. I had my time of dating the quarterback, doing normal high school things, but there was something different about me. I was always slightly strange. They called me the duchess or the queen because I always knew what I wanted to do. We are a different breed, you know! Pavarotti compared singing opera to walking a tightrope, you might fall and sometimes you do fall—in front of everyone—and there are the same kind of gasps, and it's just as horrific when it happens, it really is."

On the human voice: "Music without voice is symphony. With the voice [a piece of music] becomes a direct line to the human being who is listening...there are no curves in the road, it goes directly to you because you are hearing a human sound. What I crave in a world that is so coffee-comes-immediately, dinner's-in-the-microwave, [is that] intangible thing, which music can be, and it becomes so much more present and powerful if it becomes expressive, and not just notes on a piece of paper."

On the influence of the golden age: "I am a true admirer of the golden age, an artist imbued with the passion of the old school. I listen religiously to Tebaldi, Milanov, Ponselle. I think what I appreciate about the old school, and what I'm very honored to be grouped in with, is that they sought to express the ineffable—that which would remind people of something greater than themselves. Young students, ones who are serious I think, should know Caterina Mancini; they should know Muzio, Rosa Raisa, Gina Cigna—these names will not fade away. They weren't so much on the beaten track but their contribution to the art form was enormous. I'm just glad, for our future, that the next generation is being exposed to them."

SUGGESTED RECORDINGS

Presenting Aprile Millo

A collection of Verdi arias from *Ernani, Il Trovatore, Otello, Aida, MacBeth, Un Ballo in Maschera,* and *La forza del destino.*

Angel CD #47396

1. DIZZY GILLESPIE

The Diz

Dizzy Gillespie

© Ken Franckling.

Dizzy Gillespie was born John Birks Gillespie in 1917, in Cheraw, South Carolina, to a family of ten. His father, a local bandleader, encouraged his musical side and made instruments available to him from a young age. At four, John was playing the piano; by age twelve he had taught himself to play the trombone but soon switched to the trumpet. He received a scholarship at the Laurinburg Institute but left the school in 1935 to pursue his career, following his idol Roy "Little Jazz" Eldridge, who pioneered black musicianship in a white band. John soon earned the name "Dizzy" for his comical stage antics.

Dizzy Gillespie and Charlie Parker created a form of jazz called "BeBop," in which they broke all the rules. Up until that time, jazz was confined to big band and swing. Diz and Charlie, known as "the Bird," invented a whole other form of jazz musically, rhythmically, and artistically. Its center was 52nd Street in New York City in the mid-forties. At the time it was "hip" to be part of the bebop movement, which also sparked a fashion trend that included suede shoes, berets, and dark glasses worn at night.

Many people were turned off by the layers of harmonic complexity in this new sound…after all you couldn't dance to it; it was more like jazz concert music. Bebop was known as the first modern jazz style, seen at first as an outgrowth of swing, not a revolution. Thelonius Monk, Bud Powell, Kenny Clarke, and Oscar Pettiford were just a few of the musicians known for bebop, jamming at such renowned clubs as Minton's Playhouse and Monroe's Uptown House. Dizzy, now blooming as a trumpet virtuoso and gifted improviser, taught and influenced countless other musicians including trumpeters Miles Davis, Fats Navarro, Clifford Brown, Arturo Sandoval, Lee Morgan, and Jon Faddis.

In addition to changing the music world forever with bebop, Dizzy was a pioneer in founding Afro-Cuban jazz, which mixed Latin rhythms and African elements together with jazz and even pop music, particularly salsa. One of his most famous songs, "A Night in Tunisia," has a distinctly Afro-Cuban feel, and one of Dizzy's landmark travel events was his visit to Cuba, where he jammed with local musicians and met Fidel Castro, who was a big fan.

I first heard Dizzy in Boston in the late 1950s at Symphony Hall. He was performing as part of Norman Granz's "Jazz at the Philharmonic" series. From my seat near the front of the stage, I had a great view of Dizzy's iconic trumpet tilted up at a forty-five-degree angle. His breath came hot out of the bell of his horn, cooling into a gauzy smoke as it hit the air. I couldn't help but think that this cat's playing was on fire! Word was that his horn was damaged at a gig and he just kept it that way. Others said he saw and copied a horn like it in England: a trumpeter had it bent up like that because his vision was poor and it made reading music easier. Whatever the reason, Dizzy's inflated cheeks, horn-rimmed specs, beret, scat singing, and unique sound blew me away.

My dear friend Charlie Lake, "the Whale," was Dizzy's road manager for almost twenty years. Charlie handled all of Gillespie's business on the road, which was worldwide. He'd make sure he got the right room at the hotel, that he was on time for gigs, handled all of Dizzy's personal requests, set up the stage, and took care of his horn. Dizzy did have a habit of being absent-minded. As a matter of course, Charlie would visit his hotel room while Dizzy would be downstairs checking out. Charlie would leave the room with a huge trash bag full of forgotten items. The Diz had a way of living so much in the present that the immediate past was ancient history. In other words, he just left everything behind. Even money! Charlie swears today that Dizzy has funds abandoned in banks all over the world because he always insisted on getting paid in cash. This was a habit that persisted right up to the end of his career and wasn't just a function of being absent minded. Dizzy had dealt with one too many unscrupulous managers who stiffed him.

Dizzy had a way of charming the world around him by pretty much doing what he felt like doing at the time. According to the Whale, Dizzy once stepped on a plane carrying a watermelon that he was eating pieces of. He said something like, "hey, this is good s—t!" handed it to the flight attendant and suggested she cut up the rest of it and pass it around to the other passengers. In other airport shenanigans, Dizzy lore reports that he'd been caught a number of times going through security with a controlled substance in his pocket, but was let go when he professed complete ignorance and blew his cheeks out to full sail.

The first thing Dizzy would say to the Whale, his manager, when he arrived in Boston was "take me to see Ron." And each time he stopped by it was a celebration: it would take him half an hour to get from the front door to my studio because everybody wanted to talk to him and have their picture taken with him; all the way from the corridor, to the cafeteria, to the studio the Diz would sign autographs, albums, complying with all requests to blow out those famous balloon cheeks and a crack a huge smile.

During a 1990 interview, he shared a story that I think illustrates how the world loved him. "I was in Sicily, the morning of a gig. My cordless mic is hooked to me and my trumpet, and I just kept forgetting that, so I kept dropping it. Well, this one time, I *really* dropped it. The first valve went down and wouldn't come back up. So we're wandering around and we find a repair shop. This young Sicilian cat closed his shop just to fix my horn. We don't speak Italian; cat speaks not one word of English. He spent four or five hours on the horn. Then he had to go by boat to bring it to me, got there a minute or two before the show started."

Dizzy's sense of humor took everyone off guard. He would get onstage and make up what seemed like a real story, then spin it off into ridiculous-land, making the audience howl with laughter, then launch into these soul-searing sounds. He appeared on the *Muppet Show* once with Kermit the Frog. In 1964 he put himself forward as a presidential candidate, saying that if he were elected, the White House would become "The Blues House." His running mate would be Phyllis Diller, and his cabinet composed of Duke Ellington (Secretary of State); Miles Davis (Director of the CIA); Max Roach (Secretary of Defense); with Charles Mingus, Louis Armstrong, Thelonius Monk, and Malcolm X all holding vaulted positions.

I think to hear Dizzy at his best would be to listen to the *Jazz at Massey Hall* album that he recorded in the 1950s with Charlie Parker, when they were really into the peak of the bebop movement. Another favorite of mine is *Diz and Roy,* where Dizzy and Roy Eldrige embarked on a fierce trumpet battle. He made a wonderful album of ballads with strings called *Dizzy Gillespie and Strings* with Johnny Richards where he does a tune called "Swing Low Sweet Cadillac."

As Dizzy got older, time took a toll on his "chops," so he relied more on dancing and clowning around. But when he did play you could hear the old Dizzy in there, and he played right up until the end of his life. My son Aldo, who heard one of his last performances a few weeks before he died, said he was as kind and gracious as he always was to everyone. Dizzy seemed driven by a spiritual power that propelled him even from his earliest days of performing, at times having to confront some of the worst forms of racism. It was a very tough time for black musicians to perform, particularly in the deep South.

Drive and passion took Dizzy all over the world, until the world recognized him with countless awards including no fewer than fourteen Doctorates of Music. He became a world ambassador, sent by the State Department on tours to take jazz to Africa, Europe, and Havana. Jazz is a universal language that conveyed a freedom many were not used to hearing in their own countries. Dizzy embodied that freedom; there was nobody else like him. He was so loose and free, always unaffected, always in touch with joy.

Suggested Recordings

Dizzy Gillespie: Dizzier and Dizzier

The best of Dizzy's early recordings from 1946 through 1949. This collection is a wonderful introduction to Gillespie's days recording with other pioneers during the bebop era, including Charlie Parker, Milt Jackson, Don Byas, Ray Brown, and James Moody. We hear Dizzy in a small group setting as well as fronting his big band.

Some selections:

"Night in Tunisia"
"Jumpin' With Symphony Sid"
"Anthropology"
"Kool Breeze"
"Two Bass Hit"
"52nd Street Theme"
"Good Bait"

BMG Music 09026-68517-2

Dizzy: The Music of John Birks Gillespie

This collection surveys the full range of Dizzy's recordings from 1950 to 1963 and features classic jam sessions with jazz greats Oscar Peterson, Stan Getz, and Roy Eldridge. It also serves as a companion to the biography of Dizzy by Donald L. Maggin entitled Dizzy, *The Life and Times of John Birks Gillespie.* Maggin also provided the excellent liner notes that accompany this collection.

Selections include:

"Bloomdido"
"Africana"
"Caravan"
"Blue Moon"
"BeBop"
"I Remember Clifford"
"Exactly Like You"
"Leap Frog"

Verve B 0004133-02

I highly recommend the book *Dizzy, the Life and Times of John Burks Gillespie* by Donald Maggin.

Gentleman Ben

© Ken Franckling.

Duke Ellington once wrote: "The problem of expressing the contributions that Benny Carter has made to popular music is so tremendous it completely fazes me, so extraordinary a musician is he."[20]

Benny Carter, whose seven decades of accomplishments included professional arranger, composer, alto saxophonist, and trumpeter, was about to visit me for an interview. So it was with a minor case of nerves that I welcomed the erudite, sophisticated, crisply dressed gentleman into my studio back in March of 1988. I was struck not only by his elegant yet laid back style, but his humility when speaking of his enormous contributions to music. Along with Johnny Hodges, Carter was the model for the 1930s swing era alto saxophonists, an innovative stylist with his own signature sound not only on the sax, but the trumpet, clarinet, piano, and trombone. A much admired arranger and composer, he was known for not only setting the stage for big band jazz, but for his major contributions to the world of film and television music. His personality and musicianship—the rare ability to collaborate, juggle all kinds of music and musicians with professional grace, which was not a hallmark of jazz musicians at the time—set him apart and made him in great demand.

Plus, how can I put this? The man was just…cool. One of the coolest jazz musicians who ever sat before me.

Born in 1907, Carter was primarily self-taught except for a few piano lessons from his mother. As a young man he befriended Bubber Miley who lived around the corner from him in Harlem, and who happened to be Duke Ellington's star trumpeter. By age fifteen, Benny was sitting in at several Harlem night spots.

Again, with no formal training, he taught himself how to arrange music as a member of Charlie Johnson's Orchestra. Soon he joined Fletcher Henderson's Orchestra, then in 1932 took off for Detroit and McKinney's Cotton Pickers where he became a force not only on alto sax but on his first love: the trumpet. Compositions he wrote during this time, "When Lights Are Low" and "Blues in My Heart," have since become jazz standards.

Within a year he was putting together his own band, which included swing greats Chu Berry, Teddy Wilson, Sid Catlett, and Dicky Wells, and he and his band were often featured at the Savoy Ballroom. By the mid-thirties he was traveling through Europe, playing an inestimable role in spreading the word of jazz abroad; recording and gigging with the top French, Scandinavian, and British bands, especially as staff arranger for Henry Hall's BBC house radio band. Swarms of delirious fans would greet him at every train station. During this time he also led the first international, interracial band.

He returned home in the late thirties, jumping into the swing era in the United States. He not only found work as a soloist, composer, and arranger with Lionel Hampton, but ultimately joined forces with Benny Goodman, Count Basie, Duke Ellington, Glenn Miller, Gene Krupa, and Tommy Dorsey. In a few years he'd pared down to a sextet, which included bebop pioneers Kenny Clarke and Dizzy Gillespie. Always open to new styles of music, the band soon welcomed modernists Miles Davis, J. J. Johnson, Max Roach, and Art Pepper.

By this time Carter had settled in California, and he was steadily taking on more studio work. I asked him about his transition from arranger to composer. He said, "You know, so many things that I've done I've never considered a goal before I did them. Then they fell into my lap and I took advantage...I was lucky, I just happened to be in Hollywood playing in a club with my orchestra, and they were doing a picture called *Stormy Weather*. I was called in to do some arranging, along with a bit of playing and from then on I was stuck in Hollywood for a couple of years."

Carter was also known for securing equal opportunity and equal pay for black musicians in the entertainment business. Before Carter, black artists were restricted to playing for movie soundtracks; Carter was hired not only to perform, but to direct studio orchestras as well as write the music for dozens of films and television programs. He even waged successful legal battles to obtain housing in then-exclusive areas of Los Angeles.

Beyond scoring a number of feature films including *An American in Paris* and *The Guns of Navarone*, he has provided arrangements for nearly every popular singer including Ella Fitzgerald, Billie Holiday, Peggy Lee, Ray Charles, Lou Rawls, Sarah Vaughan, Pearl Bailey, and Mel Tormé. Though Carter gave up full-time leadership of big bands in 1946, he became even more active in the fifties and sixties as a soloist, especially with such renowned groups as Norman Granz's *Jazz at the Philharmonic*. Especially beloved in Japan, he was received there like royalty.

In the seventies he turned his talents in a new direction—education. Invited to participate in classes and seminars offered by Morroe Berger, a sociologist at Princeton University, who eventually wrote Carter's biography *Benny Carter—A Life in American Music,* Carter was inspired to share his wealth of knowledge with eager music students. Conducting workshops and seminars at universities such as Princeton, Harvard, and Rutgers earned him honorary doctorates wherever he set foot. Nominated for seven Grammys and winner of two (for "Harlem Renaissance" and "Elegy in Blue)," Benny will always be known to his fellow musicians as the "King."

Our interview took place when the man was eighty-one, and he still had his chops. *A Gentleman and His Music*, an LP featuring an all-out jam session with Scott Hamilton, Ed Bickert, Gene Harris, John Clayton, Joe Wilder, and drummer Jimmie Smith, was cut when he was seventy-eight years old. At eighty he had reunited with old friend Dizzy Gillespie for the release "I'm in the Mood for Swing."

I asked him if it was true that he needed to be cajoled to play his trumpet: "Not at all! What they have to do is wrestle it away from me. I just love to play it—I prefer it to the sax—but I just don't get to play it much, so I have to watch out. I don't think I should be assailing rather than regaling the ears of my listeners, you know?"

During his travels in Europe, Carter spent much of his time visiting good friend Coleman Hawkins. Two recordings that best reflect their synergy are "Honeysuckle Rose," recorded with Django Reinhardt, and the album *Further Definitions*, now considered a masterpiece. I asked him who might have been an influence on Coleman Hawkins: "You know, that really makes me think...today we have so much to listen to, so many choices; but back then, in 1922 when Hawkins was playing with the Mamie Smith Jazz Hounds, what tenor sax players were around? What influences could he have had? I'm telling you, what came out of him, just came out of him! He was a real giant and innovator."

Carter remarked on how much he enjoyed speaking at colleges, but lamented the utter lack of resources available to him as a teenager: "I guess the advantage was that you learned how to swing, first hand. You had to feel it; there were no books to teach you. Sure, there were books with scales and so on, but no scores with solos like a Charlie Parker solo—you couldn't put your hands on that anywhere. I would've given anything at the time to find a Frankie Trumbauer solo book! Sure I could listen to his record; I could copy "Singing the Blues" or "I'm Comin' Virginia" that I loved so much, but that was it.

"But we learned from each other. We put on these endless, no-holds-barred jam sessions. Spur of the moment, for hours right on till morning sometimes. Then they were called 'cutting contests,' but they were as much about collaboration as they were competitive. We had so much fun playing, listening and playing off of each other."

Finally I asked if there was anything in his record-breaking career that he regretted not accomplishing. He said, "Ron, there's really only one. I've been in several movies, but never have I realized my dream of being leading man to Lena Horne.'"

SUGGESTED RECORDINGS

Best of Benny Carter
This Grammy winner features Benny in performances with jazz greats Dizzy
    Gillespie, Phil Woods, Clark Terry, Harry Edison, and many others.
Selections include:

    "Lover Man"
    "Wonderland"
    "Prelude to a Kiss"
    "Remember"

Musicmasters CD 65133-2

Benny Carter: New York Nights
A 1995 release with some of Carter's favorite younger musicians including Chris
    Neville, piano; Steve LaSpina, bass; and Sherman Ferguson, drums.
Musicmasters 65154

Sax a la Carter!
A classic recording from Capitol in 1960. Benny at his very best with Jimmy
    Rowles, piano; Leroy Vinnegar, bass; and Mel Lewis, drums.

Jacquet's Got It

Courtesy of Pamela Jacquet Davis.

Born Jean Baptiste Jacquet in 1922, in Broussard, Louisiana, Illinois Jacquet was one of the true jazz giants of the tenor saxophone. His full-bodied, bluesy, rich sound was instrumental in developing the so-called "Texas Tenor Style," a way of playing the sax to bring out its big sound and biggest volume. Jacquet was known for introducing the screeching technique, as well as an original rompin' stompin' sound that's been a part of R&B ever since. His true jazz and swing fans, however, appreciate the warm, sensitive tone apparent in countless jazz ballads that communicates a sensitive side of one of the last big-toned swing tenor saxophonists.

Though he began singing and dancing to his dad's band at age three, Illinois went on to play drums as a teenager, then switched to soprano, alto, and finally the tenor sax under the tutelage of Lionel Hampton in the late 1930s. It was in 1942 with the Hampton band that he made jazz history with one of the most famous solos ever: "Flyin' Home" became his signature tune, and he included it in every performance that followed. The solo became so familiar that other saxophonists played it note for note.

In one of our interviews, he talked more about that incredible night: May 26, 1942: "I guess I was getting good at being everybody else: I could imitate Lester Young, Coleman Hawkins, Flip Phillips, lots of gifted players, and I did it out of love for their style. But just before I went on, Lionel took me aside and said, 'man, I've heard you be everybody else. Now you go on up there and play like Illinois Jacquet. Go be yourself.' And that was the moment, you know, when I heard my own sound. It was some high-spirited blowing! Anyway, you know the rest; but everywhere I go, *everywhere*, even the end of the world where I was last month: New Zealand, they know that solo. That was a stroke of luck; the grace of God gave me the originality to come up with a solo like that."

After leaving Hampton, Illinois joined Cab Calloway's Band in 1943, finally teaming up with the Count Basie Orchestra in 1945. The early 1950s began his long association with Norman Granz's *Jazz at the Philharmonic.* These concerts, also showcasing Coleman Hawkins, Lester Young, Charlie Parker, Dizzy Gillespie, Roy Eldridge, Oscar Peterson, Ray Brown, Louie Bellson, and Buddy Rich introduced jazz to millions around the world.

It was during this period that he made another one of his famous recordings, this time teaming up with fellow tenor saxophonist Flip Phillips. By this point, Jacquet's wildly swinging improvisational forays were working countless crowds into a frenzy. Their saxophone battle on *Perdido* became a classic, and was performed at every JATP concert from that time on.

I always enjoyed Illinois' visits to my show. He had an infectious sense of humor and told wonderful stories about the legends he played with. One involved Charlie Parker. Stoned and without his horn or any bread, Charlie rang his doorbell one evening. "Bird" was strung out and looking to crash for a day or two. Those few days turned out to be several weeks. Illinois said when he returned from one of his many worldwide engagements, Bird had not moved from the couch that he'd last seen him on!

My first interview with Illinois took place back in the 1970s when he appeared at Sandy's Jazz Revival in Beverly, Massachusetts. At that time I was hosting an all night jazz show called *GBH After Hours.* Sandy Berman, the late owner of the club, called and told me he was bringing Illinois down for an interview after the gig that evening. Needless to say, I knew this would be tiring for Illinois because he would not be arriving until two o'clock in the morning after his performance at the club. I mentioned this to Sandy, but he said, "Don't worry about it—everything's cool."

It wasn't until two-thirty in the morning that Illinois arrived at my studio. I could see he was tired and dragged, but I made sure the first thing he heard when he stepped into the studio was one of his most famous recordings, the original 10" LP of "Black Velvet." His eyes lit up and from that moment on, the interview went just fine. He stayed for more than an hour, told great stories, and dubbed me "Ron Delicatessen"! To top it off, I gave him the LP, which delighted him no end. From then on we became great friends; it seemed he wouldn't leave a city in the world without sending me a postcard. He also never missed a chance to visit me whenever he played in Boston. I was most flattered when he wrote a jazz chart for me called "Runnin' With Ron" (referring to my days as a marathoner) and recorded it with his big band. When my marathon days were over, I started walking for a change. Jacquet said, no problem I'll just have to write a new one for you: "Walking With Ron."

On worldwide reactions to his music: "Once we were in Perugia in Italy, which is a new city built on top of an ancient one, an incredible place. Anyway, we did a gig there, and they wouldn't let us leave the stage. People just couldn't get enough of the music. They have a way of feeling the music there, not just hearing it. I know I'm in another state of mind when I'm playing the ballads, a very soulful state of mind. Anyway, they wouldn't let me leave the stage for quite some time. Even after—I can't remember how many encores. It was getting late, you know. This happened in Spain, too: people would cry, they came up to us crying and touching us, asking for an autograph. It's fascinating how people from different countries express their love for the music."

Illinois championed the careers of many young musicians including the guitarist Gray Sargent who now works with Tony Bennett. A true jazz original, Illinois was the consummate showman who always delighted his audience with his clowning and dancing as well as his fantastic blowing. Credited with more than three hundred original compositions, he even jammed with President Bill Clinton, an amateur saxophonist, on the White House lawn during Clinton's inaugural ball in 1993.

His manager and life partner, Carol Scherick, called me with the sad news one July day in 2004 that he had died after one of his concerts with his big band at Lincoln Center in New York. It turned out to be not only his final performance, but also one of his greatest. I was privileged and honored to be one of the eulogists at his funeral at Riverside Cathedral in New York City. It was a glorious and fitting send-off to an artist revered and loved worldwide, who was finally flying home.

Suggested Recordings

Illinois Jacquet and His Big Band: Jacquet's Got IT!

One of the finest big band recordings ever. Illinois put together some of the best musicians for this session that took place in New York City in 1987. His tenor sax solos on all the selections are inspired and soulful, defining what jazz is all about.

Selections include:

"Tickletoe"
"Smooth Sailin'"
"Flyin' Home"
"More Than You Know"
"Blues From Louisiana"
"Port of Rico"
"Running With Ron"

Atlantic Jazz 781816-2

Illinois Jacquet: The Black Velvet Band

In this collection we hear one of the earliest and best of Illinois' big band sessions, performing with jazz greats Joe Newman, his brother Russell Jacquet, J. J. Johnson, Milt Buckner, and Jo Jones.

Selections include:

"Black Velvet"
"King Jacquet"
"Big Foot"
"Mutton Leg"
"My Ol' Gal"
"Blue Satin"
"Adam's Alley"

RCA/Bluebird 6571-2-RB

Illinois Jacquet Plays Cole Porter

Illinois once told me the real test of a jazz musician was playing ballads. In this all-ballad collection, backed up by a nineteen-piece orchestra of strings, woodwinds, harp, French horn, and rhythm section, Illinois proves his point with masterful performances of Cole Porter classics. I am indebted to my good friend and Illinois' #1 fan, Dan Frank, for getting this hard-to-find CD. It was Dan who brought Illinois and his great band year after year to the Barry Price Center Benefit concerts.

Selections include:

"It's Alright With Me"
"I Got You Under My Skin"
"I Concentrate On You"
"Get Out of Town"
"So In Love"
"Every Time I Say Goodbye"
"Begin the Beguine"

Argo LP-746 (reissued as a CD with original number)

Hot, Cool, and Swinging

Stan Getz, Joyce Della Chiesa, and me

Courtesy of Charlie Lake.

If Mozart could play the saxophone, he would sound like Stan Getz. It was in the early 1960s when a friend and fellow jazz enthusiast, Bob Buccini, asked me if I had heard a tune called "Desafinado." He'd heard it on a jukebox and told me to check it out; it was like no other sound he had ever heard. As one of Stan's college students Larry Grenadier remarked, "His sound was striking; it hit you over the head. His timing and rhythm were so strong; he was a master of space and silence."[21]

It turned out to be one of the biggest hit recordings of the time and popularized the Bossa nova, a brilliant blend of jazz and Brazilian rhythms. As it turned out, Stan had been playing in this style for some time. "The Girl from Ipanema," recorded with Joao Gilberto and his wife Astrud, became one of the most well known Latin jazz cuts of all time, winning two Grammys (Best Album and Best Single), sales surpassing even The Beatles' *A Hard Day's Night*. In the last few weeks of 1962, there was a national Bossa nova craze, and Stan found himself on top of the Downbeat Poll for the year.

His nearly fifty-year career began in the 1940s in New York City, when he worked with Stan Kenton, Benny Goodman, and Woody Herman's Second Herd.

While working with Woody's band, his solo on the 1948 recording of "Early Autumn" became a classic. Based on this one solo, Stan had become a star, and everyone wanted to hear him play.

Even as a child, Getz felt the need to play every instrument in sight, but gravitated toward the saxophone. His father bought him one when he was thirteen years old. Stan said, "In my neighborhood, the choice was: be a bum or escape. So I became a music kid, practicing eight hours a day. I'd practice the sax in the bathroom, and the tenements were so close together that someone across the alleyway would yell, 'Shut that kid up!' and my mother would shout back, 'Play louder, Stan, play louder!'"[22]

That unique and cool "Getz sound" was influenced by the great tenor saxophonist Lester Young, "the Prez." It was out of that sound that Stan developed his own style that could be hot, cool, and swinging at the same time.

It was the drummer Jimmy Falzone who first introduced me to Stan. Jimmy had worked with Stan when he was a teenager in the Kenton band. One afternoon in the summer of 1985, I picked up the phone at WGBH and the voice on the other end said: "Ron...this is Stan Getz...Jimmy told me to call you." Needless to say, I was delighted to invite him on my show, and that began our friendship that continued until he passed away in 1991.

He shared some thoughts on music: "It's like a language. You learn the alphabet, which are the scales. You learn the sentences, which are the chords, and then you talk extemporaneously with the horn. It's a wonderful thing to be able to speak extemporaneously, which is something I've never gotten the hang of. But musically, I love to talk off the top of my head. And that's what jazz music is all about. Nothing gives me the same satisfaction of spontaneous interaction."

Stan was known, however, for some remarkably spontaneous behavior. One night in London in 1969, while hanging out and drinking wine with Peter Sellers and Mike Milligan, the conversation turned to Stan's swimming prowess, and eventually they bet him he couldn't swim across the Thames that night. In no time Stan was walking through the lobby with his swim trunks under his terrycloth robe. Up to the very last minute the size of the bets increased, until Stan dove into the dark, cold river water. Panicking, Milligan and Sellers ran to the police to report it, but they were told to go home and sleep it off. They jumped in a cab and raced over the nearest bridge to look for Stan on the other side, where they found him calmly sitting on a bench, dripping wet but enjoying the night air. Getz turned to them and said, "What took you guys so long?"

By the time we met in person, Stan had overcome his life-long battles with drugs and alcohol and was on the road to better health that rejuvenated his playing. During one of our many interviews, he told me he met a lovely woman named Samantha in a health food store near his home in Malibu. They began to date and soon after planned to marry. At the time they met, Samantha had no idea who he was. She soon found out! She bought every Getz recording she could find and only then did she understand who this great man was.

He very much wanted my wife Joyce and me to come to his wedding. Alas, it was not to be. Stan was now battling his new demon: cancer. Though he made great strides in his fight against this disease, it finally overcame him with Samantha at his side to the very end.

Later, when my wife and I visited Los Angeles, we met Samantha for lunch at the Beverly Hilton Hotel. She told us about Stan's great stamina and will to live. After wonderful remembrances, we said our goodbyes. Wanting to see Stan's home, we took a ride north on the Pacific Coast Highway. As we approached the beautiful Malibu area, with the top down on our convertible, from the radio came the unmistakable sound of Stan's music greeting us! It was like he was saying, "Thanks for stopping by!"

SUGGESTED RECORDINGS

Getz/Gilberto

No Stan Getz collection would be complete without this one that includes the original hit recordings of the Bossa nova years from March 1963. Stan's musical colleagues include Antonio Carlos Jobim, Joao and Astrud Gilberto, Tony Williams, and Milton Banana.

Selections include:

"Girl From Ipamena"
"Desafinado:
"Corcovado"
"O Grande Amor"
"So Danco Samba"

Verve 810048-2

Stan Getz: A Life in Jazz

This CD is a companion to the excellent biography by Donald L. Maggin entitled *Stan Getz: A Life In Jazz*. The CD includes many highlights of Getz' distinguished career and collaborations with Gary Burton, Ella Fitzgerald, Chick Correa, J. J. Johnson, and Jimmy Raney. As Maggin points out in his notes, "Nature provided Stan with abundant talents for music that included perfect pitch, a photographic memory, and the ability to create fresh and beautiful melodies in his improvisations."

Selections include:

"Night Rider" (from the 1961 masterpiece *Focus*, an album featuring Eddie Sauter's brilliant compositions and arrangements)
"Summertime"
"Billies Bounce" (with J. J. Johnson and Oscar Petterson)
"You're Blasé" (with Ella Fitzgerald)

"Litha" (with Chick Correa)
"I'm in Love" (with Abbey Lincoln)

Verve 314535119-2

Stan Getz and Kenny Barron: People Time

Recorded live in Copenhagen in 1991 with pianist Kenny Barron, this duo
collection is one of Stan's last and most brilliant sessions. The two-CD
set features originals by Charlie Haden, Mal Waldron, Benny Golson, and
Eddie del Barrio along with standards by Cole Porter, Benny Carter, and
Jimmy Van Heusen.

Selections include:

"Night and Day"
"First Song"
"East of the Sun"
"I'm OK"
"Like Someone in Love"
"Soul Eyes"
"Gone With the Wind"
"I Remember Clifford"

Verve 314510823-2

Super Drummer

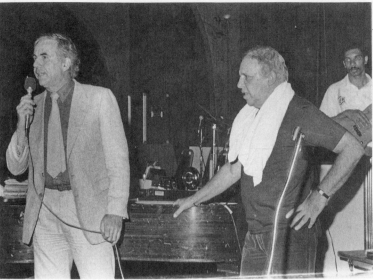

Buddy Rich
and me

Courtesy of Charlie Lake.

There's a famous story about Buddy Rich that made the rounds shortly after he died in 1987. Buddy had been in and out of the hospital for several weeks undergoing tests for a variety of ailments. During his final visit, just before surgery he was asked if he was allergic to anything. "Yeah...country western music!"

Buddy was born in Brooklyn in 1917 to parents who lived and breathed Vaudeville. Buddy's father Robert noticed that his son could keep a steady beat with spoons at the age of one. At the tender age of eighteen months, Buddy made his first appearance on stage in his parent's act, "Wilson and Rich." At four years old, he presented an act as a drummer and tap dancer called, "Traps, the Drum Wonder," performing regularly on Broadway. At eleven, he led his first band, turning into the second highest paid child star in the world (after Jackie Coogan.)

In the late thirties, Buddy's career took off in earnest when he played at the Hickory House in New York, jamming with Joe Marsala, Bunny Berigan, Harry James, and the great Artie Shaw.

Buddy became known around the world for his virtuosic power, dexterity, groove, and speed, despite the fact that he never received a formal lesson and never practiced outside of his performances. Though he typically held his stick using a "traditional grip," he was a master at the "match grip." He could pull off the one-handed-roll on both hands, do gymnastic crossover riffs, and was once clocked at twenty-strokes-per-second on a single-stroke roll. Aside from his explosive displays, he could slide easily into quieter passages and was masterful at the brush technique. Influences included: Chick Webb, Gene Krupa, Dan Tough, and Jo Jones, among others.

By 1939 he had joined Tommy Dorsey's famous orchestra before enlisting with the marines. During his years with Dorsey, his roommate was a young singer named Frank Sinatra. A volatile combination to say the least! To taunt Frank, Buddy would play as loud as he could when Frank was singing a quiet ballad. One night at the Paramount Theatre, Frank had had it. He picked up a music stand and threw it at Buddy, who luckily ducked in time. It crashed into the wall and to this day, sixty years later, the dents are still there.

During the 1950s, Rich toured with Norman Granz' *Jazz at the Philharmonic*, teaming up with greats like Oscar Peterson, Charlie Parker, Illinois Jacquet, Roy Eldridge, Thelonius Monk, Al Haig, Dexter Gordon, Dizzy Gillespie, and Ella Fitzgerald. These concerts took place at Symphony Hall in Boston, and that's where I saw him for the first time. I couldn't believe his sense of swing and his spectacular drum solos that went on sometimes for fifteen minutes, always bringing down the house.

Buddy had his own successful big band from 1966 to 1974. During that period he appeared quite often at Lenny's on the Turnpike in Peabody, Massachusetts, which is where I met him for the first time. Lenny was kind enough to set up the interview between sets in his dressing room. Stories about Buddy's temper were legendary...firing members of the band for no reason, his tremendous ego, his impatience with boring interviews. Even Dusty Springfield had allegedly slapped him after a rude remark. Needless to say, I was intimidated when I knocked on his door. I walked in and there was Buddy, in his underwear, wrapped in a bath sheet minutes after playing a dynamic drum solo that closed out the set to a standing ovation.

I was relieved to find him quite the opposite of what I expected after all the buildup. He invited me in and graciously consented to a relaxed and revealing interview. He spoke of the days when he was billed as "Traps, the Drum Wonder" and also with great affection regarding his parents who started him on the road to his career. When I mentioned the Sinatra stories, he said, "We were just kids then, and sometimes we liked to bait each other just for kicks. Actually, we're the best of friends, and there's nobody like Frank anywhere. He's the greatest singer of all time."

Later on, I learned it was Sinatra who had backed Buddy's band and was instrumental in keeping him active during an era when rock was the big thing. The story goes that Rich mentioned to Sinatra after a gig that he was interested in starting his own band. Sinatra promptly wrote him a check for $40,000, saying, "Good luck. This'll get you started.'"

At that time, Buddy's band was made up mostly of graduates from Berklee College of Music. He said that Berklee produced the best young jazz musicians of any school in the world and he was always assured of fresh, vibrant talent. It appeared that anyone who played in his band had to deal with the perfection that the leader demanded from each and every one of them. When I asked what made his band so unique, he replied without hesitation, "I do!"

Some years later, Buddy returned for an appearance at a club on the North Shore where I was asked to introduce him. As usual, it was a tour de force, again with standing ovations.

I told Buddy I would drop back to see him in the band bus where he used to ride up front with the musicians. As I entered the bus, I asked him if he'd like to meet my wife Joyce. He said of course. I brought her in and there he was again, clad only in his underwear and signature towel. I said, "Buddy, meet my wife Joyce; she's from Brooklyn like you." He smiled and she befriended him with a meatball sandwich on fresh Italian bread. He said, "Wow! You've made my day!"

Buddy's caustic humor made him a bit of a hit on several TV talk shows including *The Tonight Show with Johnny Carson*, the *Mike Douglas Show*, the *Dick Cavett Show,* and the *Merv Griffin Show*, entertaining audiences with his constant sparring with the hosts and his cracks about various pop singers of the day.

Ross Konikoff once remarked, "Never in my life have I met or heard about another human being who was more born to one task than Buddy. It was this single-mindedness that necessitated his brutal honesty. The only thing that prevented him from playing before the age of three was his inability to enunciate the words, 'Stay with me, goddammit.'"[23]

After Buddy died, I got a call from his daughter Cathy, who as a teenager had sung with her dad's band at Lenny's. I hadn't seen her since then, and she had grown into a tall, beautiful woman. She was coming to Boston to promote some recently discovered live video performances by her father. She told me that unlike all the negative stories about her dad's temper and nasty disposition, as a father he couldn't have been nicer to her or her mother. He called every night when on the road from all over the world to make sure things were going well on the home front. Cathy makes her home in Las Vegas with her husband and works tirelessly to keep the Buddy Rich legacy alive for a whole new generation.

There's a great story the late Whitney Balliett mentions in his book, *Super Drummer, a Profile of Buddy Rich.*

"I'm told I'm not humble, but who is? I remember being interviewed by a college kid once who said, 'Mr. Rich, who is the greatest drummer in the world?' and I said, 'I am.' He laughed and said, 'No, really, Mr. Rich, who do you consider the greatest drummer alive?' I said, 'Me. It's a fact.' He couldn't get over it. But why go through that humble bit? Look at Ted Williams—straight ahead, no tipping of his cap when he belted one out of the park. He knew the name of the game: Do your job. That's all I do. I play my drums."[24]

Suggested Recordings

Big Swing Face Buddy Rich

This is a live recording of the first edition of Buddy's 1966 band: arguably his
    greatest band ever. This is the band that also appeared at Lenny's on the
    Turnpike during the late 1960s and early '70s.

Selections include:

> "Norwegian Wood" arranged by Bill Holman
> "Love For Sale" arranged by Pete Meyers
> "The Beat Goes On" arranged by Shorty Rogers, vocals Cathy Rich
> "Chicago" arranged by Don Rader
> "Willowcrest" arranged by Bob Florence

Pacific Jazz CDP 7243 8379 8926

Buddy Rich Live at Ronnie Scotts

This is a later edition of Buddy's band dating from 1980 with some outstanding
    soloists like Steve Marcus on tenor sax, Bob Doll on trumpet, and Bob
    Mintzer on baritone sax.

Selections include:

> "Slow Funk"
> "Good News"
> "Saturday Night"
> "Ernie's Blues"
> "Beulah Witch"

DRG 91247

Buddy Rich: The Lost West Side Story Tapes

This DVD is every Buddy Rich fan's dream come true. He was sixty-seven at the
    time and playing better than ever. These master tapes were thought to
    have been lost in a fire in 1985 but were discovered and restored in 2000,
    thanks to his daughter Kathy. The concert includes Buddy Rich standards
    such as:

"Cottontail"

"Mexicali Nose"

"West Side Story"

In addition, there are interview segments, behind-the-scenes footage of Buddy
    and rare photos from the Rich Family achieves. For more information
    about Buddy, go to www.BuddyRich.com

DVD Hudson Music HDZWS01

The Irascible

Joe Venuti

Author's collection.

Joe Venuti claimed he was born on a ship as his parents emigrated from Italy in 1906; however, many believe and in fact records show he was simply born in Philly. Considered the father of jazz violin, Joe was almost as well known for his groundbreaking technique as he was for being one of the great jokesters and storytellers of all time. Put it this way: anyone who knew Joe has a story.

Joe studied classical violin as a child, the fruits of which he combined with his natural inventiveness on the fiddle to produce his own signature sound, including a technique that allowed him to play four note chords. Childhood friend Salvatore Massaro, better known as jazz guitarist Eddie Lang, became a cherished musical partner until Lang's untimely death. In the late 1920s, Joe and Eddie moved to New York where they became so well known for their "hot" violin and guitar solos that they were commissioned to liven up otherwise stock dance recordings with original twelve- or twenty-four-bar solos.

Many early recordings turned to classics when they teamed up with the likes of Bix Beiderbecke, the Dorsey Brothers, Frankie Trumbauer, Jack Teagarden, the Boswell Sisters, and the young Benny Goodman. Though Venuti and Lang recorded some milestone jazz records during the 1920s, Venuti's career began to lose steam after Eddie's death in 1933. His fortunes improved somewhat in the mid-thirties when he joined the Paul Whiteman Orchestra.

In the mid-fifties, Joe met Bing Crosby and they developed a friendship that continued for many years. Bing gave Joe the opportunity to appear as a regular guest on the *Bing Crosby Radio Show*. This relationship, in fact, seemed to help pull Venuti out of a rough couple of decades following Eddie's passing when he formed his own unsuccessful band and did some anonymous Hollywood studio work. On Bing's show he was able to show off his quick wit, outrageous stories, and gruff charm in the best light.

Venuti's playing was inseparable from his personality, both of which were aggressive, inventive, playful, and punchy. He became known for his "violin capo" technique and his extended swinging pizzicato solos, but his most well known invention, rarely copied because it's both very difficult and extremely wacky, was to unfasten the hairs of the bow and wrap them around the top of his fiddle, with the bow underneath. This arrangement let him play all four strings simultaneously, producing lush four-part harmonies.

Joe virtually disappeared from the music scene during the 1960s, and many people wondered if he was still alive. He put those rumors to rest when in the mid-seventies he resurrected himself and, coming back stronger than ever, appeared at the Newport Jazz Festival and recorded with a slew of pop and jazz stars including Bucky Pizzarelli, Curly Walker, Eldon Shamblin, Jethro Burns, swinging tenor saxophonist Zoot Sims; even concocting and recording "Venupelli Blues" with Stephane Grappelli.

It was around this time that I first met Joe. He was appearing in Boston at the Merry-Go-Round Room in the Copley Plaza Hotel with pianist Dave McKenna. We hit it off right away, and I invited him to be a guest on my show. I'd already heard some classic Venuti stories, such as the time a pianist bugged Joe by tapping his foot...so he nailed the guy's shoe to the floor! According to more than one source, every Christmas Joe would send Wingy Manone, a one-armed trumpet player, a single cufflink.

But my all-time favorite Venuti story reportedly happened at the Hollywood Bowl. Joe was backstage waiting to perform when he realized he was about to share the stage with Roy Rogers' famous horse, Trigger. Being Venuti, while standing next to Trigger, he took his bow and began to saw away at the horse's privates! Needless to say, the horse was turned on and exhibited his unmistakable pleasure and masculinity. You can imagine the audience's reaction when Roy called out to his famous horse to come on stage.

Other tales include Joe pushing a piano out of a fifth-floor window to see what key it would play in when it hit the sidewalk; giving a musician directions to a gig that involved a two-hundred-mile odyssey, which landed him a block from where he started; calling up forty-six tuba players and sending them to a faux gig in Hollywood; chewing up (onstage) a violin he borrowed from bandleader Paul Whiteman.

In our 1990 interview, Joe shared this story: "I was in Italy when this aficionado of jazz heard me play and said, 'Maestro, I think you should give a concert.' Problem was, he was low on cash, but he did have a cheese shop. I told him to forget it; pay me in cheese. I did four concerts for cheese. Man, I was swimming in bel paesa, parmesan, gorgonzola, mozzarella! We ate as much as we could, and I sold the rest."

I asked how he named his songs. He told me: "We made these names up at the session. 'Bullfrog Moan,' 'Jet Black Blues,' 'Going Places,' 'Doing Things,' 'Add a Little Wiggle.' Right there on the spot. One side was called 'Nothing,' the other side was called 'Something.' One side was called 'Flip,' the other was 'Flop.' And I got news for you, that one lived up to its name." Backing instruments named on these recordings include the comb, hot fountain pen, kazoo, and something called the goofus, for which I never learned the translation. He also mentioned the unceremonious way musicians were treated in the thirties: "No rehearsal, just record. Four tunes in four hours, twenty-five bucks and see ya later."

But there was a serious side to Joe that came out in our interview. He told me he started out as a classical musician and played for the great Toscanini. He had a deep love for Italian opera, especially Puccini, and could sing in that gravelly voice of his all the well known arias, as well as play them on the violin. In fact he shared with me that he'd penned an opera in the Italian buffa style, laughingly admitting that it had never been performed.

I'll never forget a lunch I enjoyed with Joe and Dave McKenna at Giro's, a once-famous Italian restaurant in Boston's North End at the corner of Hanover and Atlantic Avenue. This place had an old world sort of dignity; all the waiters wore black tie. Joe insisted on ordering "family style"...that is, everything on the menu! In the middle of this fabulous meal, who should walk in but another legend, Dizzy Gillespie with his manager Charlie "The Whale" Lake. What an unbelievable occasion that turned into when these two started telling stories! I only wish I had my tape recorder when Dizzy took out his famous upright trumpet, puffed out those cheeks, and played a duo with Joe. Everybody in the place stopped to enjoy this once-in-a-lifetime impromptu jam session.

In 1978 Venuti was scheduled to play a jazz date in a club in Chicago. The band arrived a day ahead and received the sad news that Joe had passed away the night before in Seattle, where he made his home.

On opening night, a violin was placed on a chair in front of the band: a fitting tribute to a great man. Joe wowed music fans for over sixty years, playing with breathtaking speed, but always with absolute neatness and precision. This dazzling technique as well as his irreverent, light hearted humor put jazz violin on the musical map.

SUGGESTED RECORDINGS

Joe Venuti–Eddie Lang: Great Original Performances 1926–1933

This CD includes some of their finest and rarely heard performances and is a lasting testimony to two of the greatest innovators in jazz. The vintage recordings have been digitally restored by the jazz historian Robert Parker, resulting in excellent sound.

Selections include:

"Bugle Call Rag"
"Four String Joe"
"Krazy Kat"
"The Wild Dog"
"Hot Heels"
"Running Ragged"
"Sensation"

BBC 644

The Fabulous Joe Venuti

This wonderful collection was recorded in Italy during a Venuti tour in 1971. He was over eighty and still had the swing and verve of a man decades younger. In this session, he was able to record with many of Italy's finest musicians including Lino Patruno and Giorgio Vanni.

Selections include:

"Sweet Georgia Brown"
"After You've Gone"
"Jazz Me Blues"
"Margie"
"Some of These Days"
"Sweet Sue"
"Clementine"

Omega 3019

Joe Venuti and Zoot Sims

In 1975 Venuti was in New York City and teamed up with Zoot Sims on saxophone, John Bunch on piano, Bucky Pizzarelli on guitar, and Bobby Rosengarden on drums. What a swinging session!

Selections include:

"I Got Rhythm"
"Avalon"
"Russian Lullaby"
"Where OR When"
"Shine"
"I'll See You in My Dreams"

Chiaroscuro CRD 142

A Lifetime of Swing

Lionel Hampton

© Ken Franckling.

Lionel Hampton was perhaps one of the greatest showmen in jazz: he was a vibraphonist, pianist, percussionist, bandleader, and actor. Born in Kentucky in 1908, Lionel was raised by his grandmother. After a move to Chicago in his teens, he took xylophone lessons from Jimmy Bertrand and started playing drums, jumpstarting his career as a percussionist with a group called The Chicago Newsboys.

"Hamp," as he was known by his musician friends, was a styling sort of guy. He always bought the best of everything, including the latest silk shirts and the finest suits. In the 1930s he bought his first marimba and set of drums and became accomplished on both instruments. But it was the vibraphone that brought him lasting fame. At that time, Louis Armstrong had come to California and hired the Les Hite band, enlisting Lionel to play the vibes on two songs. This performance not only galvanized his career as a vibraphonist, but it popularized the use of the instrument ever since.

In 1936 he met dancer Gladys Riddle, who became his wife and personal manager. She developed a reputation as a brilliant businesswoman, responsible for raising enough money for Lionel to start his own band. Their marriage lasted well over sixty years and was one of the most endearing relationships in the jazz world. His beloved Gladys also encouraged him to study music theory at the University of Southern California.

In November of the same year, the Benny Goodman orchestra came to the Palomar Ballroom in Los Angeles, where John Hammond brought Goodman to hear Hampton play. Goodman asked Hamp to join the Benny Goodman Trio, made up of Goodman, Teddy Wilson, and drummer Gene Krupa, expanding it into the Benny Goodman Quartet. This was the first time two black musicians integrated the all-white Goodman Orchestra.

After Lionel left Benny in 1940, he formed his own band, and what a band it was! The musicians who played with Hamp in his Lionel Hampton Orchestra were a who's who in jazz; they included Charlie Mingus, Joe Newman, Art Farmer, Clark Terry, Dexter Gordon, Illinois Jacquet, and singers Joe Williams and Dinah Washington.

In 1942 Hamp recorded "Flying Home," Illinois Jacquet's famous solo that drove audiences into a frenzy and paved the way for rhythm and blues. This recording put the band over the top, and Hamp featured it in every one of his concerts. Illinois' solo was so popular that saxophonists who followed him played his solo note for note.

Also known for his generous role as an educator, Lionel worked with the University of Idaho in the 1980s to establish accessible music education, and in 1986 the University's music school was renamed the Hampton School of Music, ensuring that Lionel's vision will live on. The sixty-million-dollar-project provided a "home for jazz," housing the university's Jazz Festival and its International Jazz Collection designed to help and teach presenters of jazz.

In a 1990 interview with Lionel, he was effusive about the quality of the program: "We've educated over twenty-five hundred students so far; can you imagine that? We present concerts all year long by professional artists. We've had Dizzy, we've had Ella, and they'd perform, then do a lecture, and the kids go gaga over it! And the professors—I've never seen anyone break down music like this—they're so thorough with these lessons, they could teach a tree. And they honor me, they do. When I was there last, an eighty-six piece choir sang 'Midnight Sun,' and you never heard anything so beautiful as the way they did it. Not just two or three part harmony, this was five, six parts—gorgeous."

When I met Hamp in the 1970s, he was appearing with his band on the north shore of Boston. I called him and he said, "Yeah, Gate...come up to my dressing room after the first set." I must say after hearing his opening performance I was a bit disappointed; I guess I expected the band to catch fire...and it didn't, and I worried that Hamp, in his late seventies, might be past his prime.

When I entered his dressing room he was sitting, relaxed and watching TV. His eyes never left the TV during our entire interview. Finally he said, "Hope you gonna stick 'round, Gate...because that first set wasn't happen'n and I'm gonna kick some butt in a few minutes." And did he ever! The second set lasted over two hours, and Hamp seemed to never tire, outplaying all the other younger musicians in the band.

After the performance I went back to his dressing room. With a big grin, he looked at me and said, "Did you dig that, Gate?" This time his wasn't watching TV.

When he died a few years ago, I recalled that evening and thought about the millions of people he had entertained all over the world. Like Louis Armstrong, Hamp was one of our great ambassadors of jazz and good will.

Suggested Recordings

Lionel Hampton and the Just Jazz All Stars

Recorded in 1947 by Crescendo

This CD features Hampton and an all star jazz lineup including Charlie Shavers on trumpet, Willie Smith on alto, and Slam Stewart on bass. Among the selections is my all time favorite instrumental performance of "Stardust."

Lionel Hampton Hot Mallets Volume 1

Lionel himself selected the best of his small band recordings from 1937 to 1939.

RCA 6458-2-RB

Lionel Hampton The All Star Groups

RCA 2433-2-RB

Boston's Own

Ruby Braff
with Gray
Sargent

© Ken Franckling.

In 1988 I was privileged to write the liner notes for a CD entitled *Me, Myself and I,* by The Ruby Braff Trio.

Here's an excerpt: "I hereby declare Ruby Braff to be a National Treasure. What other musician has such an extraordinary range of ideas, emotion, and sustained playing? Ruby is unique, not only as a performer, but as a superb interpreter of our country's musical heritage. He has recorded everything from 'America the Beautiful' to 'White Christmas.' Like his idol Louis Armstrong, Braff has great respect for the melody, embellishing it in ways others envy. Ruby has played and recorded with a multitude of jazz greats including Benny Goodman, Roy Eldridge, Coleman Hawkins, Buck Clayton, and Pee Wee Russell among many others. Very few musicians share his eclectic repertoire. He is equally comfortable talking about the wit and wisdom of Dorothy Parker as he is discussing the music of Tchaikovsky and Puccini. His iconoclasm is well known. You can't fake it with Ruby. He tells it like it is, and his artistry is a reflection of this."

Since his passing in 2003, his stature as one of the all-time great innovators in jazz has only grown. I'm still amazed at the output of classic recordings he made during the last decade of his life. Thanks to the efforts of Mat Domber of Arbors Records, Ruby was able to record prolifically, choosing his own material along with his favorite musicians.

Interviewing Ruby, however, was always an experience that kept me walking on eggshells. Here was a guy who fired his own music teacher; he was eight at the time. Ask him the wrong question, and the result could be an outburst of invectives that made you wish you could disappear!

Here are some classic Ruby quotes that still ring in my ears:

"It took civilization two thousand years to give us Louis Armstrong, and fifteen minutes for Bruce Springstein."

"Rock music is built on three chords and two of them are wrong!"

"The state of music today is so bad, even Sammy Kaye sounds good to me these days."

Stories about Ruby Braff are legendary. Here's one that has made the rounds:

While traveling in Japan, Ruby approached the front desk at his hotel to ask if there were any messages for him. Politely he was told, "No, Mr. Braff, no message today." Ruby then asked if there was any mail for him; again the polite man bowed, and replied, "No, Mr. Braff, no mail today." Fuming by now, an agitated Ruby said, "Well for Christ's sake, do you have the time?!"

A New York musician related another classic Braff story to me. After a gig, Ruby was heading home in a cab with some fellow musicians. As each musician was dropped off, Ruby bad mouthed the guy to the remaining cats with caustic remarks like, "That guy's a moron and can't play for s--t." After another musician was dropped off, Ruby said, "His chops are gone, I wish he'd take up bowling." Finally, as the last musician said good night to Ruby, he thought to himself, "I'm sure with no one left, Ruby will bad mouth me to the cab driver!"

More memorable quotes from the man himself:

"I've always hated the trumpet. I didn't choose it. I wanted the B-flat tenor saxophone. (My parents) brought home this peculiar thing with valves on it, which I hated forever. Never did care for it.

"Unfortunately, I'm mostly self-taught. I hope to fix that one of these days."

Referring to famous musicians such as Tommy Dorsey and Artie Shaw: "They looked like they were having such a marvellous, glamorous life, living in hotels, so well-dressed. It seemed like the epitome of luxury. I had no idea that they were all miserable!

"My first records were made in Boston, for a label called Storyville, and for Savoy Records, with Edmond Hall and Vic Dickenson. But they were terrible recordings—off broadcasts, mainly. Very sad things. I couldn't play, either. The one made in a club where you could hear the audience more than the music was one of the better records.

"Sure, they've made statements about my supposedly combining a modern approach with a feeling for traditional forms. Well, people say all sorts of things, because they want to categorize and label. I've only ever had two labels: Either it's good or it stinks.

"So it's silly. Is (a musician) playing good or isn't he? That's the only thing that counts. But I know a lot of people don't agree with me, particularly the critics. They must put labels on music, so they can have it like canned goods on their shelf.

"Talent is something that very few people have, really. And there are no geniuses. Maybe Louis and Duke are something in jazz. But they keep throwing these words around."[25]

All this from a musician who could be sensitive and caring when he wanted to be. He carried on a phone relationship with my mother, when she was in her nineties, until she died. She always looked forward to her extended conversations with Ruby on a wide variety of subjects from Al Jolson to the price of milk. She said he always was a delight to talk to and called her mostly when it was raining!

As Dan Morgenstern, director of the Institute of Jazz Studies at Rutgers University, has said, "Ruby was able to reach heights of artistic achievement granted only an exalted few in the final decade of his life. He put everything he could muster into his horn despite his emphysema. The strength he corralled to override his condition was truly super-human coming from such a small, and increasing frail body."

Braff's overriding love for music came through in one of our last interviews: "Every kid in school should know the names of Harold Arlen and Duke Ellington and George Gershwin, and they don't; and I think it's an awful thing. The 1930s was a unique time for our country: it was a gentler time, a gentler country; people were more innocent in a more innocent land, and with it came great beauty. That, *that* is the chunk of American music that should be cared for and loved and protected until the end of time."

SUGGESTED RECORDINGS

Ruby Braff: In the Wee Small Hours in London and New York

Recorded in London and New York in 1999, Ruby performs a collection of standards showcasing his unique sound backed up by a lush string section arranged and conducted by Neil Richardson and Tommy Newsom.

Selections include:

"In the Wee Small Hours of the Morning"
"April in Paris"
"Pennies from Heaven"
"Love Walked In"
"White Christmas"
"Old Folks"

"All Alone"
"You're Sensational"

Arbors ARCD 19219

Ruby Braff: Very Sinatra

This 1993 recording is devoted to songs made famous by Frank Sinatra. Ruby
was a great admirer of Frank's artistry both as a musician and singer.
Braff often said that he'd like to live exactly as Sinatra does, except for
two roadblocks... "I can't afford it, and I couldn't pass the physical!"
The tasteful arrangements are by Dick Hyman who plays both piano
and organ along with Bucky Pizzarelli on guitar, Michael Moore on
bass, and Mel Lewis on drums.

Selections include:

"All the Way"
"The Second Time Around"
"My Kind of Town"
"Nancy"
"Come Fly With Me"
"Lady is a Tramp"
And an original by Ruby entitled "Perfectly Frank"

Red Barron JK 53749

Ruby Braff and His Buddies

This collection won the best jazz record of 1995 by the combined critics of Jazz
Journal International and is one of the most swinging recordings that
Ruby ever made. His jazz buddies included the great Dave McKenna on
piano; Scott Hamilton, tenor sax; Gray Sargent, guitar; Marshall Wood,
bass; and Chuck Riggs, drums.

Selections include:

"It's Alright With Me"
"Ain't Misbehaving"
"Swinging on a Star"
"Them There Eyes"
"On the Sunny Side of the Street"

Arbors ARCD 19134

It's Shearing You're Hearing!

George Shearing

Courtesy of George Shearing.

It was in the early 1950s that I first heard the singular sound of the George Shearing Quintet on the radio. George was making history with his Capitol recordings that featured piano, vibraphone, guitar, bass, and drums. Later on he added Latin rhythms to shake up the group's style. His improvisations were unapologetically romantic, but I always picked up a hint of whimsy in his music, reflecting the warmth and offbeat humor of the man I had the pleasure of getting to know.

Born in London in 1919, George was the youngest of nine children. Though congenitally blind, George began learning how to play the piano at three years of age. His father delivered coal, and his mother cleaned trains at night after caring for the family during the day. With only four years of formal training at the Linden Lodge School for the Blind, George found his inventive, orchestrated jazz voice through not only listening constantly to recorded jazz musicians, such as Teddy Wilson and Fats Waller, but also by jumping into performance, joining an all-blind band while still in his teens for the sum of five dollars a week.

In 1947 he emigrated to America where he put together the George Shearing Quintet, known for its shifting personnel over the years, which has included Margie Hyams, Chuck Wayne, John Levy, and Denzil Best. Shearing became known for the lock-hands technique, which is when the pianist plays parallel melodies with the two hands, creating a full, rich sound. He was accompanied by a low-key rhythm section including guitar, bass, drums, and vibraphone. The Shearing sound commanded national attention when he gathered his quintet to record "September in the Rain," which sold 900,000 copies. Among other songs recorded by his Quintet include: "Mambo Inn," "Let's Call the Whole Thing Off" and "I'll Never Smile Again."

George's piano style was heavily influenced by the "bebop" sound created by Charlie Parker and Dizzy Gillespie in the 1940s. During his early years in America, George performed on 52nd Street in New York, known as "Swing Street," with jazz greats Oscar Pettiford and Buddy DeFranco. His U.S. reputation was permanently established when he was booked into Birdland, the celebrated jazz spot in New York, eventually inspiring "Lullaby of Birdland," composed in 1952. He acknowledged creating the piece in just ten minutes, but as he told the *Christian Science Monitor* in 1980, "I always tell people it took me 10 minutes and 35 years in the business, just in case anybody thinks there are totally free rides, there are none!"[26]

George shared some of his thoughts on his early years in New York: "Here I am this young English cat in shades, and they didn't know what to make of me. There was an obvious language barrier. I think it was George Bernard Shaw who said that the Americans haven't spoken the English language in over a hundred years. My wife reminds me of the significance of the 4th of July and I say, yes, but remember you still owe us for the tea.

"Fifty-second Street is gone now, but it was everything back then. Before the quintet, I did several months at the Three Deuces, with Oscar Pettiford on bass and J. C. Heard on drums. I had the best possible training just being opposite these giants. No better apprenticeship has ever been offered. Once we had Ray Brown on bass, Charlie Smith on drums, and one fine day, Ella Fitzgerald. I got someone to take over my intermission piano for a few nights, anything to play with Ella. We did 'Flying Home,' and we were still going at 2:30 in the morning. I'm telling you, it was like I died and gone to heaven."

In the late 1950s he began performing classical concerts with symphony orchestras all over the world with arrangements by Robert Farnon, a masterful pianist with great technique and his own sound. But with George, as many have said, you always knew, "It's Shearing you're hearing."

This was especially true because Shearing's harmonically complex style mixed swing, bop, and modern classical influences. In fact his fascination with classical music resulted in guest performances with concert orchestras in the 1950s and '60s; his solos frequently borrowing musical patterns or phrases from Debussy, Delius, Schumann, Rachmaninov, Vaughn-Williams, Elgar, and particularly, Erik Satie. Shearing's delicate touch and fanciful nature made him an ideal interpreter of Satie's work.

He commented in our 1996 interview on his tendency to incorporate classical phrasing: "I try to be diversified both in my music and my investments." His famous "Shearing sound" continued until 1978 when he disbanded his quintet and began to work in other musical contexts.

In the same interview, George commented on his relationship with Mel Tormé: "We are the best musical marriage that I know, Mel and I. We like the same composers, we feel the same way about music, and unlike many singers, Mel is also an arranger. He's not my favorite pianist, but hey, I'm not his favorite singer. He's a consummate musician. If I play something and I make a change, *within that bar*, Mel will be on it a split second after I am, real time. Therefore, he doesn't worry about me trying to memorize accompaniments so I can play the same way every night to cover up his insecurity. In other words, *I can improvise*, and isn't that what jazz is all about? Mel would never, ever ask me to play something the same way. If you can't be free to improvise, tell me, what's the point?"

George's dry wit always delighted me. In 1990 I interviewed him after an appearance at the Regatta Bar in Cambridge, where he announced the release of a solo piano CD, one of several on the Concord label. Among other topics, we discussed his countless trips performing concerts all over the world, making him one of the most frequent flyers of all time. He said, "You know, Ron, they've asked me to form 'Shearing Airlines'…of course I'll be flying blind but plan on sticking my white cane out the window to determine our wind velocity and direction."

His thoughts on jazz from our 1996 interview: "When I let the George Shearing Quintet go in 1978, it was time. But absence really does make the heart grow fonder, because by '94 I'd become recharged somehow. I'd get out of the shower every day geared up with a new arrangement for the same combination that I'd been so sick and tired of in 1978.

"But I have to say, jazz has changed: it's become so complex. I came over to this country knowing about Glenn Miller, Teddy Wilson, Art Tatum, Benny Goodman. Now I go in these clubs and hear these complex lines that Charlie and Dizzy were playing and I think, *what?* Good God, do I have to go back to school for another ten years? It's a strange feeling."

Granted an honorary doctorate of music from three universities, knighted by the Queen of England, composer of over three hundred songs, invited by presidents Ford, Carter, and Reagan to perform at the White House, and, last but not least, creator of countless terrible puns, George Shearing and his music will always be near and dear to my heart and to the hearts of millions of fans worldwide. Of his passing in early 2011, Dave Brubeck said, "George paved the way for me and (the Modern Jazz Quartet) and even today, jazz players, especially pianists, are indebted to him."[27]

SUGGESTED RECORDINGS

How Beautiful Is Night

George Shearing with the Robert Farnon Orchestra

This collection brings together the magnificent piano artistry of George Shearing with one of the greatest arrangers of our time, Robert Farnon, whose lovely arrangements provide the perfect setting for Shearing and his quintet along with Farnon's orchestra. These wonderful interpretations of great standards make for a sublime listening experience. Some selections on this CD include:

"Dancing in the Dark"
"Heather on the Hill"
"Oh, Lady Be Good!"
"Our Waltz"
"Days Gone By"
"Put On a Happy Face"

Telarc CD-8332

That Shearing Sound—The New George Shearing Quintet

George Shearing revisits his famous quintet years with a newly formed edition of the group. It's a joy to hear that famous sound once again in new versions of the classic quintet selections popularized in the late 1940s and early 1950s that made this group one of the most popular and listened to in the history of jazz.
Selections include:

"East of the Sun"
"I'll Never Smile Again"
"I Hear Music"
"Girl Talk"
"Autumn Serenade"
and Shearing's most famous composition, "Lullaby of Birdland"

Telarc CD-83347

George Shearing—Favorite Things Solo Piano

Starting in the 1970s, George Shearing started to record a series of solo performances that showcased his remarkable talents that he explored as a much younger man in his native England. In this collection we hear echoes of his love for classical composers like Tchaikovsky, Brahms, and Satie. This shows Shearing to be the true master of interpolating quotes from classical music into his solo piano performances.
Some selections from this CD:

"Angel Eyes"
"Taking a Chance On Love"
"Summer Song"
"Moonray"
"P.S. I Love You"
"It Amazes Me" (also featuring George's vocalizing)

Telarc CD-83398

Three Handed Swing

Gray Sargent and Dave McKenna

© Ken Franckling.

Pianist Dave McKenna was born in Woonsocket, Rhode Island, to a musical family. His mother played violin and piano; his father, a postman, played drums part-time; and both of his sisters were singers. As a youngster, Dave was largely self-taught and began playing weddings and bridal showers by the time he was fifteen. One of his early champions was "Boots" Mussulli who had a band in nearby Milford, Massachusetts. Boots later became a member of the Stan Kenton Orchestra and appeared frequently at the Crystal Room in Milford.

As a teen, Dave joined Charlie Ventura's band that featured jazz greats Conte Condoli (who also worked with Stan Kenton), saxophonists Al Cohen, and bassist Red Mitchell. In 1950 he played with the Woody Herman "Herd" until the army tapped him for a stint in Korea where, of all things, he became a cook! He said he learned how to make pancakes for five hundred guys but couldn't figure out how to make pancakes for one.

After the service, Dave teamed up with many other jazz greats including Gene Krupa, Stan Getz, and Buddy Rich. In the mid-1960s he settled on Cape Cod with his wife Frankie and their sons Stephen and Douglas. He made his home there for many years, becoming pianist in residence at "the Columns" in West Dennis.

I was introduced to Dave by our mutual good friend Dick Johnson, who was playing with him at that time on the Cape. He insisted I go out and hear Dave, telling me he was simply the greatest. What an understatement that turned out to be! Up until that time, no pianist I had ever heard got more out of the piano than Dave. He played swinging bass lines with his left hand while his right had the ability to play ballads, swing, or bop. Though he started out as a big-band sideman, he became best known for his distinctive solo playing, with that powerful left hand making a bass player seem unnecessary.

This technique, rooted in the jazz piano tradition of an earlier era, was built around these powerful bass lines, elegantly voiced chords, and a loving approach to melodies, especially those of the Tin Pan Alley standards that were the foundation of his playing. Unlike many of his contemporaries, he was more likely to ornament a tune with graceful embellishments than to spin off wild riffs, abandoning the melody. This "three handed swing" style brilliantly evoked the rhythmic structure normally provided by a three- to four-person band. To hear Dave play solo piano was to hear a whole symphony orchestra.

After leaving the Cape, Dave became pianist in residence at the elegant Plaza Bar in the Copley Plaza Hotel for almost ten years. He became so popular there that many of the icons of the music world such as Tony Bennett, George Shearing, and Rosie Clooney would drop by to listen whenever they were in town. In the world of classical music, André Previn, John Williams, and Kurt Musur were also great admirers. It was during this period, the early 1970s, that my wife Joyce and I made a trip to Italy with Dave. It was a long desired dream of his to sample the cuisine he loved so much.

Florence turned out to be one of the highlights of that trip. While walking past a disco we noticed an announcement in the window that jazz pianist Romano Mussolini would be playing that night. Dave had heard of Romano and mentioned he wouldn't mind seeing him. That evening we arrived to the sounds of loud, abrasive disco music. The manager informed us that Romano was running late but was on his way. Soon after that, several gentlemen showed up who appeared to be bodyguards with Romano in tow. No mistaking that this man was the son of "Il Duce"; he looked just like his father.

After the first set, I introduced Dave to Romano, who invited him to play. Dave graciously declined, but Romano insisted and Dave finally said sure, as soon as I finish my dinner. He played a heartfelt and swinging Duke Ellington medley which had the place in an uproar, as well as Romano, watching in disbelief as Dave's hands flew across the keyboard. Even the cooks came out of the kitchen when they heard his music. Afterwards, more plates of beautiful pasta arrived at our table...now Dave was in heaven!

McKenna couldn't have been happier during his later days with the success of his beloved Red Sox and Patriots. Years ago he even penned and recorded a musical tribute to his idol Ted Williams, called "The Splendid Splinter."

McKenna's fans are worldwide and his theme medleys from the Great American Songbook rival those of any other musical artist. I rarely saw him with written music at the keyboard: he'd committed thousands of songs to memory. As modest as he was, he once described his playing to me with these words, "I'm just a saloon piano player who's killing time." But what better way to kill time than listening to Dave play! His humility and laid-back style always seemed to contrast with his masterful playing. He was truly one of the all-time keyboard greats in a class with Art Tatum, Oscar Peterson, Teddy Wilson, and Nat Cole.

SUGGESTED RECORDINGS

An Intimate Evening with Dave McKenna

This collection of live solo piano performances from 1999 recorded at the Sarasota Opera House is a good example of how Dave rewrites the song without losing the melody and includes several of those famous McKenna "theme medleys":

The Thought Medley includes: "The Very Thought of You," "I Had the Craziest Dream," and "Thinking of You."

The Street Medley includes: "Easy Street," "Broadway," "42nd Street," "Beal Street Blues," and "On Green Dolphin Street."

The Change Medley includes: "There'll Be Some Changes Made," "Change Partners," and "You've Changed."

The Letter Medley includes: "I'm Gonna Sit Right Down and Write Myself a Letter" and "Love Letters."

The Time Medley includes: "Time After Time" and "Time On My Hands."

Volume 10 Arbors 19264

Dave McKenna Giant Strides

One of the best of McKenna's saloon piano recordings showcasing his great sensitivity and signature approach to standards as a master improviser and piano innovator.

Selections include:

"Yardbird Suite"
"I Got the World on a String"
"Lulu's Back in Town"
"Walking My Baby Back Home"
"Windsong" (a beautiful waltz by Bob Wilbur)
"Dave's Blues" (an original by Dave and my personal favorite)

Concord CCD 4099

Dave McKenna and Grey Sargent Live at Maybeck Recital Hall

Dave McKenna once said, "I really dig the way Grey Sargent plays. He's right up there with the best of them." McKenna and Sargent played for years around the New England area and something extra special happened when they got together as you will hear in these selections.

Selections include:

"Sheik of Araby"
"Girl of My Dreams"
"Deed I Do"

Concord CCD 4552

Born to Play

Dick "Spider" Johnson

Courtesy of Pamela Johnson Sargent.

Very few musicians I've been privileged to know were as versatile as Dick Johnson, Brockton's gift to the jazz world. In the notes for Dick's first Concord CD in 1979 I wrote, "Dick has the musical talent of three or four great players rolled up into one, and can swing mightily on alto, tenor, soprano saxophone, flute, and clarinet." Though he was affiliated with big bands for over fifty years, touring with Charlie Spivak, Benny Goodman, Neil Hefti, Buddy Morrow, and Buddy Rich, for the past twenty-five he was director of the Artie Shaw Orchestra, hand-picked by the late "King of Clarinet" himself.

His dexterity and speed on all the reed instruments earned him the nickname "Spider," and it was an album he cut for Concord Records called *Spider's Blues* that opened a new chapter in his life. His manager, Bill Curtis, sent the record to Dick's idol Artie Shaw. The response from Artie was ecstatic: not only did he say it was the best clarinet playing he'd heard, but he asked if Dick was available to lead Shaw's Band. Making his first road trip in years, Artie came to Boston to personally rehearse the band at the WGBH studios. Audiences young and old came to hear the exciting charts that had made the Shaw Band famous. The orchestra still performs regularly worldwide, bringing big band music at its best to a whole new generation.

I first heard Dick play alto saxophone at a roadhouse in Brockton called the Roma Cafe. It was back in the early sixties and he'd just come off the road with the Buddy Morrow Band. I couldn't believe my ears! On the lower registers his tones were rich, warm, and vibrant, or soaring high above the band when needed. He sounded like a combination of Charlie Parker, Lee Konitz, and Johnny Hodges. I introduced myself and we became good friends.

Dick's wit and boundless energy were an inspiration. Comfortable in any setting, Dick was always a great guest on my show. We talked about everything from favorite movies, his love of food and restaurants, to back-stage gossip, and priceless stories of life on the road. He would break me up as well as anyone else who happened to be in the studio.

Ruby Braff, always one of the most difficult musicians to please, once told me that Dick was one of his favorite players. When I told Dick, he said, "Wow... I guess I'm one of the few cats who made the cut!"

During one of our interviews, Dick shared a story of a failed attempt to snare an applause break: "We were on with Dave McKenna. We thought, how are we going to get half the applause Dave gets. Gray (Sargent) and I just pulled out some bebop tune like 'Crazyology,' hoping to dupe Dave, but then of course *we* had to hang on for dear life. I got an okay round of applause, and then Gray took off and whaled and got the same thing. Then Dave got ramped up. *While he was still playing*, he got a standing ovation. I looked at Gray and we both nodded: forget it; let's just go along for the ride."

When not performing, Dick made his home in his native city of Brockton with his lovely wife Rose. His son Gary carries on the family tradition in music and is one of the finest drummers on the scene. His daughter Pam is married to the brilliant guitarist Gray Sargent, a member of the Tony Bennett quartet.

I was honored when Dick dedicated a big band arrangement called "Spread that Gospel, Ron." I have it framed in my studio and consider it one of my greatest treasures. Thanks, Dick, for all you've done in spreading your gospel worldwide, and may you rest in peace, my friend.

SUGGESTED RECORDINGS

Dick Johnson Plays Alto Sax, Flute, Soprano Sax and Clarinet
Dave McKenna on Piano; Bob Maize, Bass; and Jake Hannah, Drums
A collection of jazz standards showcasing the versatility of Dick Johnson along with the brilliant artistry of Dave McKenna.
Concord CCD4107

Artie's Choice! And the Naturals
Featuring Dick Johnson, Lou Columbo, Trumpet; and Gray Sargent, Guitar

This privately produced two-CD collection includes marvelous Dick Johnson arrangements of "Stardust," "Waltz for Debbie," "Indian Summer," "Young and Foolish," "Emily," and other standards.

Star Dust and Beyond: A Tribute to Artie Shaw featuring Dick Johnson

Dick's loving tribute to his idol and mentor Artie Shaw that includes such classics as:

"I Concentrate on You"
"My Funny Valentine"
"My Romance"
"Gone With the Wind"

Boss of the Blues

Joe Williams

© Ken Franckling.

Joe Williams was a renowned jazz vocalist, a baritone who sang a mixture of blues, popular songs, ballads, and jazz standards. He was born Joseph Goreed in 1918, in Cordele, Georgia, to his eighteen-year-old mother Anne. Determined to make a new life for her and her son, Anne moved to Chicago and worked as a cook for four years until she could afford to send for him to join her and his grandmother and aunt.

Joe was a teenager when he began singing in nightclubs around the windy city. He reveled in the then-rebellious sounds of Louis Armstrong, Duke Ellington, Ethel Waters, Cab Calloway, and Big Joe Turner, among others, even starting up his own gospel vocal quartet called "The Jubilee Boys," as well as teaching himself to play piano. His first job was at a club called Kitty Davis's, where he cleaned latrines and sang for tips. Even though the most he took home was five dollars a night, both Joe and his family were convinced he could make a living with his voice, so he dropped out of school at age sixteen to pursue his dreams.

Word of this young man's heartfelt tone and impeccable timing spread fast, and he was soon tapped to apprentice with jazz legends Coleman Hawkins and Lionel Hampton in the early 1930s. His first real break was in 1938, when Jimmy Noone invited him to sing with his band, which soon created a reputation for Williams not only at Chicago dance halls but from coast to coast on national radio stations. Soon he was touring with the Les Hite band, which accompanied such greats as Fats Waller and Louis Armstrong.

Lionel Hampton hired Joe to fill in for his regular vocalist in 1942. By the time the band's former singer returned, Williams was in great demand. He made his first recording with Andy Kirk and His Twelve Clouds of Joy in the late 1940s. Following stints with Albert Ammons, Red Saunders, and trumpeter "Hot Lips Page," he had his first big hit with "Every Day I Have the Blues," which became his signature song.

After teaming up with the Count Basie Orchestra in 1954, he became an international star and one of the most important elements in the Count Basie Band. He stayed with Basie for seven years, recording "Every Day I Have the Blues" among countless others. Joe shared some details with me during our 1990 interview: "I needed to get out of Chicago, I'd been there all my life. Basie told me, 'Look, I can't give you what you want or what you deserve, but why don't you come with me around the country and see what people think?' Within a year's time, we did our first tour of Europe. First stop was this tiny town outside of Stockholm, where there were ten thousand people jammed into this park. When we finished, ten thousand people were standing on their chairs and cheering. I said, 'What are we going to do, Base?' And he said, 'For once, you're going to quit while you're ahead.'"

Later on, Joe toured with his own group and made wonderful recordings with other jazz giants including George Shearing, Cannonball Adderley, the Thad Jones–Mel Louis Orchestra, and the Capp/Pierce Juggernaut Band. With his good looks and charismatic presence, he became a familiar face on television, appearing on Johnny Carson's *The Tonight Show*, as well as the Joey Bishop, Steve Allen, Merv Griffin, and Mike Douglas shows; even taking a turn as father-in-law "Grandpa Al" on the *Bill Cosby Show*. Joe also spent much of his time performing at jazz festivals, appearing in movies, and playing various jazz cruises. He told me he had been on so many cruises that when in port, he never bothered to leave the ship.

Joe possessed a powerful, rich baritone capable of singing ballads, blues, and standards in his own swinging style. I'll always remember my radio conversations with him in which he expressed his great love for classical music, especially opera. He recalled to me his early days in Chicago where he never failed to miss the Saturday afternoon broadcast of the Metropolitan Opera hosted by Milton Cross. At that time, black artists were nonexistent at the Met, and I always felt that Joe would have had a great career as an opera singer if the times had been different.

Once he blew me away in the studio when he sang a few measures of King Phillip's aria "Ella giammai m'amo" from Verdi's *Don Carlo*. After hearing that, there was no doubt in my mind that he would have made a great Verdi basso!

Duke Ellington wrote about Joe Williams in his autobiography, *Music Is My Mistress*, "He sang real soul blues on which his perfect enunciation of the words gave the blues a new dimension...all the accents were in the right places and on the right words."[28]

Joe passed away in Las Vegas where he made his home. He was singing right up until the end and still in magnificent voice. His wife Jillian said he always looked forward to his visits to Boston where he had so many friends who packed the house whenever he performed here. I feel privileged to have known such a remarkable man and to be able to share his treasured legacy.

SUGGESTED RECORDINGS

Joe Williams with the Count Basic Orchestra, directed by Frank Foster

In this exciting 1993 recording, made during a live performance at Orchestra Hall in Detroit, Joe revisits some of the big hits he had with Count Basie.

Selections include:

"Hurry On Down"
"Honeysuckle Rose"
"Sometimes I'm Happy"
"The Comeback"
"Roll 'em Pete"
"Sugar"
"There Never Be Another You"

Telarc CD 83329

Jazz 'Round Midnight

A collection showcasing the matchless style of one of the great singers of blues and ballads. Joe Williams is in great company in this superb CD with vocalist Shirley Horn, the Count Basie Orchestra, pianist Norman Simmons, and "SuperSax" conducted by Med Flory.

Selections include:

"Embraceable You"
"Come Rain or Come Shine"
"Never the Less"
"Teach Me Tonight"
"When Sunny Gets Blue"
"I'm Beginning to See the Light"

Verve 314 527 034-2

Here's To Life: Joe Williams with the Robert Farnon Orchestra

Joe told me that this is one of his all-time favorite recordings, and it's one of mine as well! Recorded in London in 1993 with a full symphony orchestra and arrangements by Robert Farnon, this CD is difficult to surpass. The beauty and range of Joe Williams' voice in his interpretation of these ballads is astounding.

Selections include:

"Here's To Life"
"What a Wonderful World"
"If I Had You"
"Young and Foolish"
"A Time For Love"
"Maybe September"
"When I Fall In Love"

Telarc CD 83357

III. THE GREAT AMERICAN SONGBOOK

The John Singer Sargent of Singers

Tony Bennett, Joyce Della Chiesa, and me

© Roger Farrington.

After an appearance with the Count Basie Band at the Berklee Performance Center one snowy evening in 1982, Tony Bennett made his way to the Copley Plaza Hotel to visit his old friend, jazz pianist Dave McKenna. There he sat in with Dave and sang a few songs to the delight of the lucky people who just happened to be in the audience that evening... which included Joyce and me.

After his set, Tony joined us for dinner. This was the beginning of a long and beautiful friendship with one of the great icons of the American Songbook. During that first meal together, we touched on topics ranging from the Italian Renaissance, Frank Sinatra, John Singer Sargent, David Hockney, Dr. Martin Luther King, American and Italian film; to Martin Scorsese, Robert DeNiro, Federico Fellini, and Victorio DeSica.

All this before the gelato.

Born Anthony Dominick Benedetto on August 13, 1926, in Astoria, New York, Tony Bennett can handily be called one of the greatest friends the American Songbook has ever known. With a poet's imagination and an artist's passion, his work has endeared him to millions around the world for over fifty years.

Even after decades of worldwide acclaim, Tony has never forgotten his humble origins or his dear mother Anna, a dressmaker who was widowed at an early age and brought up Mary, John, and Tony on her own. During one of our interviews, Tony related a story that turned out to have a profound impact on his thinking and ultimately his career. One day a woman approached his mother with inferior cloth and said, "I want you to make me a beautiful dress with this." Anna gave the material back to the woman and said, "To make a beautiful dress, you need beautiful material."

Tony learned a real lesson that day! Never compromise your artistry by singing inferior songs; always choose quality and you'll never go wrong. Sinatra gave him the same advice many years later.

Bennett's father came from Calabria, Italy, and opened a grocery store in New York, but it was Tony's uncle, a tap dancer in vaudeville, who gave him an early window into show business. By age ten Tony was already singing wherever he could, soaking up the sounds of Al Jolson, Eddie Cantor, Bing Crosby, Louis Armstrong, and Jimmy Durante. At New York's High School of Industrial Art he studied music and painting (he was especially taken at the time with caricatures), but dropped out at sixteen to help support his family. Though he worked as a copy boy and runner for the Associated Press in Manhattan, he also landed several gigs as a singing waiter in Italian restaurants in Queens.

Even though he worked hard to put food on his family's table, New York's burgeoning jazz scene was an inspiration to him, and his home life felt relatively secure. He told me: "I loved my early days growing up in Astoria. It's where Woody Allen makes his films! Back then it was half Italian, half Greek, just a nice middle-income neighborhood which had a real country feeling—lots of trees—but was just fifteen minutes from the city."

Drafted into the army in 1944 during the final stages of World War II, Tony's experiences as an enlisted man read like an adventure novel. At basic training, Benedetto tangled with a sergeant from the South who lacked tolerance for Italians from New York City, assigning him backbreaking doses of KP and latrine cleaning. Assigned as a replacement infantryman for a unit that suffered heavy casualties in the Battle of the Bulge, Tony moved across France into Germany, ultimately fighting on the front line which he described as a "front row seat in hell."

In Germany, Tony and his company fought in bitterly cold winter conditions, hunkered down in foxholes as Germans fired on them. After crossing the Rhine, he and his company engaged in brutally dangerous house-to-house, town-after-town combat to smoke out the German soldiers, narrowly escaping death several times. At the war's end, he helped liberate a Nazi concentration camp near Landsberg.

Tony's dining with a black friend from high school—when the army was still segregated—led to a demotion and reassignment to Graves Registration Service duties. Subsequently, he sang with the Army military band under the stage name Joe Bari, which was a partial anagram of Calabria.

The entire experience made him not only a patriot but a pacifist, and he would later write, "Anybody who thinks war is romantic obviously hasn't gone through one."[29]

Upon his discharge, Tony learned the discipline of singing bel canto, which would, along with other healthy habits of living, keep his voice in good shape even to the present day. As he said during our 1985 interview, "I joined the American Theater wing when I got out under the GI Bill of Rights, learned popular phrasing under Myriam Speare who taught Peggy Lee and Helen O'Connell. She was right on 52nd Street, which was the land of geniuses, I'm telling you. The golden era of singing. It was the age of miracles when we saw the highest level of American music: Stan Getz, Nat King Cole, Stan Kenton, Woody Herman, Duke Ellington, Count Basie, Jimmy Lunceford."

He continued to perform while waiting tables, incorporating the style and phrasing of other musicians such as Stan Getz's saxophone technique and Art Tatum's piano, a brilliant way of helping him improvise and interpret songs. In 1949 Pearl Bailey lit up when she heard him sing and asked him to open for her in Greenwich Village where her friend Bob Hope sat in the crowd. Hope immediately took him on the road, billing him as Tony Bennett, where Mitch Miller caught his act and signed him with Columbia Records.

His first big hit, "Because of You," a ballad with lush orchestration, caught fire via jukeboxes, reached number one, and stayed there for ten weeks in 1951, selling over a million copies. His recording of "Blue Velvet" attracted screaming teenaged fans at the Paramount Theater in New York, where Bennett did seven shows a day, starting at 10:30 in the morning.

Along with the hits came Bennett's marriage to Ohio art student Patricia Beech. Two thousand female fans dressed in black gathered outside New York's St. Patrick's cathedral in mock mourning. Bennett and Beech would have two sons: Danny in 1954 and Dae in 1955.

"Rags to Riches," an uptempo big band number, was his third number one, followed by "Strangers in Paradise," which became a hit in the United Kingdom, launching his career as an international artist. Even in the fifties when rock and roll was taking hold and pop singers beginning to struggle, Bennett placed eight songs in the top 40.

In the late fifties, Bennett's pianist and musical director Ralph Sharon suggested a change in strategy. Noting a short shelf life of bubble gum material, he advised Tony to go with his instinct and record a jazz album. Tony's first long-playing album, *Cloud 7*, showcased these new jazz elements while 1957's *The Beat of My Heart* used jazz musicians Herbie Mann and Nat Adderly and Latin stars Candido Camero and Chico Hamilton. The first male pop vocalist to sing with Basie's band, Bennett followed up with *Basie Swings, Bennett Sings.* This was also a time when Tony was building up the quality of his nightclub act, staging a highly successful performance at Carnegie Hall and finally appearing on *Johnny Carson's Tonight Show.* He was, in fact, Johnny's first guest ever.

The next few years saw the release of "I Left My Heart in San Francisco," which would become Bennett's signature song, and "The Good Life" on his album *I Wanna Be Around*. But as the sixties wore on, there was no escaping the Beatles and the British invasion and with them a dimming focus on pop, standards, and jazz. Beyond some minor hits mostly based on show tunes, Bennett's star seemed destined to fade, perhaps even go out.

Bennett's marriage ended soon after an attempt to break into acting in a 1966 film, *The Oscar*, an experience he neither enjoyed nor sought to repeat. To round out the misery, Bennett cut the album *Tony Sings the Great Hits of Today!* featuring Beatles tunes and a psychedelic art cover. The fact was, Bennett became physically ill at the thought of stepping into the studio to record these songs. Years later he would equate this experience to that of his mother being forced to produce quality from cheap raw material.

Bennett married Sandra Grant, an actress he'd met filming *The Oscar*, and with her had two daughters, Joanna in 1969 and Antonia in 1974. Deciding to take his career into his own hands, Bennett started his own record company, Improv. Even though under this label he recorded classics such as "A Tribute to Irving Berlin" and "What is This Thing Called Love?" as well as two historic albums with pianist Bill Evans, Improv lacked distribution and by 1977 was out of business. Bennett hit bottom with no recording contract, no manager, a second marriage in failure mode, and the IRS trying to seize his Los Angeles home.

In 1979 he called his sons Danny and Dae and said, "Look, I'm lost here. It seems people don't want to hear the music I make."[30] Danny not only listened, but came to terms with the fact that what he lacked in musical gifts, he more than made up for in business sense, the opposite constellation of abilities his father possessed. Danny moved his dad back to New York, began booking him in colleges and small theaters to cleanse him of a "Vegas" image, and by 1986 Tony was re-assigned to Columbia Records, this time with creative control. The release of *The Art of Excellence* brought him to the charts for the first time since 1972.

Danny Bennett felt that younger audiences would connect with his dad's music if only they were given a chance to hear it. By the mid-eighties, even rock stars such as Linda Ronstadt began recording albums of standards and songs from the Great American Songbook. A younger, hipper audience caught on to Tony Bennett's magic with the help of appearances on *Late Night with David Letterman*, *Late Night with Conan O'Brien*, even a series of benefit concerts organized by alternative rock radio stations like WBCN in Boston. In 1990 he released *Astoria: Portrait of the Artist*, *Perfectly Frank* in '92, and *Steppin'Out* in '93; the latter two earning gold status and Grammys. At the MTV Music Awards he stood shoulder to shoulder with the Red Hot Chili Peppers and Flavor Flav. As the *New York Times* put it, "Tony Bennett has not just bridged the generation gap, he has demolished it."[31] At age 68, after winning the top Grammy prize of Album of the Year, it was clear that Tony Bennett had come all the way back.

I can't help but think of Tony as the John Singer Sargent of singers: the man paints portraits in song with his voice. Like a magnificent oil or watercolor, his voice evokes delicate shades of light and color, capturing the essence of the lyric and melody. That signature catch or tear in his voice seems to spring naturally from every experience the man has ever had.

The bel canto element in his singing conjures an Italian operatic style that makes each song like a mini aria. Sometimes I hear the sound of Giuseppi Di-Stefano; at other times, Claudio Villa. Occasionally Tony will simply put the mic down and sing naturally, often "Fly Me to the Moon," partly to demonstrate to the younger members of the audience the dying art of vocal projection. He shared with me that his Calabrian grandfather would stand up high on a mountain and sing, his voice carrying throughout the village.

I'll wait as you imagine *that* for a moment....

There's a song called "When I Lost You" that Irving Berlin wrote when his first wife passed away. Tony recorded one of the verses a cappella. If you aren't moved hearing him paint that picture of loss I might question your status as human. A cut on the album, *The Playground*, called "My Mom" by Walter Donaldson, a song about mothers, also never fails to get to me each time I hear it.

In a 1985 interview I asked Tony how he keeps things fresh, after having sung these tunes hundreds and hundreds of times: "It's the combination of elements: the crowd, the atmosphere of the place, the performers I'm with." We talked about his comfortable rapport with the jazz musicians he worked with at the time: Ruby Braff, Zoot Sims, Bobby Hackett, and Dave McKenna. He called Bobby Hackett: "one of the great melody players of all time. In fact, it was Bobby who introduced me to Louis Armstrong who said, 'I'm the coffee, but man, Bobby's the cream.'"

The artistry of Bennett and Sinatra have often been compared. In the early fifties when a young Bennett was first signed with Columbia, he was warned against trying to become another "Old Blue Eyes," encouraged to develop a style of his own. Both are poets, but Sinatra's sound seems more robust, almost brash at times, while Tony, who works more closely with his arrangers, is smoky, mellow, and intimate. In the end, however, the admiration between the two was mutual. Sinatra said, "For my money, Tony Bennett is the best singer in the business. He excites me when I watch him. He moves me. He's the singer who gets across what the composer has in mind, and probably a little bit more."[32]

The same kind of commitment Bennett brings to the music and lyrics of Jerome Kern, Cole Porter, George Gershwin, Johnny Mandel, Johnny Mercer, and others he brings to his more introspective passion: drawing and painting. The small boy who drew chalk pictures on the sidewalks of Astoria is alive and well in the man who picks up a paintbrush every day in quiet contemplation of the things he loves most: the rolling hills of Tuscany, the time-worn faces of jazz masters Duke Ellington and Dizzy Gillespie.

"Like music," Tony said, "art is a lifetime of study, which is the whole adventure, but it's a terrific amount of work if you are serious about it." A self-confessed "museum freak," Tony visits museums and galleries all over the world, learning the subtleties of various styles and studying the great masters, always making time to sketch the view from the window of his hotel suite, or as he told me, "photograph whatever strikes me, if I don't have time to sketch or paint. I especially love landscape painting, and there is no better day for me than one without plans, when I can wander in the countryside." We shared a laugh over an exhibit of the impressionists at Boston's Museum of Fine Arts; reviewers were still questioning whether Monet was "good" or not, since as Tony put it, "no one likes him but the public." One of Tony's favorite artists is good friend David Hockney, for whom he painted "Homage to Hockney," on permanent display at the Butler Institute of American Art in Youngstown, Ohio, where Tony was recently named one of America's greatest artists.

Tony has often said that he sees colors when he sings; that his voice is affected by the weather: even the rain or sun influence his sound. I can certainly close my eyes and see not only colors but images and often entire scenes in my mind. "Because of You," "When Joanna Loves Me," and "Strangers in Paradise" animate entire worlds inside my head. I believe his intuitive sense of the relationship between sound and image is enhanced by his daily involvement with both of those worlds.

The United Nations has commissioned his work (under his family name of Benedetto) on two occasions including their 50th anniversary, and his work, including lithographs, is part of permanent collections at the National Arts Club in Manhattan, the Smithsonian, as well as numerous galleries around the world. Among the many owners of original Benedettos are the late Cary Grant, Carol Burnett, Whoopie Goldberg, the late Frank Sinatra, Donald Trump, Oprah Winfrey, Mickey Rooney, Katie Couric, and contemporary artist Robert Rauschenberg. I am also the proud owner of a pencil sketch he did of me while at dinner at the Four Seasons with Joyce and his wife Susan. Tony carries his sketchbook and uses it everywhere he goes: airports, airplanes, restaurants, concert halls, and cafes, saying "Airplanes are best. People aren't moving too much and they're pretty much stuck there!" Many of his works are included in *Tony Bennett: What My Heart Has Seen* in 1996, as well as the best-seller *Tony Bennett in the Studio: A Life of Art & Music.*

I confess that a lot of what I admire in Tony I admired in my own father; in fact some of the similarities are striking. Both served in World War II, both stood up for African American friends. In my father's case, he vouched for a black enlisted man who was being court-martialed for setting up his tent incorrectly (using the butt of his rifle to pound down a tent stake as opposed to a rock or similar item.) The black soldiers under his command thanked my father with a shaving kit, something he treasured all his life. Shortly afterward, he was assigned to Graves Registration in Hawaii (now known as "Mortuary Affairs"), which involved everything from making identification via bodies or body parts, to recovery of bodies, to ensuring proper burial. As noted earlier, Tony was assigned to these same duties (though not sent to Hawaii) because he shared a meal with a black friend. Like Tony, my father also painted not only with his voice, but on canvas; the two men share this wonderful Renaissance quality. Both men stood up for what they believed when actions like these were certainly met with more resistance than today.

A staunch believer in the Civil Rights movement, Bennett took part in the Selma to Montgomery marches in 1965, and he consistently refused to perform in apartheid South Africa. Tony donates so much time to charitable causes he is sometimes nicknamed "Tony Benefit."

On a purely personal note, he is just a very good friend in a world where true friendship simply isn't as common as you might think, certainly not as common as it should be. A certain vulnerability based in real strength and a sense of self seems necessary, both for friendships between men and, from what I've heard, women as well. My birthday simply doesn't pass without some good wishes from him, and he asks after Joyce and our family with genuine interest. Over the years Joyce and I have become a surrogate aunt and uncle to Tony's daughter Antonia, a wonderful young singer who stayed with us a great deal, especially during her years at the Berklee College of Music.

In 2007 Tony married his long time partner Susan Crow, and together they founded Exploring the Arts, a charitable organization dedicated to creating, promoting, and supporting arts education. They simultaneously founded the Frank Sinatra School of the Arts in Queens, a public high school focused on teaching the performing arts.

Now in his mid-eighties, Tony tours steadily, doing one hundred to two hundred shows a year. He has sold fifty million records worldwide, won fifteen Grammy Awards, and released more than seventy albums. But it doesn't matter if he's singing to thousands or just a few, his voice finds you and holds you.

His persona has crossed over to the youth market like no other artist before or since, introducing millions of young people to the American Songbook not only through his appearances on MTV and elsewhere, but through the efforts of his son and manager, Danny Bennett. His encouragement of fellow singers shines through in the 2001 album *Playin' With My Friends: Bennett Sings the Blues*, which also features Stevie Wonder, k.d. lang, Bonnie Rait, B.B. King, and Ray Charles. All in all, one of the cleverest, classiest comebacks I've ever seen.

A focus on diet, exercise—especially tennis—and proper rest keeps his voice preternaturally young and able to reach the high registers, a feat that becomes more difficult with age. As he told me, "The theory is that after thirty-five your voice goes down. My idols are Ellington, Fred Astaire, Bing Crosby, and Maurice Chevalier. They sustained what they had as they got older; they hung in there. That's what I'm hoping to do; in fact I have an ambition to get better as I get older." He added that he had no intention of retiring: "If you study the masters—Picasso, Jack

Benny, Fred Astaire—right up to the day they died, they were performing. If you are creative, you only get busier as you get older. In fact, I need two lifetimes. I'll never get it finished. I have that many ideas about what I'd like to do and what I'd like to learn."

SUGGESTED RECORDINGS

Tony Bennett "The Playground"

No better way for kids and adults to come together. Some selections include:

> "Bein' Green"
> "Put on a Happy Face"
> "When You Wish Upon a Star"
> "My Mom"

Columbia CSK 41457

Tony Bennett "The Art of Romance"

When it comes to love songs, there's no better singer than Tony. This CD, conducted by composer/arranger Johnny Mandel, includes such favorites as:

> "I Remember You"
> "Where Do You Start"
> "Don't Like Goodbyes"
> "Close Enough for Love"

RPM Records/Columbia CK 92820

Forty Years: The Artistry of Tony Bennett

This four-CD boxed set, together with an informative booklet and anthology, is a must for any Tony Bennett collector. It includes just about every hit he recorded along with some lesser-known songs.
Selections include:

> "Boulevard of Broken Dreams"
> "I Wanna Be Around"
> "Maybe This Time"
> "Because of You"
> "Stranger In Paradise"
> "I Left My Heart In San Francisco"

Columbia/Legacy 46843

The Embodiment of Elegance

Bobby Short and me

Courtesy of Charlie Lake.

James Gavin sums up Bobby Short's impeccable artistry in his excellent book, *Intimate Nights—The Golden Age of New York Cabaret:* "By the early seventies, Bobby Short had become a national symbol of style, sophistication, elegance and good taste. The influences of his idols, the vivacity of Fats Waller and Cab Calloway, Duke Ellington's suave refined manner, the supreme dignity of Ellington's vocalist Ivy Anderson, combined to give Short a polish that none of his colleagues could equal."[33]

I couldn't agree more! New York's premiere cabaret singer and pianist, Bobby Short owned a charisma and presence unrivaled for the time. With his beatific smile and charm he could light up a room just by walking in it, even before singing a note. What other entertainer could get away with wearing a tuxedo with a bare chest and bow tie and look absolutely dashing? Many times interviewing Bobby in my studio, I felt I should have been wearing my tux as well.

His extraordinary career began in Danville, Illinois, in 1926, where one of his classmates was Dick Van Dyke. The ninth of ten children in a family of modest means, he began playing piano as soon as he could reach the keys. He told me that both his parents played piano, in fact "most households back then had a piano and at least one person who could play it." A child prodigy, Bobby learned to sight read stunningly early, though he would insist to host Marian McPartland, "I played by ear, Marian, I still play by ear."[34]

Though young Bobby was playing the piano and singing in roadhouses by the time he was nine, he also lived in the traditional world of family, church, and school, gaining a great deal of musical experience from glee clubs. As he said in his memoir, *Black and White Baby*, "It was all right (performing in clubs) with my mother because I was in the care of a man whose aunt was a church friend of hers."[35] On weekend nights a family friend would take him from taverns to vaudeville stages where a hat was passed as he played and sang. Two years later he left for Chicago and was managed by agents. "I had no idea the image I projected,"[36] he later recalled, but he did remember singing "Sophisticated Lady" in a high, squeaky voice.

Another formative influence was the radio. He explained: "It was very elegant. We were left alone a lot at night as kids, but there was always the radio. My great loves were Ella Fitzgerald, Art Tatum on the piano—who completely blew my mind and changed me forever—Fats Waller, and Earl Hines. I also adored Mildred Bailey, Walter Fuller, Arthur Lee Simpson, the Andrews Sisters, Fred Astaire, and Bing Crosby. They were my world."

New York came just before he turned thirteen. Though arrangements were made for a tutor, he was more excited about his first theatrical photographs that involved custom-made white tails and ankle-length camel's hair coats. Long before graduating from high school, Bobby was performing at Harlem's Apollo Theatre where he met his idols Duke Ellington, Fats Waller, Benny Carter, and the legendary pianist Art Tatum.

In our 1988 interview we talked about his first impressions of New York: "It was 1937. I was just a kid and 52nd Street *was* 52nd Street. One could hear Joe Marsala, and Adele Girard, Art Tatum, Billie Holiday, Francis Faye, Roy Eldridge. It was a jazz street. When I came back in 1945 there was still a lot of jazz, but it was starting to fall apart. Of course it's still called jazz street but it's not like it was. After gigs we musicians would leave and hang out or jam between sets at Mintons, or at the White Rose on 6th Avenue. There were smart nightclubs popping up in the 1940s: Leon and Eddies, Tony's, where Mabel Mercer sang; then across the street, Bonds and Cook, the piano team would perform." Bobby was always generous with his impromptu late-night performances at the various cafes and restaurants up and down 52nd Street.

In 1968 he was offered a two-week stint at the Café Carlyle in Manhattan to fill in for George Feyer. Accompanied by Beverly Peer on bass and Dick Sheridan on drums, Short parlayed this visit into a nearly four-decade run, becoming the pianist in residence at the Carlyle, much like Feyer had before him. Sitting an arm's reach from his audience, Bobby combined an effortless elegance, intelligent vocal phrasing (perfected at the feet of Mabel Mercer and Ethel Waters), a talent for showcasing little known songs while reinvigorating standbys, infectious high spirits, and unflagging professionalism to produce an ever growing and enamored audience.

Many have said that Short was a living library of America's popular songs, knowing more songs than even he has counted, but also who wrote them, who sang them, and when and where they were first performed. Stephen Holden of the *New York Times* wrote, "(Bobby) infuses traditional society piano with the rollicking animation of Harlem vaudeville...even sadder songs convey a high style *joie de vivre*."[37] Night after night, the rich and famous of New York society came to be entertained in what turned out to be one of the longest engagements of any performer in the history of show business. He became a symbol of Manhattan sophistication, attracting royalty, movie stars, socialites, sports figures, captains of industry, and jazz aficionados, and was a guest performer at the White House when President and Mrs. Nixon entertained the Duke and Duchess of Windsor. Woody Allen included him as a must-see for his characters' tour of his beloved city, granting him a part in *Hannah and Her Sisters*.

Our interview marked his twenty-first year at the Carlyle: "It's more than where I make my bread and butter. It's the nicest room of its kind in New York, thus in the country, so perhaps the world. There are no other rooms where one can go and be that comfortable I think, but it wasn't always like that. It took me a number of years to make it what I dreamed it could be, to make it the kind of room where people would actually come in and sit and listen to what I was doing."

He reflected on his audience: "Great saloon singers had firm blues and jazz roots. Cabaret had to get the audience's attention in a hurry, then it was always a struggle to keep their attention. You need that sense of urgency, and with a jazz background you came out prepared to entertain your audience. They didn't want to hear 'Softly As In a Morning Sunrise,' they wanted to hear something peppy. They were out there drinking, out in a bar for some kicks and to have a good time."

For me, a trip to "Gotham" was not complete without a visit to the Carlyle. Every performance Bobby gave was a master class. His dedication to the "Great American Song" made him equally brilliant at capturing the lighthearted spirit of Bessie Smith's "Gimme a Pigfoot" as he was at pouring out the honey in Gershwin and Duke's "I Can't Get Started With You." I can honestly say I learned more about a song from him that anyone else.

During our interview we often discussed his favorite composers and songwriters; he named Rodgers and Hart, Jerome Kern, Harold Arlen, Vernon Duke, Noel Coward, and George and Ira Gershwin; although Cole Porter always topped the list. The sophistication of Porter's lyrics seemed tailor made for him, and Short's playful sense of humor was in perfect sync with Porter's loaded double-entendres. He told me he was once asked what these lyrics meant from a Porter song: "I will be your broom if you'll be my dustpan." He said, "What's this song *about*? Sex! I mean, is it me? I don't think so."

He had a talent for insinuating the sensuality behind a song. As Whitney Balliett put it in a 1970 *New Yorker* profile, Short "stripped (a song) to its essentials—words lifted and carried by the curves of melody," also noting that his baritone, often tinged with laryngitis, "lends his voice a searching down sound, and his uncertain notes enhance the cheerfulness and abandon he projects."[38]

Bobby also dedicated himself to championing African American composers who contributed to New York's musical theatre, including Eubie Blake, James P. Johnson, Andy Razaf, Fats Waller, Duke Ellington, and Billy Straythorn, showcasing their work not in a didactic way, but simply as equals to their white contemporaries.

I once shared an unforgettable lunch with him and his good friend Charlie Davidson at the Ritz in Boston. Bobby would frequent Charlie's legendary "Andover Shop" in Harvard Square to augment his natty wardrobe (his name appeared on numerous "best dressed" lists). Our lunch lasted several hours and was constantly interrupted by excited fans. He was always gracious and accommodating to each and every one who stopped by.

When I reflect on Bobby, I envision a kind of intimate live performance and unabashed romance that is sadly missing today. Though he called himself a saloon singer, the world will remember him as one of the greatest cabaret performers of the twentieth century. What Fred Astaire was to dancing, Bobby Short was to American Song.

Suggested Recordings

The Café Carlyle Presents Bobby Short: You're the Top Love Songs of Cole Porter

Robert Kimball who wrote the notes for this CD said: "Seeing and hearing Bobby
  Short perform Cole Porter songs at New York City's Café Carlyle is one of
  THE quintessential experiences of Gotham Nightlife." When you listen to this
  CD, you'll know why. It was recorded live in 1998 with Bobby's marvelous
  band and wonderful arrangements. It's the next best thing to being there!
Selections include:

"I Concentrate On You"
"You Do Something To Me"
"In the Still of the Night"
"I've Got You Under My Skin"
"You're the Top"
"You're Sensational"
"Can-Can"

Telarc CD 83463

Bobby Short: Late Night at the Carlyle

This collection captures Bobby in a more intimate setting with his trio. It was recorded in 1991, live at the Carlyle with Beverly Peer, bass and Robert Scott on drums. In addition to being a great singer, Bobby gives us a chance to hear his expertise on the keyboard playing some familiar and less familiar selections from the American Songbook.

Selections include:

> "Do I Hear You Saying I Love You?" (A lesser know Rogers and Hart tune from 1928)
> "Body and Soul"
> "Street of Dreams"
> "Paradise"
> "Satin Doll"
> "Love is Here to Stay"
> "After You, Who?" (A rare Cole Porter tune dropped from the 1934 film version of the *Gay Divorcee*)

Telarc CD 83311

Bobby Short: Swing That Music

This recording came about when Bobby rediscovered favorite music from his early days; it reminds me of the classic Teddy Wilson sessions with Billie Holiday. All the arrangements are by trombonist Dan Barrett who teams up with Howard Alden, guitar; Chuck Wilson, reeds; Frank Tate, bass; and Jackie Williams, drums. The music is irresistible, infectious, and a delight from beginning to end.

Selections include:

> The Title Song: "Swing That Music"
> "Tenderly"
> "Drop Me Off in Harlem"
> "If Dreams Come True"
> "Gone With the Wind"
> "Sleep Baby Don't Cry" (A haunting lullaby by William Archibald and my personal favorite)

Telarc CD 83317

3. FRANK SINATRA, JR.

His Own Way

Photo courtesy of Frank Sinatra, Jr.

As the only son of larger-than-life icon Frank Sinatra, Frank Sinatra, Jr. was dealt a complex hand that he has played out with dignity, his own native talent, and a kind of learned elegance for over fifty years.

Born in Jersey City, New Jersey, in 1944 to Frank and Nancy Sinatra, young Frank rarely saw his famous father who was either on the road nonstop or making films. Keenly interested in music as far back as he can recall, Frank Jr. began performing in local clubs by his early teens. By age nineteen he'd been enlisted as the vocalist for Sam Donahue's band (Frank called Sam a "musician's musician") and spent a good deal of time learning the business from Duke Ellington who had taken the young man under his wing.

Around nine o'clock one evening in 1963 at Harrah's Tahoe Lounge in Nevada, nineteen-year-old Frank was finishing up a room-service chicken dinner with John Foss, 26, a trumpet player with the Dorsey band. There was a knock at the door; Frank invited the visitors in. After announcing themselves as delivery men, Barry Keenan with his friend Joe Amsler (both 23 and greenhorn criminals) whipped out a gun, tied up Foss, and forced young Frank, blindfolded, into their beat up Chevy. In minutes they were navigating their way through a blizzard in the Sierra Nevadas toward a hideout eight hours away. Two days later, a $240,000 ransom was paid just before the two young men were arrested and ultimately sentenced to short prison terms. Though it was soon shot down, a rumor circulated that the whole thing had been a publicity stunt to juice up Frank Sinatra, Jr.'s career.

By his early twenties, Frank Jr. began life on the road. In fact by age twenty-four he'd performed in 47 states, 30 countries, and been a guest on several TV shows: everything from *Family Guy* to a role on *The Sopranos* where it was unclear if he was riffing on or confirming all the lore involving his father and the mob, and where Paulie Walnuts calls him "Chairboy of the Board." Despite being offered the role of Vic Fontaine on *Star Trek: Deep Space Nine*, a show he admired, he declined, saying he only would accept a role as an alien.

He'd also advanced to becoming the opening act for several bigger names at various casinos. All the while his reputation preceded him: a consummate performer with exacting musical standards for his musicians, including nonstop rehearsals till they got it right.

In 1988 Frank Jr. put his own career on the back burner to act as his father's musical director and conductor. Poet/vocalist Rod McKuen said, "As the senior Sinatra outlived one by one all of his conductors and nearly every arranger, and began to grow frail himself, his son knew he needed someone he trusted near him. (Frank Jr.) was also savvy enough to know that performing was everything to his dad, and the longer he kept that connection with his audience, the longer he would stay vital and alive."[39]

Frank Jr. recalled the life-changing moment this way: he was socializing with friends in Atlantic City when his phone rang. It was his father, asking him to conduct for him. "After my friends revived me with smelling salts, I said, 'Why do you need me?'"[40] The answer was simple: he couldn't get a conductor to understand what he wanted done; he thought another singer might understand it best. Skeptics have cried nepotism, but nobody knew Frank Sr.'s music like Frank Jr. So for the last seven years of Frank Sr.'s career, his son was there as collaborator and confidante. "It (also) meant," Frank Jr. said, "that for the first time in my life, I spent time with him. And it was a gift from heaven."[41]

A year before his last performance, Frank Sr. told his son he wanted to put together an album of ballads with real swing, featuring the best soloists. Young Frank agreed and asked if there was anything else. The answer was "No. Get outta here."[42] One of the songs he brought his father was "The People You Never Get to Love." The elder Sinatra was delighted with the song, but age caught up with him and he never recorded it. So Frank Jr. sings the Nelson Riddle arrangement with the big orchestra every chance he gets.

No doubt there have been endless hours of barstool philosophizing over whether there is room for two Sinatras in this world: a worshipped legend and the phenomenal living talent. One was born in a world where people flocked to big band and swing; the other strives to continue a legacy against a tide of rock, pop,

R&B, and Lady Gaga. In the end, I really believe each Sinatra will find his own place in musical history.

But the fact remains, even though he passed in 1998, Frank Sr. is still everywhere you look, or listen: "weddings, cocktail soirees, movie soundtracks, TV commercials, elevators..."[43] It can't be easy to establish your own identity in the shadow of this mountain, especially when you've inherited such similar abilities. Regarding the doors that have swung open for Frank Sinatra, Jr. all his life, he has remarked, "A famous father means that in order to prove yourself you have to work three times harder than the guy off the street."[44]

It hasn't been easy. He's heard his own show referred to as "Jurassic Park." In a 2006 *Washington Post* article, Frank Jr. himself says, "There is no demand for Frank Sinatra, Jr. records. There never has been. Rod Stewart's now doing the Great American Songbook. So is Harry Connick Jr. and Michael Buble. The truth is, Frank Sinatra, Jr. has been doing it for forty-four years."[45] He said all this without a shred of self pity or irony, then turned on his heels to warm up his band for a two-night gig at the Hilton on the Boardwalk.

The "strip" in Vegas will certainly never be the same. It's about making the most amount of money with the smallest investment possible, and entertainment, per se, is just not the primary draw any longer. Frank commented: "You know what the big draw is in Vegas today? The shopping centers in the malls."[46] These days, a New Year's gig for Frank is more likely to happen in Spokane than anywhere else.

But he has persisted in being one of the few big bands still touring, even though there aren't many clubs still booking. They don't have the room or often the money it takes to make the numbers work all around, yet the man is still out there, still filling the 1,450 seats at the Atlantic City Hilton where New Jersey is still "Sinatra country," as he put it. At a 2006 show the line formed a couple of hours before showtime, filled with, among others, the aging but devoted members of the "Sinatra Social Society."

In my interviews with Frank Jr., it's clear to me that a number of factors keep him going despite what he may interpret as a lack of success: his access to hundreds of his father's arrangements and his entire musical library, his decency and generosity to all his sidemen—a well known fact in the music business. Saxophonist Terry Anthony, who has played with both Frank Sr. and Jr., has only the highest praise for not only Frank Jr. the man, but for his treatment of band members. "He's a great musician and bandleader," Frank's guitarist Jim Fox said, "He takes us to dinner...the best restaurants in town. He says it's the best thing for him—to get us all out on the road, get us all together. Now, how sweet is that?"[47] And the checks always arrive, whether a gig was missed or not.

But what impresses me when I speak with Frank is his intensity and passion for music, igniting a lifelong flame of curiosity that has probably carried him through some tough times as well as turned him into a wealth of knowledge. He not only knows every third trombone part, every cello part of every arrangement, but he studies jazz history with the ferocity of a scholar.

Frank is an aficionado of the Eddie Sauter and Bill Finnegan orchestra of the early fifties; in fact that post war period seems to interest him the most. He told me he worked with Sauter and was a student of Bill Finnegan, who "taught me more in about six lessons than three and half years of music school." As he described the orchestra in our 1997 interview, "They took the big band, trumpets, trombones, sax, plus the rhythm section, and they luxuriated that sound with a French horn, percussion, and just a few symphonic touches. This was the Sauter–Finnegan sound."

We also talked about Tommy Dorsey crashing the color barrier with his recognition and selection of Sy Oliver for his band: "In 1961 my father was very sentimental so he made an album called *I Remember Tommy*. Back in 1937 black musicians only played with blacks and whites with whites. Dorsey said, What difference could this make? If I want somebody from the black bands, I don't particularly give a damn. So he hired Sy Oliver who was the man who'd written almost the entire book for a man named Jimmy Lunceford, who took all the credit for it. Later Dorsey used Ernie Wilkins and others, but Sy Oliver broke the color barrier for white jazz bands over seventy years ago."

In 1997 I had an unparalleled opportunity to speak with Frank about George Gershwin, for whom "there has never been a bigger fan." He told me his father was also fascinated with the man, but Gershwin died just as Sinatra senior was getting into the business.

Along with his orchestra, Frank Sinatra, Jr. traveled to ten cities to celebrate the centennial of the Gershwin brothers: Ira, born in 1896, and George, born in 1898. Bringing his own core players, Sinatra Jr. engaged local musicians in each town to perform *Porgy and Bess* as well as a number of Billy May, Don Costa, and Nelson Riddle arrangements.

Frank called Gershwin "the man who took jazz out of the gutter. He did it in 1916 with a little ditty he called, 'When You Want 'em You Can't Get 'em; When You Got 'em You Don't Want 'em,' which was a failure till his next song, 'Swanee' that Al Jolson made into a monster hit in 1920. Soon after that, Gershwin wrote *Rhapsody in Blue*, and at that moment jazz began being taken more seriously."

Many great composers of the time, including Rachmaninov, came to hear this music, and they were enraptured. Frank said, "Ravel wrote his *G-Major Piano Concerto* after meeting Gershwin. With the trombone slurring and everything, that was *his* jazz! And so it went on—Paul Hindemeth, Francis Poulenc—all of them so taken by this new music. George Gershwin made an honest woman of jazz—to quote many sources!"

I pointed out that *Porgy and Bess* debuted in Boston at the Colonial Theater in 1935, forging a good connection to the city, then traveled on to the Alvin in New York for its debut in November of that year. Frank reminded me that the reception was anything but smooth: "Gershwin paid through the nose for the blasphemy of creating something like *Porgy and Bess*! The things they said about him: that he was a sinner trying to become a saint, that he gave up writing good songs to write bad concert pieces; they called him a vulgar composer. Then again they slammed Beethoven, Wagner, Stravinsky—who nowadays is called the greatest musical mind of the twentieth century. The late George Gershwin is in excellent company.

"Irving Berlin, Gershwin's friend, said he was the only songwriter who became a composer. Here was a man who wrote piano preludes, concertos, rhapsodies, symphonic tone poems—then suddenly out of nowhere—here comes an opera."

Before his tragic death at age thirty-nine, Gershwin often rhapsodized about the music that surrounded him, saying that he could never get enough of it and that he wanted to write a ballet and a string quartet among other things. Frank said, "So many times I've asked myself what we did *not* get because Gershwin didn't even live to be sixty-five. I can only speculate on the masterpieces we will never hear.

"We do have the arrangements of Gershwin songs written for my father by Nelson Riddle, Billy May, and Don Costa. Ella Fitzgerald, who we lost in 1996, gave her music to the Library of Congress, and the Gershwin curator there got us the Gershwin arrangements from her album, the one she made with Nelson Riddle, so from that we've scavenged together our program."

Though Frank named "Fascinating Rhythm" the quintessential Gershwin song, he had a real story about "The Man I Love," the Gershwin song torch singer Helen Morgan crooned one sultry evening in New York. Evidently the song was a hit in England, but they couldn't give it away in the States until the cabaret song-stress began singing it in clubs across the country.

Frank said, "I had the incredible opportunity of meeting Ira Gershwin, who signed his book to me: *Lyrics on Several Occasions*. People who knew both Ira and George said they were a hundred and eighty degrees out of phase. George was very gregarious: if he wasn't playing tennis he was taking boxing lessons to stay in shape. He loved going to people's homes and playing piano. He'd go to his friends' homes and play the songs, and by the time the show hit Broadway every-one thought it was a revival; they already knew the music.

"Ira was very quiet; he'd sit in his chair, observing, making notes. The opposite of his brother. But Ira was very kind to me when I met him—I actually spent an evening with him. I was singing in a dance band with Helen Forest who at the time sang with Harry James, Benny Goodman, and Tommy Dorsey.

"I was just twenty years old. Helen got up in her sequined gown and sang the torch song 'The Man I Love' as only she could. In the audience a nice-looking middle-aged man in a well tailored grey suit took his glasses off and started to cry.

"After the show I introduced myself to him and learned who he was. I brought him backstage to meet Helen. She took his hand and said, 'You're that man who wept when I sang 'The Man I Love.' I hope I didn't bring up any bad memories.' I told her that she was speaking to Mr. Ira Gershwin.

"'Oh,' was all she managed to say, as all the color drained from her face. After a moment he embraced her and said, 'Young lady, I've never heard it sung any better since George and I wrote it over forty years ago.'"

The great jazz historian Nat Hentoff basically ignored Frank Sinatra, Jr., assuming he'd be a pale shadow of his father, until he heard his most recent CD, *That Face!*, released on Rhino in 2006. "Backed by an invigorating swing band, his singing made me feel good with his personal, signature sound, infectious jazz timing and conversational phrasing."[48] Frank's fifteen minute song and monologue *Over the Land*, inspired by the nation's bicentennial in 1976, describes "how that flag grew in impact, where it went and the troubles it survived during its travels'"[49] since the war of 1812. After the piece was performed by the U.S. Air Force Symphony Orchestra, a U.S Marine officer visited Frank Sinatra, Jr. in his office with a warrant that commandeered the piece for placement in the National Archives. I have to agree with Hentoff who remarked "that beats a Grammy."[50]

Frank Sinatra, Jr. endures. A passionate devotion to the Great American Songbook—to music—has drawn him to stages worldwide for decades. "I think the dirtiest word in the English language is retirement," he said. "This is my job, and I've been doing it for 47 years."[51]

In our interviews, through his dry wit, charm, and direct manner, Frank Sinatra, Jr. has simultaneously addressed and diffused comparisons with his father. He names the gorilla in the room and we all can relax, but there are times this deference comes at his own expense—or at the expense of his own talent. So many times I've wondered what better, more respectful ambassador his father could have asked for. During one interview, Frank told me of a performance in Canada that changed his mind about performing "My Way." Out of respect for his father, he had never before sung it in concert. It made me wonder if his father would have had the same consideration.

Frank said, "I had never performed 'My Way.' I thought it was presumptuous of me to do it. But by the end of this concert, the audience was chanting 'My Way, My Way!' and they weren't stopping. My guys asked what to do, and I said send out the arrangement and let's see what happens."

At that moment Frank paused and seemed to light up from within. "They loved it. So now we do 'My Way' everywhere we go. You know, Ron, I just never believed that they would accept it from me."

SUGGESTED RECORDINGS

That Face! Frank Sinatra, Jr.

Selections include:

> "Spice"
> "Cry Me A River"
> "You'll Never Know"
> "Feeling Good"
> "Girl Talk" (Duet with Steve Tyrell)
> "Walking Happy" "What a Difference a Day Makes"

Orchestra conducted by Terry Woodson.
Reprise CD R2 70017

Style's Back in Style

John Pizzarelli

© Ken Franckling.

Born in Paterson, New Jersey, on April 6, 1960, jazz guitarist, singer, and bandleader John Pizzarelli is one of the hottest acts in jazz today. Internationally known for classic standards, he combines his hip, swinging style with contemporary sophistication to create his own unique sound. A veteran radio personality, Pizzarelli hosted *New York Tonight* on WNEW from 1984–88, recently launching *Radio Deluxe with John Pizzarelli,* a nationally syndicated program co-hosted with his wife, Broadway star Jessica Molaskey. Josh Getlin of the *L.A Times* says that John and Jessica's relaxed, off-the-cuff show "combines the retro feel of a 1940s living room broadcast with a boomer's passion for the Great American Songbook,"[52] bringing warmth, humor, and that long-lost "live radio" feel back.

Born into music, John is the son of jazz guitarist "Bucky" Pizzarelli and the nephew of Peter and Bobby Pizzarelli, both virtuoso banjo players. John told me that some of the great musicians of the day visited his home, recalling especially a Christmastime jam session with Zoot Sims, Joe Venuti, and Les Paul playing the old standard "Out of Nowhere." When John was just six, his dad began taking him to recording sessions where he met jazz greats Dave McKenna, Slam Stuart, Dizzy Gillespie, and Erroll Garner; he even sat in with Marian McParland during her decade-long reign at the Hickory House, a New York city jazz spot.

All this great music had a profound impact on young John. His eclectic record collection included not only the music of his generation: the Beatles, James Taylor, and Billy Joel, but also *Sinatra and Strings,* Billie Holiday's *Lady in Satin,* and Clifford Brown's *At Basin Street*. These artists were an inspiration to him, and in turn he integrated elements of their style into his music. He told me, "I'm very lucky to be able to perform the music I loved and learned as a child to express myself not only as a singer and player, but also as a composer."

Along with Ray Kennedy on piano, John's brother Martin Pizzarelli on bass, and drummer Tony Tedesco, this current edition of the John Pizzarelli Trio is one of the finest since the late Nat Cole, entertaining people from Berlin to Istanbul. In fact, two albums: *Dear Mr. Cole* and *P.S Mr. Cole* are musical tributes to a man John credits as the one who inspired him to pursue jazz. The trio swings hard and plays ballads beautifully.

John shared with me that he's recorded twenty-three albums of his own, as well as other joint recordings with his father, and appeared on more than forty albums by other artists including James Taylor, Natalie Cole, Rickie Lee Jones, Dave Brubeck, George Shearing, Rosemary Clooney, his wife Jessica Molaskey, even the Boston Pops with Keith Lockhart. John has also appeared on Broadway, numerous TV shows including *The Late Show With David Letterman*, and a well known Fox Woods Casino commercial, "The Wonder of it All."

Another passion the Pizzarelli family shares is their love of Italian cuisine. At home, the combination of good times, homemade pasta, particularly gnocchi, and fine wine was a tradition the family shared with all their guests from the music world.

I looked forward to John and his father visiting me at the studio, not only for the music and the company, but because they always brought a calzone or pepperoni and cheese pizza to a hungry and appreciative DJ! Our conversations always turned to food: where to get it, which cities had the best restaurants, what they served, and especially, where the best pizza could be found. With a name like Pizzarelli, they should know! Top on their list is Pepe's Pizza in New Haven, Connecticut, best known for their white pizza. In Boston it's the original Regina's in the North End, or Santarpio's in East Boston which they were partial to since that was Sinatra's favorite when he was in town.

John and his trio love to entertain not only musically but with their witty banter and infectious humor. One of their most requested numbers is John's own loving tribute to New Jersey, his home state. With his clever composition "I Like Jersey Best," John gives us a long overdue tribute to the much-maligned state. During one of our interviews he said, "When you consider what New Jersey has given the country—Bucky Pizzarelli, Bill Evans, George Van Epps, Fort Dix, Wildwood, Atlantic City, Route 22, the Polaski Skyway, Abbott and Costello—this was a song that had to be written!"

He shared with me how the song came to be: "Actually, it was written in 1981 by Joe Cosgriff, on a whim, in about forty minutes at a diner. He gave it to a mutual buddy, Phil Bernardi. We recorded it in 1983, then played it before the New Jersey state assembly in the state house in 1985. The goal was to make it the official state jingle.

"That day it was the first order of business. They slammed the gavel down and there we were, my dad watching from the balcony. Joe Peterro, the guy who was sponsoring the bill to make it the official state jingle, stood up and said, 'Before I start, John's father is a very famous guitar player named Rocky Pizzarelli, and we'd like him to stand up and take a bow.' Anyway, I sang and they were very receptive, they stood up and applauded. And now it's *still* the unofficial state jingle. But it's funny, crowds get on their feet for it here. It's twenty times more popular in Boston than in New Jersey. In New Jersey, they don't get it."

A huge Red Sox fan, John has played baseball most of his life. In April of 2007, his trio played at a BLOHARDS luncheon at the Yale Club. John said, "It's the Red Sox Nation chapter in New York, stands for the Beloved Loyal Order of Red Sox Diehards, something along those lines. Every time the Red Sox play in New York these fans meet at the Time Life building, and they sure know their stuff. I want to wear my Sox hat, but Jessica won't let me wear it in New York City."

A lighter-than-air jazz guitarist, John teases easy swing and Bossa nova pulses from his guitar creating a sound that melds the virtuosity of George Benson and Les Paul with the soul of Django Reinhardt. Any time you have the opportunity to catch a Pizzarelli performance, do it! A consummate entertainer, he is quite simply one of the best of his generation.

Suggested Recordings

John Pizzarelli Trio . . . Live at Birdland

This 2-CD set, recorded at Birdland in New York City, captures a live performance of the trio at its very best. It includes not only outstanding interpretations of standards and originals, but also John's delightful commentary on a wide range of topics from Dizzy Gillespie to Frank Sinatra.

Selections include:

"Three Little Words"
"I Like Jersey Best"
"Just You, Just Me"
"Manhattan"
"Isn't It a Pity"
"Only a Paper Moon"
A James Taylor Medley

Telarc 2CD-83577

John Pizzarelli: Dear Mr. Cole

John and his trio in a loving tribute to Nat Cole.
Selections include such Cole favorites as:

"Nature Boy"
"Route 66"

"Sweet Lorraine"
"Straighten Up and Fly Right"
"Little Girl"
"Unforgettable"

Novus 63182-2

The Rare Delight of You . . . John Pizzarelli with the George Shearing Quintet

This collection offers the opportunity to hear the musical magic of Pizzarelli's
voice and guitar combined with the legendary sound of the George Shearing
Quintet . . . a match made in heaven!

Selections include:

"September in the Rain"
"Indian Summer"
"Everything Happens to Me"
"Be Careful, It's My Heart"
"Lulu's Back in Town"
"Shine On Your Shoes"

Telarc CD 83546

5. MEL TORMÉ

"Don't Call Me the Velvet Fog!"

Mel Tormé

Courtesy of the Tormé Estate.

In my mind, Mel Tormé defines multi-talented more than any other artist in the history of American music. Born in Chicago in 1925 to a career that spanned some six decades, he has been respected as a jazz singer, actor, composer, arranger, pianist, drummer, author, child radio performer, and raconteur.

From childhood, his hobbies and interests were numerous: he was an aficionado of World War 1 aircraft, American movies, and the so-called "Little Books." A child prodigy, he sang for his supper at four years old in Chicago's Black Hawk restaurant with the Coon-Saunders Orchestra, and was working the vaudeville circuit soon after that.

In his early teens he was already writing original songs and acting on radio shows such as *Little Orphan Annie* and *Jack Armstrong.* His first big break came in 1942 at seventeen when he joined the Chico Marx orchestra as a singer, arranger, and eventually as the band's drummer. He made his first film, *Higher and Higher,* with Frank Sinatra in 1944.

His recording career ramped up in 1946 when he took over a vocal group which he named, "Mel Tormé and his Mel-Tones," modeled on Frank Sinatra and "The Pied Pipers," and started recording for Decca and Music-Craft. Hits included Cole Porter's "What Is This Thing Called Love?" but his best-known song, which became a classic, written with partner Robert Wells, was "The Christmas Song." Inspired to write the tune in order to cool off on a hot July day, Mel and Robert dashed off the song in a mere forty minutes.

I first interviewed Mel on the radio on July 2, 1985. He commented on his early influences as a singer: "Listening very early on to Ella Fitzgerald, Duke Ellington, Connie Boswell and the Boswell Sisters, the Mills brothers; a little later on to the Andrew Sisters, all influenced my intonation and phrasing. These were the groups that helped me formulate ideas for the Mel-Tones, the ones who got me to the place I am today, from how I interpret a song or add my own filigree to a phrase. And I have to say, (alto saxophonist) Phil Woods is the greatest, and Artie Shaw blew my mind as a bandleader."

We also talked about his favorite composer: "Johnny Mercer was my number one lyric writer of all time. The great thing is the admiration went both ways: he'd always wanted to compose something just for me. Unfortunately, we talked about it but never did it, which is a big regret of mine."

I've also been struck by Mel's self-deprecating sense of humor. Though he never loved his nickname, "The Velvet Fog" (which often morphed into "The Velvet Frog"), he had a wonderful openness to reinvention. Mel took advantage of opportunities to appear on TV even when the roles had a tongue-in-cheek reference to what was perhaps his fading star. The irony is, these many appearances led to an even greater following among Gen-Xers who learned about him in a series of Mountain Dew commercials and on an episode of *Seinfeld* where Mel dedicates a song to Kramer. He even made nine appearances as himself on the 1980s situation comedy *Night Court*, whose main character Judge Harry Stone (played by Harry Anderson) was painted as an unabashed Tormé fan, which in fact was true in real life as well.

Like Tony Bennett, Mel never sold out in the 1960s when rock music started to take over; in fact he referred to rock and roll as "three chord manure." This period was perhaps his roughest time, so challenging in fact that he considered changing professions and becoming an airline pilot. But slowly, through a series of club performances, he began to reconstruct his following. He stayed with the classics from the Great American Songbook, commenting during our interview, "As time went on, I literally recorded the entire American songbook. I grew up during the depression—I learned these songs when they came out, which was kind of nice. I *lived* them, I grew up with them. I didn't turn thirty and say hey, time to learn these songs. They are part of me."

In 1982 Mel began a long association with Concord Records, helping to pioneer jazz. While at Concord, he worked with jazz greats Marty Paich, Rob McConnell and the Boss Brass, the Frank Wess/Harry Edison Orchestra, and perhaps most fruitfully with jazz pianist George Shearing.

The excellent albums *An Evening With George Shearing and Mel Tormé* and *Top Drawer* earned Mel the Grammy for Best Male Jazz Vocalist in 1982 and 1983. In the course of our interview, Mel had this to say about his special musical relationship with George Shearing: "George Wein—the entrepreneur who put together the Newport Jazz Festival—he was the one who got the bright idea of putting us together, and George Shearing and I have been friends since the fifties. And yes, it was life-changing to finally win two grammys after thirteen nominations, but I am upset that George was never recognized in this way. It took working with George to make this happen, period, and he wasn't even nominated. I share those two awards with Shearing; he is, at minimum, half the reason I won them. As George says, we breathe together, we literally think identically on a musical plane, and that's why I think the records are so successful."

Though a stickler for maintaining and protecting his voice—Tormé insisted on eight hours of sleep before every performance, never smoked, avoided drafts, and rarely drank—he was obligated to perform for the London Sessions after an eight-hour flight during which, tormented by a painful divorce, he didn't sleep. I'm so glad he relented and recorded anyway. His performance of "All in Love Is Fair," set off by Phil Woods on alto sax solo and accompaniment, never sounded so emotive, so heartbreakingly beautiful, as if he truly was confessing his own personal story in that song.

The author of five books, including a biography of drummer Buddy Rich, a remembrance of Judy Garland's controversial television series, an autobiography, as well as a loving tribute to singers who influenced him: *My Singing Teachers,* Mel was nothing if not terrifically gifted. But I've always felt that Tormé was unrivaled singing ballads and "scatting"—he was simply one of the best jazz singers in the business. His 1962 hard-driving R&B song "Comin' Home, Baby" prompted gospel singer Ethel Waters to say, "Tormé is the only white man who sings with the soul of a black man."[53] Composer and lyricist of over three hundred songs, he was blessed with a lush sound along with perfect pitch and brilliant intonation... simply put, Mel never sang a bad note!

Mel performed worldwide in concerts and jazz festivals throughout the world until the time of his unfortunate stroke in 1996 that ultimately took his life. I treasure the many times he came to visit me in the studio. His broad range of musical knowledge was always refreshing, and I knew of no one else who could carry on conversations about so many other topics relating to the history of entertainment in America.

SUGGESTED RECORDINGS

The Mel Tormé Collection: 1944–85

This four-CD collection represents Mel Tormé's collaboration with the greatest songwriters, arrangers, and musicians in this four-decade history. Also included is an extensive photo biography of Mel together with a complete discography and recording history of all of the songs included in this collection.

Among the selections:

"Night and Day"
"Blue Moon"
"All of You"
"It's Delovely"
"Lullaby of Birdland"
"Cheek to Cheek"
"Sunday in New York"
And a knockout Gershwin medley that includes twenty songs!

Rhino R271589

Mel Tormé: The Best of the Concord Years

This two-CD collection picks up from 1985 and presents some of the finest recordings that Mel made during the last two decades of his phenomenal career. During this period, Tormé was in his vocal prime. This collection includes performances with George Shearing, Cleo Laine, the Marty Paich Dek-tette, Rob McConnell and the Boss Brass, and the Frank Wess/Harry Edison Orchestra.

Some of the selections included:

"Stardust"
"The Carioca"
"Born to be Blue"
"These Foolish Things"
"Pennies from Heaven"
A Duke Ellington medley
And Mel's version of his own "The Christmas Song"

Concord CCD2-4871-2

Mel Tormé–George Shearing: A Vintage Year

Recorded live in concert.

Selections include: "The Midnight Sun," "When Sunny Gets Blue," "Someday I'll Find You," "The Way You Look Tonight," "Bittersweet," "New York, New York" (medley), and "Little Man You've Had a Busy Day."

Concord CCD 4341

The Thrush of Columbus

Nancy Wilson

© Photofest, Inc.

Nancy Wilson began her career singing in church choirs and dance bands as a teenager, though she'd made the decision to be a singer by the age of four. Some of the greats who influenced her during those formative years included: Carmen McRae, Sarah Vaughan, Dinah Washington, LaVerne Baker, Ruth Brown, Nat King Cole, Louis Jordan, and Lionel Hampton's Little Jimmy Scott. Every spare moment was spent either listening to the radio at home or at "the juke joint down the block."

Over the years her repertoire has included jazz and blues, show tunes, standards, even gospel and R&B. She's been described as a "storyteller," "a professor emeritus of body language," a "consummate actress," and "the complete entertainer."[54] She prefers the term "song stylist," and explained why in our 1991 interview: "I never sing standards the same way twice because each time it's a separate performance. 'Song stylist' is more me than anything else because I'm interpreting the lyrics as well as acting. I like to put myself into a song so that it will touch you, not to impress you with my voice. I want it to mean something to you ten years from now. Each song is a vignette, a little play. For me, it starts with the lyric."

After touring with Rusty Bryant's Carolyn Club Big Band in her late teens and early twenties, she made her first recordings in 1956 under Dot Records, joining the ranks of Capitol Records in 1959. There was no question that this was the label to be with at that time. Capitol had become one of the most popular and best selling record companies in America; their roster of singers included Nat Cole, Peggy Lee, Dean Martin, Kay Starr, and Frank Sinatra who joined the label in 1953.

Touring with Rusty's band brought her to New York where she met and became great friends with saxophonist Cannonball Adderley. Nancy allotted herself six months to achieve her goal of having Cannonball's manager John Levy sign her, and Capitol Records as her label. When she got the call to fill in for Irene Reid at the Blue Morocco, she called Levy to let him know, and he showed up for the gig. John called the very next day, recorded a demo with her, and within five days Capitol was on the phone.

About her early days she told me, "I made it a point to be on the spot when anyone ever needed a singer. I finally quit college and starting singing full time all over the west." She had everything going for her: she was young, beautiful, and gifted with her own unique sound, but at the time of her Capitol contract, she was up against the rising tide of rock and roll. This did not stop Ms. Wilson from turning out albums that became classics. In all she recorded over seventy albums—virtually the entire American Songbook—and worked with the best arrangers in the business including Nelson Riddle, Billy May, and Oliver Nelson.

Her move to New York gave her access to regular work in jazz clubs around the city where she came to the attention of George Shearing, among others. They hit it off right away when she sat in with his group at New York's Basin Street East. The result was one of the most successful Capitol albums ever, called *The Swingin's Mutual*. It was a great success commercially, artistically, and musically. The jazz critic Leonard Feather called it one of the most logical and successful collaborations of the year.

Her debut single "Guess Who I Saw Today?" was so successful that between 1960 and 1962 Capitol released five Nancy Wilson albums.

She shared with me the special significance of "Guess Who I Saw Today?" during one of our interviews: "The first time I heard the song was in 1952, in Ohio, when I was fifteen. Carman McCrae sang it, then Eydie Gorme. I ended up singing that song every night I performed for as long as I can remember. I think it struck a chord as the ultimate song about betrayal. It was the song John Levy heard when I came to New York, and I know he signed me because of it."

In the late seventies, Nancy acted in a variety of television shows including the *Andy Williams Show*, the *Carol Burnett Show*, and the *Flip Wilson Show*, while sales of her albums with Capitol were second only to the Beatles, surpassing even Frank Sinatra, Peggy Lee, the Beach Boys, and early idol Nat Cole.

Nancy never compromised her talent with inferior material or arrangements. She exuded class, making everything sound smooth and effortless and choosing to work with the best musicians of the day: Benny Carter, Harry Edison, Pete Candoli, Dick Nash, and Shelley Manne, to name a few.

When I introduced Nancy from the stage of Symphony Hall in the mid-eighties, she turned in one of her finest performances singing and swinging as only she could. She sang many of her signature songs, including "Guess Who I Saw Today?," "Now I'm a Woman," "Peace of Mind," and "How Glad I Am," which won her a Grammy in 1964. My wife Joyce has always been one of Nancy's biggest fans and was very excited about meeting her backstage before the concert. Joyce's big thrill came when Nancy asked her to zip up her dress, and they enjoyed a little repartee. She was on cloud nine all night!

Recently a friend gave me a DVD of a live performance of Nancy in the 1970s when she sang in a concert with the Count Basie Band and the great Joe Williams. I was knocked out by her dynamic stage presence and her ability to relay the lyrics so purely as to make you swing, swoon, or cry. She not only inspired the musicians, but the audience as well. *Time* magazine said after her career-launching turn at the Coconut Grove, "She is, all at once, both cool and sweet, both singer and storyteller."[55]

After an appearance in Las Vegas, she confessed to me how privileged she felt to work with so many legends in the music business. Nancy singled out pianist/arranger Jimmy Jones who she described as one of the greatest and most underappreciated arrangers and conductors she had every known. We also talked about her successful radio stint when she hosted *Jazz Profiles* for National Public Radio in 1995. She said how much she enjoyed presenting the music and the artists she loved so dearly. Her casual conversational style with the musicians made the series great listening and a highly informed history of jazz.

I asked what she thought made the greats great: "They had energy and wonderful voices of course, but there was a freedom about Ella Fitzgerald that you will never hear today. It's never going to be that good again. There's not enough room; we don't give them the space. We don't give young singers the opportunity to be Lena Horne. But the music will be heard on a radio dial somewhere. In the air someplace, the music is still there."

However she's known, as "Sweet Nancy," "Fancy Nancy," or "The Girl With the Honey-Coated Voice," Nancy Wilson continues to delight and captivate us. She's still active today as a performer, educator, and simply a hard worker for all sorts of charities, including the National Minority AIDS Council. Of her 2005 award where she was inducted into the International Civil Rights Walk of Fame at the Martin Luther King Jr. National Historic Site, she says, "This award means more to me than anything else I have ever received."[56]

Though she's the winner of three Grammys and countless other honors, I think it takes a certain kind of courage to look inside the lyrics of a song and bring out its heart, and for that kind of joy I'd like to offer her my personal thanks.

SUGGESTED RECORDINGS

The Best of Nancy Wilson: Ballads, Blues and Big Bands

Quite simply, this three-CD set is the definitive collection of Nancy's Capitol recording years. It includes an excellent discography by Pete Welding and is a must for lovers of her music.

Selections include:

"When the World was Young"
"Nearness of You"
"Midnight Sun"
"Satin Doll"
"Willow Weep For Me"
"Fly Me to the Moon"
"Angel Eyes"

Capitol CDP 834886

Nancy Wilson Turned to Blue

www.mcgjazz.org

One of Nancy's most recent recordings, this collection features a chamber music quartet with pianist Billy Taylor as well as an all-star big band. The lovely arrangements are by Jay Ashby, John Wilson, and Llew Matthews.

Selections include:

"This Is All I Ask"
"Be My Love"
"Taking A Chance On Love"
"Old Folks"
"I'll Be Seeing You"

MegJazz MCG J1022

Nancy Wilson's Greatest Hits

This CD is a wonderful collection of the best of her Columbia songbook recordings.

Selections include:

"Guess Who I Saw Today?"
"The Two of Us" with pianist Ramsey Lewis
"Loving You" duet with Peabo Bryson
"Hello Like Before"
"When October Goes"

Columbia CK 65542

Blue Rose

Rosemary Clooney

© Photofest, Inc.

I had the opportunity to interview the woman Tony Bennett called "the most beloved singer in America" over thirty years ago during one of her many appearances in Boston. Though her life was marked with both personal and professional struggle, her voice was a source of joy and comfort for countless fans, and her fortitude an inspiration to all of us.

Her decades-long mastery of America's popular song was preceded by a life of poverty in Maysville, Kentucky. As she describes in her first memoir, *This For Remembrance*, Rosemary's earliest years were rocked by an emotionally unstable and alcoholic father, and a mother who took off for California taking her brother Nick but leaving Rose and Betty behind. One night after celebrating the end of World War I, their father took off—household cash in hand—never to return. To eat, Rose and her sister collected soda bottles. When the girls left home one evening to compete at an open audition at a Cincinnati radio station, their rent was past due, their utilities about to be cut off, and the phone disconnected. "The Clooney Sisters" won the audition, jump-starting their career in 1945 at WLW in Cincinnati with a twenty-dollar-a-week late-night gig.

Though Betty left the act in 1949, their work had caught the attention of bandleader Tony Pastor. At the time, Tony was handled by Joe Schribman, who was Charlie Schribman's nephew, booker for Glenn Miller as well as all the major big bands around New England. Summers she'd perform at "The Surf" at Revere Beach and "The Pier" in Old Orchard Beach, while in the winter, there were enough good ballrooms in the area to keep her singing.

In the early fifties, Rosemary left the area to try her luck in New York City. Her arrival there was perfectly timed: World War II had depleted personnel for many bands, and audiences were coming out in droves to listen to the likes of Bing Crosby, Doris Day, Frank Sinatra, Peggy Lee, Ella Fitzgerald, and Dinah Washington.

Rose was signed immediately with Columbia Records, and it was there that Mitch Miller, her agent, convinced her (she actually had no choice—do it or she was gone) to record "Come On-A My House." She resisted cutting the song with every fiber of her being, citing everything from how uncomfortable she was with putting on an Italian accent, to calling the double entendres in the song a cheap lyrical device. Richard Harrington of the *Washington Post* said what bothered her most was the "deliberately disordered phrasing, so antithetical to her instinctive devotion to craftsmanship."[57] Just like "A-Tisket, A-Tasket" proved for Ella Fitzgerald, this "pop fluff" (as Michael Feinstein put it) she hated morphed her into a star, topping the charts with gold, making "Rosie" a household name and landing her on the cover of *Time* magazine—the first female singer ever to do so. Rosemary followed up with other hits: "Hey There," "You'll Never Know," and "This Ole House," as well as a popular television show.

These milestones set off a successful twenty-year cycle, made more so by her beloved friend Bing Crosby who signed her to co-host a songfest radio show on weekday mornings on CBS. Film roles abounded, including *White Christmas*, a white-hot hit that featured Bing, Danny Kaye, and music by Irving Berlin, and where Clooney was lauded for her sultry performance of "Love, You Didn't Do Right By Me." She also toured for six years with her own group, "Four Girls Four," which included singing stars Margaret Whiting, Rose Marie, and Helen O'Connell.

Rosemary shared with me her great admiration and love for Bing Crosby. "I learned so much from Bing about being a true professional, as an actor and singer. He was the most relaxed and casual performer I've ever known. Nobody worked harder to get things absolutely correct, which I think enabled him to be relaxed and casual onstage." She also named Sinatra as one of her biggest influences; his ability to reach out and touch his audience seemed to leave its mark on every singer who came after him.

To the amazement of her family and friends, Rosemary eloped with actor Jose Ferrer, sixteen years her senior, in the summer of 1953. The marriage thrilled the tabloids—Ferrer was quite the ladies man—but was not easy for Rosemary. They moved into a glamorous Beverly Hills home once owned by George Gershwin (and as she reminded me—next door to Ira) where she and Jose entertained the toast of Hollywood: Jack Benny, Nat King Cole, Billie Holiday, and others with opulent poolside galas. Their first child was born in 1955; by 1960 they had five children. They divorced in '61, then married and divorced again in '67.

In the midst of all this turmoil, Rosemary made her signature album called *Blue Rose*, a collaboration with Duke Ellington and Billy Strayhorn. Not well received at the time, it has since become a jazz classic, proving she could cross over into the world of jazz as a singer with popular hits. She told me a bit about how she prepared to sing the title song: "Duke wrote that for me; Billy produced it. He said to sing it as if I was listening to Duke on the radio and getting ready for a date; putting on makeup, fixing my hair; and it was such a wonderful word picture for me. That's the rendition you hear on the album."

Meanwhile, pressures mounted for Rosie that would have toppled anyone. The stress of raising five children on her own while pursuing careers as a TV, movie, radio, and recording star fueled an addiction to tranquilizers and sleeping pills. She recalled in her autobiography feeling prey to the "fifties myth of family and career."[58]

Her house of cards came crashing down in 1968. When close friend Bobby Kennedy was assassinated in Los Angeles, she was standing only yards away. As she said in 2002, "I had my nervous breakdown the same time the country did."[59] This tragedy, compounded with her split from Ferrer, resulted in a mental collapse that took her years to work through and eventually emerge from. Later she would touchingly revisit and possibly expunge this pain through her recurring role as an Alzheimer patient on *ER* opposite nephew George Clooney, her moving performance winning her an Emmy nomination.

She launched her comeback at a performance at Tivoli gardens in Copenhagen in 1972; but in essence she had to start all over again, taking humble gigs and counting on help from old friends. In 1975 Bing invited her to appear with him in concert at the Los Angeles Music Centre. The duo took it on the road to Chicago, New York, London, even to Ireland, and finally Rosie's career was reborn. Playing "How Are Things in Glocca Morra" on *MusicAmerica* inspired Rose to share this story with me: "Bing asked me to go, and it was the perfect time. He supported an orphanage in Dublin—they had a band—and the children came out to the tarmac when we arrived. These little tiny kids played, 'Where the Blue of the Night Meets the Gold of the Day'—the oldest was just sixteen. When we left Ireland and they met us at our plane in the morning with the fog rolling in and they played, 'Come Back to Erin,' there wasn't a dry eye on the tarmac, let me tell you."

Each year for the next two decades she made a new album on the Concord Jazz Label run by Carl Jefferson, the sweetness of her voice mellowing to a more golden tone, with a touch of swing. Her popularity also surged in supper clubs across America. She had a chance to get back in the studio and work with musicians like Scott Hamilton, Dave McKenna, and Warren Vache as well as the bands of Woody Herman and Count Basie. In fact, her second professional life was built around making some of her finest recordings by master composers Irving Berlin, Cole Porter, Harold Arlen, Johnny Mercer, Ira Gershwin, and arranger Nelson Riddle, all who happened to be friends of hers. As she said in an interview with *Lear's* magazine, "I can even pick the songs. The arranger says to me, 'How do you want it? How do you see it?' Nobody ever asked me that before."[60]

I always felt that Rosie had the ability to sing the lyrics of a song as if she had lived the experience. Her voice had humor, honesty, and heartbreak in it, caressing you completely. Stephen Holden of the *New York Times* said: "An audience became her extended family, encouraged to rest its collective head in her lap as she poured out musical bedtime stories for grownups. Though written by others, those stories, told in her voice, came across as nuggets of personal experience."[61]

John Pizzarelli said: "She was a great person to eat and drink with, and she was a wonderful presence when she held court."

Barry Manilow: "She comes from that great time when singers respected the songwriter and music arranger more than anyone, and their interpretation showed that!"

Michael Feinstein: "Humor was a Clooney trademark, and she laughed abundantly. She also cried abundantly and had sadness...I wish I could have eased (some of that) for her. But no one could. If she only knew how much she gave to others...how we treasured the expression of her personality through her voice."

Diana Krall: "The best piece of advice she gave me was, 'Just sing the damn song, honey, it's all right there!'"[62]

As for myself, she was constantly thanking me for supporting her career, but the truth was she was just as supportive of mine. I suspect she felt in some sense like a lot of people's favorite aunt, the one who loved you no matter what. Always self-deprecating, she could tell a funny story about meeting the pope as well as tales of her stay in the Mayo clinic. I also felt that a big part of her legacy was perseverance: her return to stardom in the fickle world of show business was a triumph.

In 1997 she married long time love, dancer Dante DiPaolo, who said he fell for her on the set of the 1953 film, *Here Come the Girls*. *Girl Singer*, her second autobiography, was published in 1999 and like her singing voice, it's warm, free of bitterness, and full of love for her family and life. Recording steadily until her death of lung cancer in 2002, she made a total of twenty-five albums for Concord. The inscription on her award in 1995 for the ASCAP Pied Piper Award called her: "an American treasure and one of the best friends a song ever had."[63]

SUGGESTED RECORDINGS

Rosemary Clooney: 16 Biggest Hits

In a career marked by an incredible number of hits, Rosie was tops! During this time, she led the charts with the selections included in this CD. Among them:

"Tenderly"
"Hey There"
"Blues In the Night"
"Memories of You"

"Botch-A-Me"
"From This Moment On"
"Mambo Italiano"

Columbia/Legacy CK 63553

Blue Rose: Rosemary Clooney and Duke Ellington and His Orchestra

This reissue of a late 1950s session came to me from my good friend, Sal Ingeme. For many years Sal was the gentleman responsible for introducing many of the artists who recorded for Columbia Records, including Tony Bennett, Johnny Mathis, Barbara Streisand, and Rosie Clooney. This historic 1956 collaboration of Rosie and Duke Ellington showcases the talents of two musical giants. The original LP was unavailable for many years until it was restored and remastered on this CD in 1999.

Selections include:

"Blue Rose" (Title song)
"Mood Indigo"
"I Got It Bad, and That Ain't Good"
"Don't Mean A Thing If It Ain't Got That Swing"
"I'm Checkin' Out, Goombye"
"Sophisticated Lady"
"Hey Baby"

Columbia/Legacy CK 65506

Rosemary Sings Rodgers, Hart and Hammerstein

Backed up by a swinging group, including Scott Hamilton, tenor sax, John Oddo on piano, Jack Sheldon on trumpet, and vocals, Rosie takes us on a journey featuring marvelous interpretations of classics by Richard Rodgers, Lorenz Hart, and Oscar Hammerstein.

Selections include:

"Oh What a Beautiful Morning"
"The Lady Is a Tramp"
"My Romance"
"I Could Write a Book"
"The Sweetest Sounds"
My personal favorite, "People Will Say We're in Love"

In the above selection, Rosie shows off her great sense of humor teaming up with Jack Sheldon. Their banter is infectious!

Concord CCD 4405

A Song's Best Friend

Frank Sinatra,
Sammy Cahn,
and Paul Weston

© Photofest, Inc.

Sammy Cahn always had a way with words. Even as a scrawny kid in wire rims it kept bullies off his back and got him out of countless scrapes with his parents. His gift turned him into one of the most prolific and beloved lyricists of all time, responsible for putting more words in Frank Sinatra's mouth than anyone else.

Born Samuel Cohen in 1913 in New York City's East Side, Sammy described his childhood to me as having an idyllic quality: "those images from the movies— kids playing in the streets, the pushcarts—that's really the way it was.

"I came out of the lowest part of the lower East Side. If you take one step back you're in New Jersey. I was born on 10 Cannon Street. I've been asked if they ever put a plaque on the building. Not only did they not do that, they removed the building, the street, *and* the neighborhood. Gives you an idea how fleeting fame is.

"When I think of the East Side," Sammy continued, "I can't help laughing because it reminds me of the day I met Cole Porter. I was at a party and someone said Cole Porter wanted to meet me. Next thing I know Cole Porter's coming at me, this man on crutches, but instead of me rushing to meet him, I go immobile. I'm so stunned I can't move. He said, 'Sammy Cahn, I've always wanted to meet you.' All I can say is, '*You* wanted to meet *me*?' He said, 'Yes, because I've always envied you.' Echoing everything he says like an idiot, I say, '*You've* always envied *me*? Why would you envy me?' He said, 'Because you were born on the East Side.' So I asked him, 'What's the big deal with that?' and he said, 'If I'd been born on the East Side I'd be a true genius.'"

Not the most diligent of students, young Sammy (always with a good story for his parents) would cut classes to see movies or go to vaudeville shows. He played violin as a hobby but realized it was possible to make money at it when he saw his mother pay the musicians at his bar mitzvah, so at just fourteen he took off with the Pals of Harmony, the very band his mother had hired. He did local gigs, then took off with the band, playing shows from Atlantic City to the Catskills.

He wrote his first song at age sixteen, describing the experience in his autobiography, *I Should Care*: "It was actually Jackie Osterman at the Academy of Music on 14th Street who inspired my song-writing career...In the middle of the act, [Osterman] took a change of pace and said he'd like to sing a song he'd written. It was a fascinating thing for me to be actually looking at a songwriter—in person...walking home...I began to frame a song in my head. By the time I reached home I had actually written a lyric...The song was a piece of idiocy called 'Like Niagara Falls, I'm Falling for You—Baby!' But if, as...somebody said, a journey of a thousand miles starts with the first step, that was the first step."[64] It was Saul Caplan, the pianist from the Pals of Harmony, who joined forces with Sammy and formed his first songwriting team.

Vaudeville embraced them, but their songs languished. One day in 1935 their luck changed. During our 1985 interview, Sammy explained: "We wrote the song 'Rhythm is Our Business' for Jimmy Lunceford as an opening song, and through the popularity of this one song, we became known as band songwriters. We started writing for all the big bands: Glen Gray, Glenn Miller, Jimmy Dorsey. That was the turning point, the catalyst." At this time the duo was also welcomed into ASCAP, the American Society of Composers, Authors and Publishers.

But it was the song "Bei Mir Bist Du Schon" (means that you're grand) which sold a million copies, that made Cahn wealthy enough to buy his parents a new house. At first he had trouble selling the idea, but a then-obscure sister act from the Midwest happened to cross his path: "One day Lou (Levy) brought the Andrews Sisters: Patty, Maxene, and LaVerne up to our apartment. On the piano was this copy of a song in Yiddish. Patty asked...'How does it go?' I played it for them, and they started to sing right along and to rock with it. 'Gee,' said Patty, 'can we have it?'"[65]

Twice in his life Sammy Cahn changed his name: first to Kahn to avoid confusion with actor Sammy Cohen, and from Kahn to Cahn, some say to avoid confusion with lyricist Gus Kahn. In our interview, he explained another reason for the second name change: "At the time I was working with Saul Caplan. I said: 'Caplan/Kahn,' it just doesn't work. It sounds like a dress firm—you're gonna have to change your name. He said if I change my name you're gonna change your name. So he went to Chaplan and I went to Cahn."

In the thirties Cahn and Chaplan wrote for New York's Vitaphone Studios, a subsidiary of Warner Brothers. Artists such as Betty Hutton, Bob Hope, and Edgar Bergen sang lyrics they'd written, but by 1940 Vitaphone was shuttered. The duo moved to Hollywood still under contract, but the work dried up and they parted ways. Just as desperation began to kick in, Cahn was asked to write a song with composer Jule Styne. "From the beginning it was fun," he remembered. "Jule went to the piano and played a complete melody. I listened and said 'Would you play it again, just a bit slower?' He played and I listened...then I said, 'I've heard that song before'—to which he said, bristling, 'What the hell are you, a tune detective?' 'No,' I said, 'that wasn't a criticism, it was a title: 'I've Heard That Song Before.'"[66]

Styne's collaboration with Cahn proved incredibly fruitful; together they composed songs for nineteen films between 1942 and 1951. Year in and year out, these songs captured top ten spots. *Time* magazine compared their synergy to that of Rodgers and Hammerstein.

Sammy explained to me how "Let it Snow!" came to be: "It was one of the hottest days of the year, even sitting in our studio on Hollywood and Vine to be exact. And I said to Jules, Why don't we get out of here; everybody else has. Let's hit the beach and cool off. And he said, Why don't we stay here and write a winter song. Seemed like a reasonable idea. I went to the typewriter and typed 'oh the weather outside is frightful, but the fire is so delightful, and since we've no place to go, let it snow, let it snow, let it snow.' Just like that.

"After we came down to earth from that hit, Styne looked at me and said, Why don't we write a summer song? And we wrote 'The Things We Did Last Summer.'"

Cahn's recounting of the scoring for the title song of the film *Three Coins in a Fountain* painted a quintessential picture of 1950s Hollywood:

"We were working on a film called *Pink Tights*. Styne wrote a marvelous score, but you're never going to hear it. The film got dumped because Marilyn Monroe ran off to Japan with Joe Dimaggio.

"So there we were at the studio with nothing to do. One afternoon, the producer breezed in and said can you write a song called 'Three Coins in a Fountain'? I looked at him and said I could write a song called 'Eh' and he said don't be funny, we need a song called 'Three Coins in a Fountain' and we need it *yesterday*. I said can you at least tell us what it's about? He said three girls go to Rome and hope to fall in love so they throw three coins in a fountain. And then he was gone.

"So we had a title and a clue. I went to the typewriter, Styne went to the piano. Coming up with the lyrics took five minutes. I handed them to Styne who came up with a theme in half an hour. Still, it was hell coming up with the bridge, but we got it done, not before getting a little salty with each other. In an hour the producer comes back to check on us. Actually, I think he said, 'Okay, let's hear it.' I sang it, he loved it, then he rushed down and sang it for Zanuck, who loved it, then zipped back to me and asked me for a demo. *Me? A demo?* I said. Look, Sinatra's wandering around the halls getting paid millions for not making *Pink Tights*, why not ask him? Long story short, Frank said yes. In the end, it was that very demo record that became the one used for the film."

A collaboration with Nicholas Brodsky for "Be My Love" brought about a remarkable afternoon with Mario Lanza. Cahn said, "The music came before the words for this one, and even though he really was the Irving Berlin of Budapest, Brodsky was a waterfall pianist: I could never hear the melody under all that sound. So I had to take it apart and put it back together. I ended up singing it for Mario Lanza, if you can imagine, who stared at me the whole time with this bemused expression. Then Lanza sang it back, not to me, but *at me*. It was one of the most stunning experiences of my life; he nearly cracked my glasses. Listening to him electronically could never match being in the same room with him."

Though Cahn had met Sinatra back in Frank's early days with Tommy Dorsey, their collaboration intensified when Sinatra introduced Sammy to composer Jimmy Van Heusen, and another songwriting duo was born. Cahn said, "Through Tommy came the enduring and perhaps most satisfying relationship of my lyric writing career—Frank Sinatra."[67] Over time, the men were practically considered Sinatra's personal songwriters. Frank recorded eighty-nine of Cahn's songs including "Love and Marriage," "Come Fly With Me," "My Kind of Town," and "The Tender Trap."

Since Cahn had been Sinatra's roommate at one time, it's possible he had more than the usual insight into the man's quirks and character in general, not to mention his phrasing and sense of timing. Cahn explained, "My wife asked me all the time: Sam, tell me the truth; who came first, you or Sinatra? And I always told her: the song came first.

"The first time Sinatra heard (a song I wrote)," Sammy continued, "was when I sang it to him. It's great fun to sing to him because he's such a marvelous audience; he sits and listens and he takes the back of his thumb and rolls it over his lower lip, and when you finish he just looks at you. No comment. But he's never turned a song down. Crosby's the same way."

Other collaborators included Sammy Fain, Arthur Schwartz, Sylvia Fine, Vernon Duke, Gene de Paul, Paul Weston, and Axel Stordahl. Cahn had especially kind words for these last two: "One of my favorite arrangers in all the world is Axel Stordahl. Sy Oliver was a marvel—what a great, great talent—Paul Weston too. Arrangers are truly the unsung heroes; they paint with sound."

Cahn also proved to be a survivor, nimbly adapting to the changing tastes of a nation as he moved from the musical tunes of the 1940s to the ballads of the '50s. In 1992 he told *Pulse!* magazine that he would love to write songs for contemporary singers like Michael Bolton or Madonna: "My opinion of the music of today is simply put: Whatever the number-one song in the world is at this moment, I wish my name were on it."[68]

At one time, Sammy Cahn was considered the nation's highest-paid songwriter, often earning more than a thousand dollars a word. Over a span of thirty-three years, twenty-six songs with Cahn's lyrics were nominated for Academy Awards for best songs of the year, winning four times. He also won an Emmy for

"Love and Marriage." He even starred in a one-man show on Broadway called *Words and Music*, which critics adored.

I would place him up in the stratosphere with '40s and '50s songwriters Johnny Mercer and Harry Warren, a prolific contributor to the Great American Songbook. His delight in his lifelong involvement in songwriting was palpable during our interview: "Songwriting is one of the great joys of my life. And I've been blessed: if you're a man who puts words in people's mouths, the trick is to get them in the mouths of those who are extremely talented. And that's the kind of incredible luck I've had."

SUGGESTED RECORDINGS

An Evening with Sammy Cahn

Sinatra Sings Select Sammy Cahn

An absolute must for lovers.
Selections include:

> "Come Fly With Me"
> "Time After Time"
> "The Tender Trap"
> "Love and Marriage"
> "All the Way"
> "Three Coins in the Fountain"
> "High Hopes"
> "All My Tomorrows"
> "Five Minutes More"

Capital CD# CDP8380942

Ralph Sharon Swings the Sammy Cahn Songbook with special guest Gerry Mulligan

Wonderful jazz interpretations of Cahn classics including:

> "Be My Love"
> "My Kind of Town"
> "Teach Me Tonight"
> "Call Me Irresponsible"
> "The Things We Did Last Summer"
> "The Second Time Around"
> "I Should Care"
> "It's Magic"
> "Guess I'll Hang Out My Tears to Dry"

DRG CD 5232

IV. CONDUCTORS AND COMPOSERS

1. ARTURO TOSCANINI

The Maestro

Arturo Toscanini

© Robert Hupka. Courtesy Estate of Robert Hupka, Arthur Fierro, Executor.

Through serendipity, WBCN, and WGBH, respectively, my life has intersected with three generations of Toscaninis: the world-famous conductor Arturo, his son Walter, and Maestro's grandson Walfredo.

One Saturday in 1948, when I was ten years old, I dragged my father to an RCA Victor trade show at the old Mechanics Hall on Huntington Avenue in Boston. Why? One word: television. I'd never seen one but wanted one with every cell of my being, so I finally convinced my dad to at least have a look at these magical new inventions. We wandered around the showroom, utterly wowed by these cumbersome boxes glowing with small black and white screens. Repeated a hundred times around the hall was a single image: the white-maned conductor himself climbing to the podium and lifting his arms. The first glorious notes of the overtrue to Verdi's *La forza del destino* thundered to life. You could feel the man's intensity and passion blasting through the cathode rays as he chopped his baton through the thick air surrounding his spellbound musicians. They knew what was expected of them, as well as the consequences for not providing it: the wrath of Arturo Toscanini.

Already steeped in opera through not only my father who sang arias while shaving, but through Saturday afternoon Metropolitan opera broadcasts, I could already quote you the liner notes off all the Puccini LPs at home. But this sound—this was a *new* sound! Violins as sweet as voices, crashing timpani, a tremendous energy just under the surface that this wild man on the podium seemed to have tamed with just a stick. I not only had to have the TV, I had to hear *every* piece of classical music on earth.

More than two decades later, in the early sixties, I found myself at WBCN, when those call letters meant "Boston's Concert Network." In tribute to the impact this man had on my life, I decided to put together an all-Toscanini series. I wrote to Arturo's son Walter about the concept. His response was to immediately start mailing me a different set of reel-to-reel tapes each week. I knew what these tapes meant to Walter; he'd worked with his father during the last years of the conductor's life helping edit tapes and transcriptions of performances with the NBC Symphony. The energy that blasted out of these tapes was just as alive and powerful as what I'd heard and seen in 1948 as the awestruck kid in front of my first television.

It wasn't easy letting Walter know about WBCN's decision to stop playing classical music and become an all-rock station, something that happened just a few months after I'd started the series. Walter's reaction to the disappointment was to invite me to the Toscanini homestead in Riverdale, New York. In the basement of his home, which he'd converted to a recording studio, I was treated to rarely heard reels of Toscanini in rehearsal as he chastised members of his symphony, indulging his constant reach for perfection.

A good thirty years passed. In October of 1993, many years after Walter's passing in 1971, I reached out to his son, Walfredo, after learning he'd spent some time accompanying Arturo during one of his last tours in the states when Walfredo was twenty-one and the maestro in his early eighties. Walfredo granted me the opportunity of a series of interviews for *The Classical Hour* on WGBH, lending myself and our listeners fantastic insights into his famous grandfather.

Born on March 25, 1867, in Parma, Italy, Arturo Toscanini is widely considered to be the greatest conductor of the late nineteenth/early twentieth century. A combination of elements set him apart from all who came before: his celebrated interpretations of Beethoven, Brahms, Wagner, and Verdi, his photographic memory, his phenomenal ear for orchestral detail, his passionate swings from rapture to despair, and his sexual voraciousness are just a few. Radio and TV broadcasts as music director of the NBC Symphony Orchestra from 1938 to 1954 made him a household name.

At age nineteen, Arturo played cello and acted as Chorus Master with an opera company on tour in South America. After several lackluster performances of *Aida* in Rio de Janeiro, the musicians completely lost patience with their conductor who'd apparently been doing such a terrible job that they went on strike, forcing the company to find a new conductor. After no fewer than two replacements were booed offstage, the company turned to their Chorus Master, who knew the whole opera cold. With zero conducting experience, Arturo took up the baton, tossed the score to one side, and led an astounding performance, going on to conduct eighteen more operas with the company.

Back in Italy, he continued to conduct but also returned to the cello, playing in the world premiere of Verdi's *Otello* in 1887 under the composer's supervision. Impressed by Toscanini's faithfulness to the score, Verdi knew he was dealing with no ordinary cello player when Arturo suggested an *allargando* for the Te Deum where it was not in the score; Verdi responded that he'd omitted it for fear "certain interpreters would have exaggerated the markings."[69]

Word of Arturo's brilliance spread. The next decade saw Toscanini not only entrusted with the world premieres of Puccini's *La Boheme* as well as Leoncavallo's *Pagliacci*, but conducting symphonies worldwide. He became the resident conductor at the La Scala Orchestra, leaving for the Metropolitan Opera in 1908, but returning in 1920 to tour with La Scala in the states. In 1930 he toured Europe with the New York Philharmonic to fantastic acclaim from both critics and audiences.

Toscanini initially supported Mussolini in 1919, along with many other bourgeois Italians at the time. By 1923 he had come around to a complete opposite point of view, at one point refusing to play their national hymn at concerts. He became the first non-German conductor to appear at Bayreuth in 1930, while the New York Philharmonic was the first non-German orchestra to play there. In 1931 he was assaulted by Fascist thugs in Bologna, and thereafter refused to conduct in Italy until a new regime was in place. He cursed other musicians, such as Richard Strauss, who continued to perform in Italy after 1933: "To Strauss the composer I take off my hat; to Strauss the man I put it back on again."[70] To a friend he said, "If I were capable of killing a man, I would kill Mussolini."[71]

Exiled from not only from Bayreuth, Salzburg, and now his own country, Arturo conducted with the Vienna Philharmonic in Vienna and the BBC Symphony in London, and what is now known as the Israel Philharmonic in Tel-Aviv, Jerusalem, and Haifa, even traveling with this company to perform in Alexandra and Cairo.

That said, the maestro was limited in where he could go and was at a crossroads of sorts in his career. In 1937 the NBC Symphony Orchestra was created for him, and he returned to the states to embrace this opportunity. The acoustics of the custom-built studio were a bit dry; however, remodeling in 1939 added reverberation to the space now used for NBC's *Saturday Night Live*. During our 1993 interview, Walfredo recalled, "NBC had the idea of promoting classical music as well as sales of radios and recordings. So it wasn't about giving concerts for audiences in the hall, but rather for the millions of people listening at home...no matter how long (Toscanini's) career had been up until that point, in one day more people would hear his concerts than in the past fifty years of his career. So I think that really appealed to him."

Though criticized for ignoring American music, in 1945 Arturo led the orchestra in recording sessions of Gershwin's *An American in Paris* and *Rhapsody in Blue* with soloists Earl Wild and Benny Goodman, as well as Copland's *El Salon Mexico*; he even penned his own orchestral arrangement of "The Star Spangled Banner," which was later incorporated into NBC performances of Verdi's *Hymn of the Nations*.

Toscanini the man has been called incredibly private for such a well known figure; he left no memoir and refused most interviews, and it wasn't until Harvey Sachs' stunner *The Letters of Arturo Toscanini* hit the stands in 2002 that much of the man was revealed. These letters showcased his fantastic energy and complexity: his perfectionism, his quick temper, and boundless sexuality. Some of the most eye-popping letters, both in content and number, are to Ada Mainadi, wife of a well-known cellist. This was when he was in his seventies and she was half his age, and counts as one of untold numbers of liaisons. Keep in mind he was married with four children (though his son Giorgio passed at age five.) His grandson Walfredo put it this way: "he cast his nets wide." Though apparently not a Maestro in the love letter department, he still wrote thousands of them, a fair number to the singer Jane Lawrence Smith, a woman he had never met, but had only spoken to over the telephone.

His conquests read like a punch list of late nineteenth, early twentieth century sopranos including Lucretia Bori, Rosina Storchio, and Geraldine Farrar. Though his wife Carla intercepted a few of these steaming missives, after a while she gave up doing anything about the situation, though the letters to Mainardi take up more than two hundred pages of Sach's book. In them he begs for clippings of her pubic hair ("tiny flowers")[72] and a handkerchief stained with her menstrual blood. In his early seventies the letters devolved mostly into speculation about amorous rendezvous instead of the meetings themselves. He would dash them off after performances as if they were excess creative energy he needed to release. In notes to various lovers he often compared sex to music: "Music has the same effect on me that you have."[73]

But there is no summarizing the man. Did drama come to him or did he create it in life or on the podium for his own enjoyment? "My God, what a life!" he wrote in 1936. "And to think that people envy me! They see nothing but the exterior, which glitters in appearance, but a person's interior, soul, heart? What unknown, unexplored things they are!'"[74] As Michael Kimmelman intuited in his review of *The Letters of Arturo Toscanini*: "You sense him playing a role, the Great Maestro. Life seems to have been a Puccini opera for Toscanini...his ego clearly thrived on excess."[75]

At the same time, he was known for his generosity: he left instructions with Clara, to aid, financially, any member of the La Scala orchestra who approached her, no explanations needed. In 1936 he paid his own expenses for a trip to Palestine to conduct an inaugural concert. The musicians consisted of Jewish refugees from Central Europe, a group that ultimately became the Israel Philharmonic.

Walfredo's recollections in our interview revealed yet another side to the man: "I knew he was (famous) because he had a big Cadillac and a chauffeur, and he had a big house with a marble staircase in Milan, but I didn't know what he did until I went to Salzburg and heard him perform there. So, to me, a seven-year-old kid, he was just this nice gentleman who had these beautiful villas and was very interested in me. The funny part is that no one had seen that side of him. Here he was: this stern and forbidding figure, and suddenly there was this little boy in his arms; and he was just my grandfather, and we were having fun. He had a very relaxed side to him not many people saw."

Though even at family events, his controlling nature came to the fore at odd times: "We'd have these big meals (after a performance) in Riverdale: sometimes eighteen to twenty-four people, sitting down to a very sumptuous meal. But Grandfather himself ate very little: just some soup and a tiny piece of veal, something like that. He'd look at everyone else's plates and say 'How can you eat all that?' At first the women thought it was a great honor to sit next to him, until they discovered they couldn't enjoy their meal because of the constant criticism."

Like many of his contemporaries, Toscanini never took to Schoenberg or Mahler; however, he was ahead of his time in admiring Debussy. He also instigated changes in the physical presentation of symphonic music that would be taken for granted today: he insisted on dimming the house lights during performances, and that audiences refrain from eating, talking, playing cards, and wandering around. Theater in the early 1900s was more a casual gathering place than anything else. He also insisted that musicians adhere to the score, which sounds rather obvious, but his letters tell of a rampant sort of sloppiness that was the rule rather than the exception at the time. His critics have said he pushed things too far the other way: that his performances felt metronomic and too brisk at times.

Another huge innovation Toscanini championed was the creation of the orchestra pit; in fact he installed the first one at La Scala in 1907. Before this time the orchestra played at the main floor level. His biographer Harvey Sachs wrote, "He believed that a performance could not be artistically successful unless unity of intention was first established among all the components: singers, orchestra, chorus, staging, sets and costumes."[76]

Walfredo shared his thoughts about the lowering of the pit: "It was Wagner's idea that there should be a mystic gulf between the audience and the stage and not hundreds of people sawing away or blowing at instruments, and a man waving his hands. So, he was happiest when the orchestra and the conductor didn't exist, but the sound and music and spectacle did. When (my grandfather) caused the pit at La Scala to be lowered, he was concerned that he would be perceived as a prima donna, or that people would think this was a foolish expense. In fact there was a cartoon showing members of the orchestra being lowered into a pit, because Toscanini wanted it down, as far as it could go."

Much has also been said about the differences between Arturo at rehearsal screaming profanities at his musicians in a perhaps consciously theatrical way of extracting "perfection," in contrast to his still passionate but controlled presence during performances. Long stretches of Toscanini on film via NBC cameras captured the piano-wire tight tension between conductor and musician. Walfredo noted that during rehearsal, his grandfather would "make swoops down almost to his feet with his baton...but in concert he limited his motion because (he thought) the audience should be listening to the music, not watching the conductor." Part of what made Toscanini so modern, though, was his constant propulsion even through slower passages, while never neglecting the more subtle layers of the score. His melodramatic flourishes were evident when he left the stage in 1926 during the premiere of *Turandot* precisely at the point Puccini left off due to his death. The maestro simply stated, "Here, Death triumphed over art,"[77] and left the pit. In moments the lights came up and the hushed audience filed from the hall.

Walfredo recalled a few highlights of one of his grandfather's final tours through the states: "After playing something like four concerts a week—this is after full rehearsals—the next morning he'd be awake and ready to tour whatever city we were in: New Orleans, Houston, San Francisco...and I'm telling you we were dead tired but he was always energized by his ability to lead the orchestra and make music for people, many of whom had never seen him in action. It was a triumphal tour for him...and an astonishing thing for me to experience first hand not only his intellectual and musical talent, but his physical resistance and strength as well. It's a little like Nolan Ryan pitching for twenty-seven years. Grandfather pitched for sixty-eight years on the podium, and his intensity never diminished."

I asked Walfredo about his grandfather's pet canaries, a story I'd heard only bits and pieces of before: "He had this enormous cage of canaries, maybe eighteen or twenty of them in there, and he'd set it near the radio and turn it on. In a few minutes they'd perk up and start to sing in sympathy with the music. He loved to see that: these birds just chirping and cooing, flapping their wings with excitement. He told me that he felt that if people heard the best music—the best compositions of his beloved composers played in the best way, such as with the NBC orchestra—then maybe they would feel it too, and they'd be moved to sing along as well."

SUGGESTED RECORDINGS

Toscanini Conducts Favorite Overtures Including Works by Mozart, Weber, Verdi, Rossini, and Other Composers
RCA CD 09026 60310-2

La Boheme by Puccini

Licia Albanese, Jan Peerce, and Francesco Valentino are featured in the cast of
this historic 1946 broadcast with the NBC Symphony Orchestra. Toscanini conducted the world premiere at Teatro Regio in Turin 50 years earlier
on February 1, 1896.
RCA CD 60288-2-RG

Tchaikovsky: Symphony No. 6 "Pathetique"

Toscanini conducts The Philadelphia Orchestra in a performance recorded in
1942.
RCA 60312-2-RG

**The Pines of Rome, The Fountains of Rome, and Roman Festivals by
Ottorinio Respighi**

Arturo Toscanini conducts the NBC Symphony Orchestra
RCA CD 60262-2-RG

**Symphony No. 4 " Italian" and Symphony No. 5 "Reformation" by Felix
Mendelssohn**

Arturo Toscanini from a broadcast with the NBC Symphony Orchestra in 1953
and 1954.
RCA CD 60284-2-RG

"Where the Word Ends"

Author's collection.

Gunther Schuller, Joan Kennedy, and me

A man of endless musical pursuits, Gunther Schuller is also a joy to not only interview but to spend an evening with over wine and good food. I'm either laughing or learning with him, many times both at once.

Born in New York City in 1925, the son of a violinist with the New York Philharmonic, Gunther is the sort of wunderkind you might imagine composing a score in diapers. The fact is, except for an episode his dad recalls where five-year-old Gunther sat in his bathtub splashing his rubber ducky while humming *Tannhauser*, the musical side of the young composer's brain didn't really light up until a bit later. At age eleven, he became obsessed with a toy xylophone his younger brother Edgar was given for Christmas and composed his first score: thirty bars for xylophone, flute, violin, and piano. He still has it in a notebook somewhere. Some years later he was, as he put it: "bowled over by the *Rite of Spring* in *Fantasia*. For two or three weeks after seeing that I wasn't myself. That [movie] transformed my life, turned me into a musician."

Once the floodgates opened, Gunther worked at nothing but music for up to nineteen hours a day, many times forgetting to eat. He devoured music by Beethoven, Schoenberg, Ravel, and Stravinsky. But when he discovered Duke Ellington and told his father that jazz was just as great as the classical music he'd been listening to, his dad nearly fell off his chair. Statements like these at the time were practically heretical, and presaged Gunther's rebellious, independent, ultimately groundbreaking style of thinking about music.

He began his professional life as a sixteen-year-old principal horn player in the Cincinnati Symphony in 1943, later holding that position with the Metropolitan Opera Orchestra. Of that era, he said: "I feel so fortunate to have been in on that whole decade from 1945 to the beginnings of Bebop, and into the modern jazz period. Those fifteen years were spectacular. Not only were Mario Del Monaco and Lily Pons at the Met, but all I had to do was walk five minutes up Broadway to find at least twelve Jazz clubs, starting with the Aquarium on 52nd Street...all the way up to Birdland, Bop City, and Basin Street East. I met Dizzy in 1948 at the Aquarium, then Ray Brown, John Lewis, and J. J. Johnson. In fact that's how I got to play with Miles Davis—they ran out of horn players."

At this point, equally at ease working with Miles as with Toscanini, the young Gunther was invited by Davis to record sessions that evolved into the classic album, *The Birth of the Cool*. Meanwhile, back at the Metropolitan Opera Orchestra (where Gunther stayed until 1959,) his enthusiasm for jazz was met with a bit less excitement. He told me: "Bob Boyd used to play jazz during intermission at the Met, and it used to infuriate the players who thought jazz was disgusting. We were the young Turks."

When the director of the New York Philharmonic broadcast Schuller's "Music for Brass" in 1956, the floodgates opened. Letters arrived from Aaron Copland, Samuel Barber, and others, all welcoming him into an elite musical society. In the fifties he began conducting a range of contemporary works—including his own—at most of the major symphony orchestras in the world. His term "Third Stream," coined while lecturing at Brandeis in 1957, refers to the "totally logical" stylistic marriage of jazz and classical music, which he developed further while working with the Modern Jazz Quartet and John Lewis. To the critics he said, "'My God, [here are] these two great musics and they are in separate camps—they don't talk to each other, they hate each other, they vilify each other. We've got to get these two musics together.'"[78] Ran Blake, an improvisation-based pianist who became Gunther's student, pointed out that though the term "Third Stream" was new, musical examples such as *Porgy and Bess* were not uncommon. Together, Schuller and Blake created the Third Stream Department at the New England Conservatory. Original jazz compositions "Teardrop" and "Jumpin' in the Future" epitomize the Third Stream approach, blending classical structural sophistication with the swing and fluidity of jazz.

By the early sixties, Schuller had turned away from performance to devote himself to teaching, writing, and composition. An influential and elegant educator, Gunther has been on the faculties of the Manhattan School of Music and Yale University where he succeeded Aaron Copland; Director of the Tanglewood Music Center; and President of the New England Conservatory. In the late seventies he started GunMar and Margun music publishing companies (now part of G. Schirmer/Music Sales/AMP) and the GM Recordings label. The author of more than 180 works ranging from solos to concertos, symphonies, opera, and other works that simply don't fall neatly into any genre, Gunther continues to keep a grueling schedule even well into his eighties.

"Spectra," an orchestral work commissioned in 1958, rearranged musical space by dividing the larger orchestra into smaller chamber groups; at the same time drawing out each instrument's character in such a way that hadn't been considered before. "An Arc Ascending" (1996) was inspired by the photographs of Alice Weston. Other compositions drew on Impressionist and late Romantic tone poems of Debussy and Schoenberg. "Of Reminiscences and Reflections," one of Schuller's two memorials to Marjorie Black, his wife of forty-nine years, won him the Pulitzer Prize in Music in 1994.

Gunther also composed a stunning variety of concertos for solo or small ensemble with orchestra, bringing to the forefront less commonly championed instruments such as contrabassoon, organ, double bass, and alto saxophone. His "Grand Concerto for Percussion and Keyboards" uses more than one hundred percussion instruments. Schuller's two operas include *The Visitation* (1966) based on a Kafka story and an hour-long 1970 children's opera, *The Fisherman and His Wife,* that features a libretto by John Updike, drawn from a Grimm fairy tale.

Schuller's chamber music also embraces traditional and non-traditional trends, from four string quintets, brass and woodwind quintets, to works for solo instrument or voice with piano, and mixed ensemble pieces.

In February of 2009, the Boston Symphony Orchestra and James Levine premiered the very well received "Where the Word Ends," a single movement, twenty-five minute piece, which was also heard on one of our live BSO broadcasts. For someone with little patience for lofty titles, Gunther was especially proud of this one. He said, "[Composers] write a piece and slap some title on it and it's usually something like 'The Moon is Drifting Under the Bridge' or 'The Trees are Falling to the Left'... I'm just not into that. Regardless of whether my music is any good, I think the title is really one of the most beautiful definitions of music itself.'"[79] He shared with me the fact that the composition came to him in a rush—that he couldn't have spent more than twenty or thirty hours on it. "It was almost eerie... Maybe it's ancient age, but for 'Where the Word Ends' I almost didn't have to think about what the next note would be. It was like an improvisation.'"[80] Considered by many to be his best work, *Globe* jazz writer Bob Blumenthal called the piece a "time capsule" of his career, noting echoes of Stravinsky as well as Miles Davis.

Schuller's brilliance exists on many planes, but most strikingly, in my opinion, in his utter openness to the ultimate harmonic marriage of musical styles, philosophies, even instruments. His arrangements of classic jazz, standards, and ragtime music by Paul Whiteman, Duke Ellington, Jelly Roll Morton, and Dizzy Gillespie mesh with his realizations of music by Charles Ives and Thomas Tallis. The author of two books on jazz, Gunther is also the recipient of the MacArthur Foundation's genius award in 1991, the William Schuman Award in 1988 and 1993, Downbeat's Lifetime achievement award for his contribution to jazz, and two Grammys.

We spoke about the process behind writing *The Swing Era*, just how much research was involved and a few of the secrets revealed in the process: "It became a humungous book. Well over a thousand pages, dealing with that era from 1930 to about 1948. The index alone has four thousand words, and something like five hundred musical examples, all of which I transcribed from recordings. All in all I listened to thirty-five thousand records writing this book. I made it my philosophy that if there was anybody I was going to mention in the book, I was going to listen to every recording (they made) that I could lay my hands on. My son George ferreted out all these recordings, and, of course, I begged, borrowed, stole, bought, and copied the rest, so now we have a pretty darn good collection."

Gunther also discovered, through painstaking cataloging of the Ellington manuscripts at the Smithsonian, that a lot of the solos by Johnny Hodges, Harry Carney, and others were actually compositions written by Ellington himself. Gunther explained, "We always marveled about the high integrity of the composition of these solos, but assumed they were improvised out of plain cloth. They were not! Of course they were embellished in a free or personal way, but there they were, right there in Duke's own handwriting." Other surprises included a new appreciation for John Nesbitt, a jazz trumpet player who influenced, ultimately, Benny Goodman and the swing era. Only by actually listening to these countless recordings could he have heard this influence and been able to posit a different place in history for Nesbitt. Cab Calloway was "treated kind of negligibly by jazz historians because he was a comedian...but when you really listen, his singing is so exquisite...he could sing anything from bass to soprano; he had something like five voices in him."

These days Gunther's life is almost exclusively focused on music, though he used to travel the world with his wife Marjorie Black. He still relishes spending time with his two sons: jazz percussionist George Schuller and bassist Ed Schuller. Two young women he calls his secretaries take care of quotidian concerns like groceries and trips to the bank.

Gunther spoke to me a bit about music then and now: "Anything we wrote in those early days, no matter how far out it was, it still had to be danceable. That's all changed now of course. So, it's a different feel, but I love that old feeling. I mean, I'm certainly an avant-gardist in many ways, but there's something to preserving that sense of swing and that style. I don't think we should ever lose that. And I know that's something you agree with, Ron."...and of course he's right about that!

"Where are we headed? Change is exploding all around us, but certain principles remain. Synthesizers are just instruments and not inherently creative; though they're a whole world of sound, they don't guarantee quality. The older I get the more I realize how much there is to do, to learn, how much more music there is to appreciate and understand, especially the ethnic, world music, with record companies catching on. I love the cross fertilization between world musics and jazz and popular music. It's all seething and bubbling...really, who knows what will happen next?"

SUGGESTED RECORDINGS

Happy Feet: A Tribute to Paul Whiteman

The New England Jazz Repertory Orchestra conducted by Gunther Schuller, GM 3048

I love this recording! I wore out my LP copy, so I'm delighted to have it released on CD. Whiteman was one of the great figures in American Music, and this collection lets us hear why. There's even a cameo appearance by the legendary jazz violinist Joe Venuti.

Gunther Schuller: Orchestra Works

A collection of some of the best orchestral writing of the twentieth century including Schuller's most popular work, "Seven Sketches on Themes of Paul Klee."

GM 2059

Jazz Compositions and Arrangements by Gunther Schuller

A must for jazz lovers that showcases masterpieces from the "Cool Jazz Era."

GM 3010

3. HARRY ELLIS DICKSON
Wild About Harry!

Author's collection.

One of the most joyful occasions during my years at WGBH was in 1998, when we celebrated Boston's beloved conductor Harry Ellis Dickson's ninetieth birthday. After sharing some of his wonderful stories during a guest appearance on *Classics in the Morning,* we enjoyed a huge birthday cake, provided by my then-producer Leslie Warshaw. The greeting on the cake expressed the feelings of everyone who ever came in contact with this charismatic and dynamic gentleman of music: "We're All Wild About Harry!"

Born in Cambridge, Massachusetts, in 1908 to Russian immigrant parents, Harry wasn't at first considered the gifted child in the family. He told me: "It was my sister who got the lessons. She had no interest in the violin, but I couldn't get enough of it. I'd sit in during lessons and when the teacher asked a question, I'd answer. Finally he told my mother he'd give me lessons for nothing, so she took the fiddle from my sister and handed it to me. I was six years old."

From then on young Harry barely put the instrument down: "I had a recording of Mischa Elman playing Massenet's *Elegie,* and I played it over and over and over again on our Victrola. I thought if I could ever make a sound like that, my life would be complete. That's when I fell in love with the violin. It was a glorious era of violin playing: I remember especially Jascha Heifitz and Fritz Kriester. Isaac Stern and Itzhak Perlman weren't yet on the scene."

Dickson went on to study at the New England Conservatory, later living in Berlin from 1931 to 1934 where he studied at the Hochschule fuer Musik. By the age of fourteen, he was a professional musician and soon went on to play under such storied conductors as Serge Koussevitzky, Pierre Monteux, Charles Munch, William Steinberg, Eric Leinsdorf, and Seiji Ozawa, as well as meet and study with Bartok and Sibelius.

Beginning in 1938, he played violin with the Boston Symphony Orchestra for forty-nine years, regretfully retiring just before the fifty-year mark. Over the years he took part in several historic events in Symphony Hall, such as the world premiere of Bartok's "Concerto for Orchestra" in 1944 and some of the first years at Tanglewood, the summer home of the orchestra.

Though few can boast of such a superior musical resume, Harry the man was also charming, self-deprecating, and a lot of fun to be around. I always considered him "Maestro" and introduced him as such on the air, but he winced a bit each time, saying, "I'm just Harry, okay?" In 1999 after being named music director laureate of the BSO, he said of his time there: "I've been around so long that all the statues in Symphony Hall were little boys when I started."[81] Harry once told me of a musician he played with in his early years who himself was as old as Methuselah and had actually gone out on a bar crawl with Brahms!

In 1955 Harry began another decades-long musical relationship: this time with the Boston Pops, where he stepped in as assistant conductor for Arthur Fielder. This partnership lasted forty-four years and inspired Dickson's 1984 book, *Arthur Fiedler and the Boston Pops: An Irreverent Memoir*. In one interview Harry said, "I was as close to Arthur Fiedler as anybody ever got, and that wasn't very close."[82]

One evening, Harry observed an interaction between Fiedler and Dizzy Gillespie, probably the most polar opposite musicians in the world. After handing Gillespie the score, Fiedler began to conduct as Dizzy started to float away from the notes on the page, as usual. Fiedler said, "What are you *doing?*" Dizzy said, "Man, you just keep going, never mind about me." So they started again, and Dizzy spun off somewhere into the stratosphere while Fiedler gave him one dirty look after the other, but Dizzy was in his own world.

Harry said, "Later I wondered if any of Dizzy's band read music. I asked his bass player, who was studying the score very intently, if he did. He said, 'Not enough for it to bother me.'"

The story I remember best was when Dizzy put his funky, used handkerchief on Fiedler's podium. Eyeing it as if it were a dead rat, Fiedler knocked it off with his baton. Dizzy put it back. Fiedler knocked it off. Finally Dizzy gave in and held on to it for the duration of his performance.

Harry elaborated about life with Fielder: "Over the years, I wondered how the public could so ceaselessly love Arthur. I realize now it was more than his showmanship, more than the music. Arthur's image was lovable; he had a wolfishness about him, but it was a vulnerable wolfishness. Beyond that, little else mattered to the public about his private life. His eccentricities merely added to the fun."

Speaking of eccentricities, there was always the fire-chasing thing. When not involved in music, Fiedler spent most of his spare time as a "spark," one who learns about fires and races off to witness them. At the time of his death, he had one of the largest collections of honorary fire chief hats of anyone in the country.

Several years ago I attended the dedication of the "Harry Ellis Dickson Park" located on Westland Avenue and not far from Symphony Hall's stage door. It was a gala occasion with Harry's son-in-law, former Governor Michael Dukakis, his daughters Kitty and Ginny in attendance, along with many other dignitaries. When it came time for Harry to speak, the wailing sirens of fire engines speeding by drowned him out. Harry commented, "Just like Arthur to try to upstage me again...but that's OK, he's got a statue on the Esplanade, and now I've got a park next to Symphony Hall."

Appearing with Harry on numerous occasions when he was guest conductor of the Boston Pops afforded me the pleasure of getting to know him even better. Some of my best recollections come from our New Year's Eve celebrations. In addition to hosting the evening, one of my jobs was to count down the last minute to midnight with the audience. Once, during these last dramatic seconds of the year, the huge clock above the stage stopped, cold. Somebody had accidently pulled the plug with seven seconds to go. Harry covered up the goof and we kept on counting down. Afterwards, he had a bit of a meltdown backstage. "This guy has one job to do all year and he screws it up! Imagine...no clock for New Year's Eve...what's *wrong* with these people!" But Harry was not one to hold a grudge; soon we were toasting each other with champagne and welcoming in the new year with our guests.

In 1959 Harry founded the Boston Symphony Youth Concerts. He talked a little about the earliest days: "In the late fifties we were doing some young people's concerts in Brookline with about twenty-five or thirty musicians from the BSO, and they'd been going well. My wife and I tossed around the idea of starting a few in the hall itself; pretty soon they just took it over. We used to have auditions from high schools—just a few would apply—soon we had hundreds of applicants. Ninety-five percent of those we've chosen have gone on to become professional musicians.

"Before our youth concerts there were sporadic ones put on by the BSO, even Koussevitzky did a few. Wallace Goodrich of the New England Conservatory narrated some, but they were pretty stultifying. Wheeler Beckett's were too long. I don't believe there's special music for young people—you can play anything for them—in fact what their parents may feel is too far out they take in stride. The only concession I make is a listening span; they'll just tune out if it's too long."

Even by this 1989 interview, Harry estimated these youth concerts had reached more than three-quarters of a million youngsters. His hopes were not so much that they become professional musicians, but that they become, as Aaron Copland put it, "talented listeners."

In addition to his consummate musicianship both as violinist and conductor, he authored three very irreverent, entertaining books. His witty anecdotes—some hilarious, some serious—illustrate his days working with everyone from Danny

Kaye to Fiedler, Serge Koussevitzky, Seiji Ozawa, John Williams, and Igor Stravinsky. There are also moving reflections on his wife Jane and daughters Kitty and Ginny, and the effects on his family of the failed presidential campaign of his son-in-law Michael Dukakis. Of Dickson, Dukakis once said, "No one on this planet could wish for a better father-in-law."[83]

In *Gentlemen, More Dolce Please*, he described the era of Koussevitzky as an exciting but turbulent one. Dickson couldn't remember a concert under him when in the end each player wasn't soaking wet and as emotionally spent as the conductor. "Gentlemen," Koussevitzky once explained, "You play all the time the wrong notes not in time! And please, made important, you play like it is something nothing!"[84] To a string player he raged, "How can you play with died fingers?"[85] Another story involved an older woman who said to him after a concert, "'Dr. Koussevitzky, to us you are God,' and he answered, 'I know my responsibility.'"[86] Although Koussevitzky murdered the English language, he became, according to Harry, the conductor by whom all others would be judged.

Of all the many honors bestowed on him, Harry was especially proud of being awarded the title of Chevalier of Arts and Letters by the French government. His longevity also amused him; when asked his age he would say: "I've been through four ages in my life: childhood, youth, middle age, and *you look marvelous!*" His youth concert series has been the pattern for many others and continues to change the lives of millions of children and young adults. Other honors include the Harry Ellis Dickson Center of Fine Arts and Humanities in the Winter Hill Community School, and the Harry Ellis Dickson Orchestral Suite at Madison Park High School in 1983, as well as a scholarship under his name at the Boston Arts Academy.

These days when I think of Harry, I remember a Fourth of July many years ago. I'd left the studio late that afternoon and treated myself to a long walk along the Charles River toward my home in the South End. It was a perfect summer afternoon, hot but dry, and the sun seemed to backlight everything with an orange glow. Soon I was joined by hundreds of people also walking along the banks of the river, young and old all making their way with blankets and picnic baskets as we listened to the oddly pleasing sounds of the Pops warming up. I couldn't believe how many boats were in the river; it looked like you could walk across it just by jumping from boat to boat. As I reached the Esplanade, I could just make out the tiny figure of my friend lifting his arms in welcome as the crowd, now stretching for miles, broke into joyous applause.

SUGGESTED RECORDINGS

Harry Ellis Dickson, a member of the Boston Symphony for some fifty years, participated in just about every recording session with the BSO and the Boston Pops. He conducted hundreds of "Pops" concerts at Symphony Hall, the Esplanade, and on tour.

Suggested Readings

Gentlemen, More Dolce Please: An Irreverent Memoir of Thirty-five Years in the Boston Symphony Orchestra

> Published in 1969 by Beacon Press
> Drawings by Olga Koussevitzsky

Arthur Fielder and the Boston Pops

> Published by Houghton Mifflin Company Boston, 1981
> Introduction by Ellen Bottomley Fielder
> Epilogue by John Williams

Harry Ellis Dickson ... Beating Time, A Musician's Memoir

> Published by Northeastern University Press, 1995
> Forward by John Williams

Grandfather of Film Music

David Raksin

© Photofest, Inc.

When asked to name his favorite song, Frank Sinatra said, "Laura," without hesitation. A gentleman known as the "Grandfather of Film Music," David Raksin, composed the song for the 1944 movie of the same name.

Born in Philadelphia in 1912, David was raised in a musical family. His father, Isador, played clarinet in the Philadelphia Orchestra and composed and conducted music for silent films and vaudeville. By age six David was at the piano; soon after his dad gave him a clarinet and instructed him on wind instruments. Twelve-year-old Raksin not only had his own dance band, but played in all the dance bands in his high school. He worked his way through UPenn, teaching himself composition and playing in radio orchestras, then moved to New York City where he discovered Broadway and began arranging for record companies.

In the thirties David headed to Hollywood where he studied composition with Arnold Schoenberg, a man of genius but not known for patience. Once Raksin made the error of asking how to compose music for an airplane sequence. Schoenberg replied, "Like music for *big bees*, only *louder*."[87] David also shared with me the infamous Raksin/Hitchcock exchange: Hitchcock didn't want music for lost-at-sea drama *Lifeboat* because he worried audiences would wonder where the music was coming from in the middle of the ocean. Raksin said to pass this on: "Ask Hitch where the cameras are coming from."[88]

He summed up his early days in our 1984 interview: "I got involved with Howard Lanin and his band, but for a while things were slim. I nearly starved to death. Finally, Roger Wolfe Kahn and Al Goodman heard my arrangements. We had Artie Shaw on sax, Tommy Dorsey on second trombone. Gershwin heard me and put me on staff. I think I was nineteen at the time."

Impressed by the ingenuity of Raksin's arrangement of "I Got Rhythm" for Jay Savitt's band, composer Oscar Levant contacted his friend George Gershwin and suggested they meet. Not at all thrown by the gravity of having lunch with Gershwin, Raksin said, "He recognized that I was a colleague who knew what I was doing. He played 'Love Walked In' for me. Didn't sing, just played the melody."

Gershwin recommended Raksin to Harms Music, who drafted him to be Charlie Chaplin's assistant on the landmark 1935 film, *Modern Times*. Notoriously tough on musical partners, Chaplin never had the same assistant two movies in a row. He was also a "hummer," that is, he was unable to transcribe his scores by himself. Chaplin hummed, tapped, and whistled his musical ideas, including the three-note blast of the factory. Unfazed by Chaplin, twenty-three-year old Raksin voiced his own musical opinions. Chaplin fired him, then rehired him after Alfred Newman, a renowned film scorer, told him he was nuts to give him the axe. The score took four months to complete and included the song "Smile" for which Chaplin received total credit. As Raksin said, "There wasn't any point in making a big deal out of it; that's just the way things were back then."

In fact for his work on forty-eight films through the 1930s at Universal Studios, Columbia Pictures, and Twentieth Century Fox, Raksin received not a single credit, since that was reserved at that time for the studio's music department head. Because of his association with Schoenberg, Raksin's music was considered avant-garde by the studio system, and he was commonly relegated to low budget horror flicks such as *The Undying Monster*.

One brief collaboration was with Igor Stravinsky, whose "Circus Polka" Raksin arranged for the elephant ballet. Choreographed by Ballanchine, it was staged by Ringling Brothers and Barnum & Bailey. The troupe bellowed and stampeded on hearing Raksin's work, which he and Stravinsky interpreted as a big thumbs up.

By the time I interviewed him in September 1984, David had well over a hundred film scores and three hundred television scores to his credit. He told the story of how he landed the job composing the music for *Laura*, one of the all-time great film classics. Studio scuttlebutt at the time was that the movie was troubled, "and everyone wants to stay away from a picture with problems because you become a part of those problems." So when director Otto Preminger asked both Alfred Newman and Bernard Herrmann to compose the score, they turned him down, and Raksin was next in line. The very next day Preminger announced he wanted to use Duke Ellington's "Sophisticated Lady" for the film. Raksin told me, "I saw the picture and fell in love with it. I was horrified by the 'Sophisticated Lady' choice. When I told him it wasn't right for the picture, Otto and I had a big blowout. You don't need a tune that already has a past. You need a tune special for your picture." The argument was finally settled when Preminger said, 'Well alright, it's Friday. Show up Monday with something else or we use 'Sophisticated Lady.'"

Raksin continued, "I went home, and it's sort of a corny story, but as a result of receiving a letter from a lady who told me to get lost, I was suddenly improvising at the piano and out came this tune. I'd spent the whole weekend sweating, nothing coming out of me until I read that letter. Lose a lady, gain a tune, was one way of looking at it."

I asked David if he realized what sort of worldwide impact and reception "Laura" would receive even as he was writing it. He said, "I'm ashamed to say I predicted something like it. When you hit something that's really you, you feel it, you know it. Of course that's common, that delusion, for songwriters and composers. But hell, we stayed on the hit parade for twelve weeks."

Raksin told me that when he played it for Preminger, Otto loved it right away. David got to choose his own lyricist, so he chose the best: Johnny Mercer. In the first week after the movie's release he received over seventeen hundred letters.

I listen to "Laura" and I hear a sexy, eerie, beautiful tune. Raksin told me he wrote the entire score around a single haunting melody that he never used in its entirety, creating a sense of yearning; as he said, "the ephemeral girl and the interrupted melody."[89] The idea was to highlight the lingering impact a murdered woman had on those lives she touched while living and breathing. Even Cole Porter said it was the tune he would have most liked to have written. Hedy Lamarr, among those who turned down the script for *Laura*, remarked, "They sent me the script, not the score."[90]

With the composer sitting in the studio in front of me, I played three back-to-back versions of "Laura" (out of four hundred which exist!) first with the composer conducting the New Philharmonic Orchestra, followed by Vic Damone in a vocal version with lyrics by Johnny Mercer, and finally a jazz version by Charlie Parker with strings. Each arrangement evoked a slightly different mood.

David said "Laura" was his biggest breakthrough as a Hollywood composer because it freed him from being typecast for "B" movies. On the other hand, he said, "I actually loved doing those movies because I was never under the gun to write pretty music, and I could compose things that were at the time rather avant-garde."

His score for the movie *The Bad and The Beautiful* almost never happened. At the time he was at MGM with a great production team and a marvelous cast that included Kirk Douglas, Lana Turner, Dick Powell, and Walter Pigeon. Raksin told me Producer John Houseman "kept saying, 'we need a siren song!' But it was another weekend thing, so I was down for the count. I knew what I needed to do: create music that would persuade people that this ruthless studio bigwig was the real McCoy to people he subsequently betrayed—this music needed *charisma*. Anyway, I made a demo of the theme, played it for Vincente Minelli and John. A shrug. Lukewarm reception, to say the least. The two people who saved that tune, championed it, kept it from getting thrown out were Bette Comden and Adolf Green (screenwriters for *Singing in the Rain*) who loved it. They kept saying play it again, and again, until finally, the whole mood changed in that room."

When I asked him if he harbored nostalgia for this period in film making, he said, "This was a great time for the movies, but I don't feel nostalgic about it. Nostalgia is a word that has fallen into evil hands; it's a word exploited by marketers. I prefer to think that if something had merit, and if there are people around who have the ears and eyes to understand it, it will be understood and appreciated.

"The thing I love best about that period is the wonderful time we had. Sounds crazy but we had a ball working under such duress. We'd spend all night working, come in the next day and there was something marvelous to show for it."

He shared his thoughts on altering original scores: "Jerome Kern never liked tunes to be messed with, neither did Dick Rogers. I don't mind, especially if they improve on it. A tune is a vehicle, a mode of self-expression. Actually, I'm amazed Charlie Parker stuck so close to the tune, very unusual for him. For me, as long as tune is in there somewhere, I'm okay with it."

David never won an Oscar, though he did receive two Academy Awards nominations, for *Forever Amber* in 1947 and *Separate Tables* in 1958. He also composed film scores for *Carrie, The Force of Evil, The Secret Life of Walter Mitty, Too Late Blues, The Redeemer,* and *The Day After* in 1984. His three-year radio series, "The Subject Is Film Music," was hosted by NPR and is held by the Library of Congress, which has proclaimed the series "the finest oral history of the (film composing) profession."[91]

Themes for television included *Wagon Train, Ben Casey,* and *Medical Center.* David served from 1962-70 as president of the Composers and Lyricists Guild of America, but his later years were spent teaching composition at the University of Southern California and composing several concert pieces ultimately performed by the New York Philharmonic, the Boston Pops, and the London Symphony. He died on August 8, 2004, in Los Angeles at the age of 92. I was glad to learn that he had completed his memoirs, *If I Say So Myself*, before his passing.

Having David Raksin as a guest certainly rates as one of the highlights in my radio career. He was a warm, witty, and humble man who made an immense contribution to the world of film music.

I cherish his final comments from our interview: "Jerome Kern originally turned me on to composing. I was just a kid hanging out with my dad and they played 'Look for the Silver Lining.' And that was my inspiration. I thought if someday I could compose a piece that does for people what that song does, I will have lived a life worth living. The only other thing I learned later was necessary was to be in love and have children, so when you've done all three you've made it."

SUGGESTED RECORDINGS

David Raksin Conducts the National Philharmonic Orchestra in His Film Music

This is the CD I played during my David Raksin interview from *Laura, Forever Amber,* and *The Bad and the Beautiful* RCA disc

The entire film score for *The Bad and the Beautiful* has been released on a Rhino CD. Hard to find, but well worth having.

Musical Wunderkind

Photo by A.P. Mutter. Reprinted courtesy of IMG Artists.

André Previn is a musical polymath: the rare artist who has "successfully made the transition from the podium to the pen."[92] In over sixty years of his professional life he's been a pianist, conductor, composer, and pedagogue. He's written for Broadway, concert and opera houses, led most of the world's major orchestras, won Oscars for film scores, and been knighted by the Queen of England. I had the privilege of only one interview with him; it seemed I could have done twenty more and just scratched the surface of his life and accomplishments.

Most sources state that Previn was born in Berlin, Germany, to a Jewish Russian family in 1929; however, he states the year was 1930. Birth records were lost when his family left Germany in 1938 to escape Nazi persecution. He moved to Hollywood with his family, where as a ten-year-old he steeped himself in film via ten-cent tickets at Graumann's Chinese Theatre down the street.

After an upbringing of classical music study, teenaged Previn fell in love with jazz, emulating and eventually playing with Dizzy Gillespie and Charlie Parker. As a sixteen-year-old he was already composing and arranging music for MGM, bringing to life some of the great musicals: *Kiss Me Kate*, *Gigi*, and *Silk Stockings*. Stage-to-film adaptations included *Kismet*, *Porgy and Bess*, *Paint Your Wagon*, and *My Fair Lady*.

André shared the story behind the creation of the jazz version of the broadway score for *My Fair Lady*. One night in 1956, along with drummer Shelley Manne and bass player Leroy Vinegar, Previn assembled in a little warehouse where Contemporary Records (a small jazz label) was housed. Previn told me, "Shelley was tossing around this idea of recording the score for *My Fair Lady*. I reminded him the only tunes we knew were 'The Street Where You Live' and 'I've Grown Accustomed to Your Face,' so I had my doubts. We had to send somebody to an all-night record shop and buy the cast album. We played one tune at a time—figuring out what each one was all about, changing it around if we wanted to—then recorded it. It took all night, but we started after dinner and by breakfast we'd finished the whole album. I thought it was the most elaborate private album ever made; I never thought anyone would be interested in the jazz meanderings of that kind of show music. It sold a million copies, which was a big deal at the time, especially considering we made that *before* all the songs were a big hit."

Though André confessed fond memories of working in the film industry, he told me it was nothing he wanted to do again. We talked about the impeccable quality of so many of the films made in the thirties and forties: "The reason these movies hold up so well is because technically they're so remarkable; they're perfect. I don't know about the other elements of them as movies, but the sound and music and arrangements—sets, camerawork—they're fun to look at if it's even for that. It's interesting how people dissect things, though; there are these long PhD dissertations on Esther Williams...to us it was just a job."

Part of the reason for the quality of sound was, according to Previn: "these musicians came from the greatest symphony orchestras and dance bands in the world! They just opted for a bit of an easier life, sitting around playing in soft shirts, but it was a great time."

Previn spent decades both conducting symphony orchestras and composing classical music including vocal, chamber, and orchestral music, holding chief artistic posts at the Houston, London, Los Angeles, and Pittsburgh orchestras, and guest conducting with the Boston Symphony Orchestra, the New York Philharmonic, and Vienna Philharmonic among others. During his Los Angeles Orchestra tenure he appeared on televison in the program: *André Previn's Music Night*; in turn he had a series named *Previn and the Pittsburgh* during his time at the Pittsburgh Symphony Orchestra.

Of the Boston Symphony Orchestra he commented, "To make music with the BSO is easier than in most places because they're so wonderful, such a joy, and of course you have the best hall in America. That's not even an opinion, that's a fact."

We discussed the joys and terrors of live performance: I asked him if when a piece was going well, there was any settling into a kind of groove. He said, "That's an extremely dangerous thought! The moment you go there something terrible will happen...you really don't have time to think except for the moment at hand." At the same time he lamented that recordings will of course always sound the same, while "every performance of every piece is different. Anna-Sophie (Mutter) played Tchaikovsky's *Violin Concerto* for a week—the structure was the same, but details were different every night—even the tempo changed slightly. But I think if you 'fix' something to the point of inevitability you're going lose a lot. I like gambling with the unknown during a performance. Things can go either very, very well or quite dreadful, and there's nothing you can do."

Quite a lot can go wrong on the podium, too. He shared some advice from Bruno Walter: "He said no matter how long a piece is, it has only one climax, and your job as a conductor is to figure out where it is and don't arrive at it too quickly. That is just very, very good advice. With some repertoire, it's easy to explode the whole thing one minute in; then there's no place left to go."

Previn knew Benjamin Britten very well, another musical chameleon: composer, conductor, pianist, and violist. When Britten was ill, and had trouble concentrating on books, André told me he offered to send him some records, asking him "what he wanted to hear, and he said what about some Tchaikovsky ballets. I thought he was kidding—you don't really think of Benjamin Britten sitting around listening to the *Nutcracker*, but he thought it was an immortal masterpiece."

Several critics have attempted to sum up Previn's "sound" or at least his musical leanings, even though he's not a man easily summarized. The majority acknowledge his distaste for the dissonant along with his affection for the gorgeous sounds of the French and late Romantic composers: "He's like Richard Strauss with palm trees."[93] Underneath his musical choices and expression lives a cell-deep understanding of how orchestras work, something he learned through coming at music through every possible direction. He's like an anemone that keeps sprouting beautiful growths here and there: he recorded Gershwin standards with bassist David Finck; composed two operas: *A Streetcar Named Desire* in 1998 with Renee Fleming as Blanche Dubois and *Brief Encounter*; a cello sonata for Yo-Yo Ma, a music drama called *Every Good Boy Deserves a Favor* for the London Symphony in collaboration with playwright Tom Stoppard, and in 2009 composed and recorded the jazz album *Alone: Ballads for Solo Piano*. And he's not done yet.

André Previn was also one of the wittiest musicians I've ever had the pleasure of interviewing. His one appearance as the conductor "Mr. Andrew Preview" who struggles with a comically inept soloist on a 1971 British Christmas show was referred to for years. His 1991 book (one of four) *No Minor Chords: My Days in Hollywood* is full of candid stories of his MGM days and called "hilarious" by *Publisher's Weekly*. A memo from Irving Thalberg explains the title: "No music in an MGM film is to contain a minor chord."[94] Previn also had the presence of mind to make note of such priceless quotes as this one from Sam Goldwyn: "My wife's hands are so beautiful I think I'll have a bust made out of them."[95] On Previn's website he answers a series of short questions:

> My motto: "A day without music is a wasted day."
> What I would like to be: "I'm working on it."
> Favorite bird: "Charlie Parker."
> Military deed I most admire: "I don't admire anything military."
> How I would like to die: "Later."[96]

Previn's been to the altar five times: with Betty Bennett, Dory Langdon, Mia Farrow (he is the adoptive father of Soon-Yi Previn), Heather Sneddon, and finally, with the German violinist Anne-Sophie Mutter, who he divorced in 2006, but with whom he maintains an amicable relationship. Known as someone who likes to compose for specific musicians, he composed a Harp Concerto for Pittsburgh Symphony Orchestra's harpist Gretchen Von Hoeson, among many others. In a 2004 performance, Previn's conducting style for his violin concerto *Anne-Sophie,* the rhapsodic piece he named after her, seemed to personify an artistic tension between them. Mutter embraced the sentimental spirit of the piece, which was "surprising, given her fondness for abrasive musical scores....Love, these two experienced musicians seemed to be saying, is a complicated thing."[97]

Previn is the winner of four Academy Awards and several Grammys, as well as countless honors for his stunning musical accomplishments. Just a few include the Austrian and German Cross of Merit, the Kennedy Center's Lifetime Achievement Award, and the Glenn Gould Prize.

But more than his awards and accomplishments, Previn is defined by his love of music every waking moment of the day. He even confessed to being a bit phobic about not having his own music in the car: "Who knows," he told me, "you could be assaulted by a country western station and plough into a truck."

I shared with him a story I'd heard about Aaron Copland: while shopping in a supermarket one day he heard his own music piped in overhead. Someone approached him saying, Isn't it wonderful that your music is playing? His answer was: not really; I have to be in the mood to hear that sort of thing. Previn said, "I agree! It's everywhere: elevators, waiting rooms, shopping malls. It's as if everyone is afraid of silence, whereas I think occasional silence makes the music that much more wonderful."

SUGGESTED RECORDINGS

Symphonies Nos. 1–3 by Rachmaninov
The London Symphony Orchestra conducted by André Previn.
EMI CD 7 64530-2

Symphonies Nos. 1–9 by Vaughan Williams
The London Symphony Orchestra conducted by André Previn.
RCA CD 82876 55708-2

Shelly Manne and His Friends Play Music from My Fair Lady
Shelly Manne, drums; André Previn, piano; and Leroy Vinnegar, bass.
(This is the recording I discussed with Previn during our interview.)
Contemporary CD 7527

Uptown with André Previn, piano; Mundell Lowe, guitar; and Ray Brown, bass
Songs of Harold Arlen, Duke Ellington, and others.
Telarc CD 83303

1. JEAN SHEPHERD

A Voice in the Night

Jean Shepherd

"Okay, gang, are you ready to play radio? Are you ready to shuffle off the mortal coil of mediocrity? I am if you are. Yes, you fatheads out there in the darkness, you losers in the Sargasso Sea of existence, take heart, because WOR, in its never-ending crusade of public service, is once again proud to bring you...*The Jean Shepherd Program!*"[98]

Like thousands of other fatheads out in the darkness, I went under the spell of Jean Shepherd in the early fifties. To this day I remain enchanted. When I first heard his voice on the radio—the first time I erupted in helpless laughter at one of his stories—I knew this was a different kind of talent: one-of-a-kind, brilliant, American, endlessly creative, and entertaining. And like so many have said before: I felt as if he were speaking to *me*, talking about *my* past history with girls, the time *I* bought the ten-cent X-ray vision tube to see through my crush's blouse, the time *I* was invited to the rich girl's house and ate snails and sipped martinis for the very first time. His meandering fables, laced with sardonic wit, filled New York's air waves, permanently shaking radio free of its news/sports/music/call-in straitjacket. A master story teller in the league of Mark Twain, S. J. Perlman, and P. G. Wodehouse, Jean Shepherd took pieces of his own life, endlessly spinning and weaving them into stories that proved pain is often found in humor, with truth not so very far behind.

As a boy, Jean Shepherd or "Shep" as he was later known, would lie in his bed in industrial Hammond, Indiana, listening to the trains rumbling by in the night, "longing to be anywhere else."[99] In our 1985 interview he talked about the trilogy he wrote for PBS and the American Playhouse, how the setting and characters were rooted in his past: "This is urban America, like Detroit or Newark, or a place where everybody works at the plant, lots of railroads, refineries in the distance; there's not much written about places like this and I don't know why, because most of America is this industrial world."

His "old man"—never named in Shep's radio life—was a rabid White Sox fan, beer drinker, and disenchanted political cartoonist for the *Chicago Tribune* before he abandoned his family and fled to Florida. "Profanity was his medium," Jean said, "he hated to hear amateurs swear."[100] Jean described the father in the PBS series to me as follows: "he works at a place he just calls 'thedamnedoffice.' One word. Mother says, how'd it go today? And he always said, whaddya mean, 'how'd it go'? It's 'thedamnedoffice!'...My father always generically referred to it that way. His boss was named Fogarty; he'd simply say: 'thatdamnedFogarty!'"

Shepherd's mom, a perennial presence in his radio dramas, was a "'real mother' who wore a rump-sprung, Chinese red chenille bathrobe (with the petrified egg on the lapel), kept her hair in rollers, and ground out endless meals of meatloaf, red cabbage, and Jell-O."[101] Other characters—in real life and spun into radio tales—included younger brother Randy, eternally whining in the background, as well as assorted bullies, crushes, and neighborhood kids including Flick, Schwartz, and Brunner. When asked if he missed Hammond, Jean said, "That's like asking, 'Do you miss the cold sores you had last week?'"[102]

Ham radio became an obsession with Jean, and in his teens he played the role of Billy Fairfield, Jack Armstrong's sidekick on Chicago's radio show of the same name. He was constantly in trouble during his early stints as a DJ at WCKY, WKRC, and WSAI because he never stopped talking long enough to play records.

In our interview he shared a telling story about growing up in Chicago's south side: "Actually, we were right across the line in Indiana, and we'd go on these field trips. I was seven or eight going to the Warren G. Harding School, so of course I had no idea I was going to a school named after the worst president in history—'course there've been a few contenders since. Other kids were going to the George Washington School, the Lincoln School, but nope, it was the Harding school for us! Mrs. Robinette took us on a field trip to the first national bank, we drove for hours and hours to this bank...we get there and she shows us all these holes in the building; it was shot by John Dillinger. And that was it, that was our field trip, and to this day this is a big sightseer thing. When you grow up with this kind of historical perspective you can see that the star-crossed romance of Josephene Coznowsky is a Wagnerian tragedy."

Shep served two years in the Army Signal Corps where he developed a rollicking distaste for authority, honed his fine sense of the absurd, and stowed away a rich source of material for years to come. He attended Northwestern, the University of Chicago, and Indiana University but never graduated. After a stint at Goodman Theater drama school and selling cars, he broke in to radio on WSAI-FM with his own show hosting a hillbilly jamboree and interviewing wild animal acts. He also hosted a nightly comedy show called *Rear Bumper*. After a brief move to Philadelphia, he finally landed in New York in 1956, where he began his stormy, twenty-one-year career at WOR with an all-night show involving lots of commercials, jazz, and jug music.

Quite a bit later, in 1971, we started rerunning his WOR radio shows along with the groundbreaking PBS television series *Jean Shepherd's America*, produced by my colleague and friend at WGBH, Fred Barzyk. Those radio shows could be quite a lot of editing for me. I had to cut out as many as twenty-two commercials from a show that ran forty-five-minutes, but what a pleasure to finally work so intimately with Jean Shepherd! That voice of his, cozy but full of mischief: an Indiana twang crossed with a New York toughness. His meandering style had often been compared to jazz; his verbal riffs turning and following the muse wherever it went, whether it be his tenure in the Army, druids, the inner workings of a steel mill, King Tut, his boyhood in Hammond's industrial wasteland, or a break to perform a kazoo solo; perhaps 'Yellow Dog Blues.' In between tales, he'd sing along to bad old records or play the Jew's harp. He also liked to break things up by asking his "night people," his "gang," to put their radios in the window at two o'clock in the morning, then crank the volume to ten while he played incredibly loud recordings of train whistles, or yell things like, "You filthy pragmatists, I'm going to get you!"[103]

As Donald Fagen put it, listening to Shep, "I learned about social observation and human types; how to parse modern rituals (like dating and sports); the omnipresence of hierarchy; joy in struggle; 'slobism'; 'creeping meatballism'; 19th-century panoramic painting; the primitive, violent nature of man; Nelson Algren; Brecht, Beckett, the fable of George Ade; the nature of the soul; the codes inherent in 'trivia'; bliss in art; fishing for crappies; and the transience of desire."[104]

A typical Shepherd story began with a throwaway remark about what a "slob" he was as an adolescent. He goes on to describe the endless meatloaf dinners he had growing up: "could have been: meatloaf with carrots and mashed potatoes, or meatloaf with red cabbage and mashed potatoes, or meatloaf with peas....we thought everybody lived this way..."[105] Sure, he'd read about clam dinners—even raw oysters—and collectively gag along with his family: did people actually *live* this way? No *meatloaf*? Unthinkable...until one day in college a girl invites him to dinner, saying, "don't bother to dress..."[106] Not sure what she meant by this, he still dons his best: Penney's sport coat and Montgomery Ward slacks. As he approaches her home the lawns get bigger and bigger, until the houses are completely out of sight down gently curving drives. At a brass-knockered door a butler greets him and the girl, Nancy, rushes up to welcome him, planting a kiss on his cheek—an act never quite as casual in his circles—he takes a long stemmed glass from a tray and promptly breaks it. He learns these are martinis...he says, "My old man would only say, 'How about some booze?' We didn't have any actual names for it—it was just called booze."[107]

Along with the other guests, Jean and Nancy move to the linen and china bedecked table, where she queries him: "Have you had any fresh escargots this season?" Shepherd: "...my meatloaf insides were churning...I couldn't chicken out...so with this little fork, I fished it out...and, Oh my God! It was fantastic! I made a total pig of myself and went slurp, slurp, slurp...and then it hit me...what other things did I think are awful? Late that night...lying in the dormitory room and I can feel them snails, there's an aftertaste, and I begin to suspect...there was a fantastic unbelievable world out there. And I was just beginning to taste it, and God knows where it would lead!"[108]

Through these tales he warned about what life had in store for you: endless discovery, but also loss and betrayal, and somehow it was a comfort. I could, and did, listen for hours, in awe of what came out of him with no script, no preparation of any kind.

I actually watched him do his show a couple of times. In some interviews, Shep claimed he prepared for hours on end, but that's not what I witnessed. In front of him were just a few notes, handwritten, about how he would open and where he was going to land, but there was no script whatsoever. Nothing close to what someone without his sort of mind might have needed to spin off a three-and-a-half-hour show, five nights a week! A show with no guests, and whatever spots he did included well-aimed barbs at the sponsors. He had his stories framed in his mind as well as a sketchy outline to light his way on a path that forked and switchbacked—yet he'd always end the piece exactly on time—a feat of radio engineering that still floors me. He liked to be alone in the studio, and he never liked being interrupted for any reason. Herb Squire, Shepherd's longtime engineer at WOR, learned very quickly he'd better be able to work the board while being Shep's audience for the duration of the show. He said, "You had to react and become very animated in your reactions...because like any performer, if he didn't get a response, he'd feel up the creek without a paddle."[109]

Shepherd hated the word "nostalgia" and balked each time his work was described with that term. He didn't even like to be called a "radio personality." His stories were fetched from his past, but they were no Norman Rockwell renderings; they were more like jumping-off places for hilarious spins on "the absolute certainty of daily humiliation in life,"[110] as one astute Wall Street journalist wrote. Shepherd even bristled when Studs Terkel posited that Jean covered the collective American past; Jean said: "You think it's the past...I'm writing about American *rituals*...the two-week vacation, the graduation, the Sunday afternoon dinner, the prom, the coffee break, which is as ritualistic from one end of the country to the other...in Tacoma they're sitting around with the same looks on their faces as everywhere else."[111]

Even at the height of his popularity, however, Jean never felt as accepted or valued as he would have liked, insisting that WOR would have enjoyed nothing better than for him to play the top twenty songs and otherwise shut up. His show was never listed by the *New York Times*, and he made a big deal of that on the air. Someone at the *Times* claimed it wasn't a music show, therefore there was no category for him.

In what can only be called a brilliant coup, Jean single-handedly created demand for a book that he'd not only not written, but that hadn't been published. He jump-started a mammoth buzz for a pseudo-book he called *I, Libertine* that wound up on the 1956 *New York Times* list of new books. *Publisher's Weekly* frantically called for information on this hot new release. Egged on by Shepherd, listeners flocked to bookstores to buy the nonexistent novel by the fictitious Frederick R. Ewing. Set in England during the 1700s, *I, Libertine* followed the bawdy adventures of Lance Courtnay—by day a respected citizen, by night loutish rake. In the final irony, Ballantine Books, who'd been after paperback rights, persuaded Jean to actually write the book together with author Theodore Sturgeon.

Many times I saw Shepherd perform Saturday-night gigs at the Limelight Café where he held sold-out crowds in the palm of his hand. He would pace around, work himself up, really get into character. A New York critic called him "often brilliant and sometimes a trifle mad."[112] He did hundreds of live shows at colleges across the country and played to throngs of excited fans at Carnegie Hall as well as Boston Symphony Hall. Excerpts from his radio shows turned into essays that showed up in everything from *Playboy* to the *Village Voice* to *Car and Driver*. His four books, *In God We Trust, All Others Pay Cash*, *Wanda Hickey's Night of Golden Memories and Other Disasters*, *The Ferrari in the Bedroom*, and *A Fistful of Fig Newtons*, all drew on his radio monologues.

In our interview, we discussed the roots of his 1983 classic movie, *A Christmas Story*, a sardonic look at a holiday he'd hoped to call *Satan's Revenge*: "(The script) was taken from the first chapter of my novel, *In God We Trust, All Others Pay Cash*. I wrote the script based on that one chapter, where Ralph is waiting in line to see Santa Claus. He had this fantastic hangup about owning a Red Rider Model 200 single shot BB gun. It originally ran in *Playboy* as an antiwar parable, that's how they read it in Europe. It's interesting that they got it in Europe, but not here. Everyone at MGM was shocked by how commercial it was; it led the box office for five weeks; this was when *Yentl* was out, *Tender Mercies, The Right Stuff*. Now I'm working on a sequel, called the *Revolt of the Mole People*, which eventually became *My Summer Story*.

"Ralph is dragooned into going to summer camp—he doesn't want to go—and he's put in a cabin called the Mole cabin, and all the other cabins have names like Leopard, Tiger, Wolf, Moose. He's in the Mole cabin with a bunch of little fat guys with thick glasses. The high point comes when Ralph finishes his leather wallet on which he's carved the face of Roy Acuff and presents it to his old man."

In the mid-seventies, problems began to surface at WOR. Just when Shep was about to be released from the show for not being commercial enough, he did an impassioned commercial for Sweetheart Soap, which happened not to be a sponsor.

When his listeners learned he'd been canned, they reacted in such numbers that not only was he reinstated, Sweetheart Soap signed up as a sponsor. In fact so many sponsors wanted in that once again Jean's show felt too packed with ads, and eventually WOR cancelled the show in 1977.

A year after WOR dropped him, he advertised in various interviews that he was glad to be free of radio, insisting that his best work was as a screenwriter and novelist, therefore undermining work that he was surely proud of. At a public radio convention he was asked to address, there was a question and answer period following one of his typically brilliant monologues. A young man stood up and said "Mr. Shepherd, you must be in love with radio," Shepherd bristled and said, "No, you got that backwards. Radio should love me." He continued to trash radio with his signature wit: "all the girls in school who wouldn't let you copy their algebra papers are now wearing granny glasses and running public-radio stations."[113] He was finally able to complete the sequel to *A Christmas Story*, which was called *My Summer Story*, released in 1994, as well as the PBS *American Playhouse* TV series, which also featuring the Parker family. Episodes included: *Ollie Hopnoodle's Haven of Bliss*, *The Great American Fourth of July and Other Disasters*, *The Star-Crossed Romance of Josephene Cosnowski*, and *The Phantom of the Open Hearth*, all produced by Fred Barzyk. Jean also did *Shepherd's Pie* for New Jersey Public Television.

He talked in detail about the series in our interview: "The first one, *Phantom of the Open Hearth*, covers the life of one family over one summer. I've always been a real believer in the seasons: I believe the seasons play a great role in our lives; you're not the same in December as you are in mid-August. This one takes place in June just as the school year is ending and Ralph is about to go to his junior prom. There's the whole business of the early summer; the old man is walking around outside having his first bout with crabgrass; there's a certain meanness in the house.

"The second was the *Great American Fourth of July and Other Disasters*. Now Ralph is involved in the big Fourth of July parade and all that business, and it's July and its hot and the meanness is worse, 'cause if you know anything about Midwestern heat in an industrial town in mid-July you know that heat is an entity, so you can hear the mosquitoes buzzing outside, fist fights breaking out...

"In the *Star-Crossed Romance of Josephene Cosnovsky*, Ralph's a senior, a very different kind of guy now that it's November; he's gripped by his first truly serious girl madness coupled with the underlying theme that the grass is always greener, that you're always excited by things foreign. For him it was Josephene, a Polish girl who moved in next door. She had mysterious overtones of Heddy Lamar, Ingrid Bergman; there was an aura of stuffed cabbage about her, which is very exciting since he comes from a meatloaf family, so when he kisses her for the very first time it's something cataclysmic, the music just rises enormously..." Cue the Warsaw Concerto...

Losing Shep in 1999 was a shock to the system. How unlikely that someone so full of life could be silenced. He had also become a dear friend to both myself and Joyce. In the end he was living with his fourth wife Leigh on Sanibel Island, where he told me, "You could hear nothing but the grunting of the alligators in the bayous...."

Uncertainty shrouded much of his personal life, including circumstances around earlier marriages and his refusal to acknowledge two children born to his first wife. Bitterness characterized his later years, possibly because he never felt appreciated until *A Christmas Story*, which had been a major turning point in his life.

In my mind, without Shepherd, it's hard to picture Spalding Gray, Garrison Keillor, or even David Sedaris coming onto the scene. Bill Griffith, creator of the comic *Zippy the Pinhead*, said he'd lie awake nights listening to Shep spin his tales, and credits Jean as one of his major inspirations. Media critic Marshall McLuhan called him "the first radio novelist."[114] Five thousand hours of radio in New York is an accomplishment not realized by many.

The truth is, I still get excited when I hear the show's opening bars: the trumpeting silliness of "The Bahn Frei Polka" by Eduard Strauss. Whenever I need a Shep fix these days, I visit www.flicklives.com where I can listen to such classics as: "Taxi! Hey You, Taxi!," "Super Fink Is Here," or "Salute to Slobs."

I like to think I "got" Shepherd, through all the walls he might throw up, despite his tendency to relentlessly be "on"; that I understood the chronic need, in this business, to be appreciated and heard. During one interview, Shep recalled our phone conversation after an American Playhouse episode had just aired. He said, "Leigh and I were drinking champagne, and she sighed and said, it's over now, which I knew because the PBS plant lady had come on; and the phone rang, and I thought, who could it be, my manager, my agent? Our director? I rushed to the phone and it's you, Ron, and you said, without any preamble, 'You've created an unrivaled American classic; it reminded me of the *verismo* quality in Italian opera.' There's only one other critic who picked that out, this guy in Los Angeles: he said, 'Shepherd is the only guy working in movies who uses Wagnerian operatic themes in an American setting.'"

After I told him I remembered our conversation very well, there was a pause.

Shep said, "But did you laugh?"

I assured him we were laughing nonstop.

Just like all of us, I believe—in radio or not—Shep needed to know that he wasn't just a voice in the darkness, but that someone was out there, listening to every word he said.

SUGGESTED READINGS

All Shepherd lovers should be familiar with the book, *Excelsior, You Fathead! The Art and Enigma of Jean Shepherd*, by Eugene B. Bergmann, Applause Books, 2005.

This is the definitive book on the artistry of one of America's greatest humorists. Bergmann includes interviews with people who knew his subject including yours truly. With verbatim transcripts of Shepherd's radio shows and rare photos, the author offers a fascinating insight into the life of a complex and creative genius. Bergmann dedicates his book: "To the memory of Jean Parker Shepherd, who gave so much of his real as well as imagined self to us all."

For more on this icon of American radio, visit: www.FlickLives.com: A Salute to Jean Shepherd. The site includes biographical information as well as a large collection of Shepherd's works, including hundred of hours of radio shows, images, and writings. Through this site, where you can order his recordings, it seems as though his work is almost bigger in death than in life, and I'm heartened to know that his work is being introduced to a whole new generation.

If You're For It, I'm Against It

Author's collection.

Mort Sahl and me

Mort Sahl made his inauspicious debut on Christmas night in 1953 at a San Francisco club called the Hungry i. Dressed in a cardigan sweater, slacks, loafers, and open collar, and holding a rolled up newspaper, he walked onstage and launched his comic career using material inspired by politics of the day. Just by being Mort, he broke the mold: that of the slick nightclub comedian telling canned wife jokes and oozing show-biz smarm. His delivery was nervous and staccato; the content full of tangents, asides, and digressions, yet somehow he always circled back to make his brilliant, often stinging point. From that night on he was considered the premier satirist of our time, influencing, among others: Lenny Bruce, Dick Gregory, Woody Allen, Jay Leno, George Carlin, and Shelly Berman.

Born in Montreal in 1927, Mort and his family soon moved to Los Angeles. His mother said that he was talking at seven months and "spoke like a man of thirty" at age ten.[115] Hoping to go to West Point, Sahl was drafted instead and ended up in the Alaskan Air Force, where he got into trouble for editing the newspaper "Poop From the Group," and was given eighty-three consecutive days of KP for editorials about alleged military payoffs. After his service, he went to the University of Southern California "to please my father,"[116] majoring in city management and traffic engineering, and graduated in 1950.

After a few fruitless years trying to find writing gigs, Sahl was broke and starving. His girlfriend suggested he try the "Hungry i," which meant "hungry intellectual." She said, "The audiences are all intellects, which means if they understand you, great, and if they don't, they'll never admit it…"[117] Though the crowd threw pennies and peanuts at Mort, the owner saw something in him and kept him on. Instead of "how-fat-is-my-wife" jokes, Mort put it on the audience to connect a few more dots than they were used to; in other words: think. Satire forces the listener to consider the object being satirized in order to laugh along. He told the crowd that conservatives were now dressing in charcoal gray suits "because modern science was looking for a color more somber than black."[118]

The audience started to catch on, not only at the Hungry i, but at legions of hip clubs and with the liberal press. That said, Sahl was never someone to be pigeonholed politically. Behind his genially rumpled manner, he insulted everyone including Senator McCarthy, and presidents from Eisenhower to Nixon to Obama, even nabbing a *Time* cover story which was unheard of at the time. He fearlessly tossed out lines like, "I'm not so much interested in politics as I am in overthrowing the government,"[119] and "If you were the only person left on the planet, I would have to attack you. That's my job."[120]

Sahl became not only the first comedian to make a comedy album, but one after another they became best-sellers; this at a time when topical humor simply wasn't to be found on television. He also worked as a speechwriter for John F. Kennedy, Ronald Reagan, Ross Perot, George Bush, and Alexander Haig, and as a script doctor during the early eighties.

I met Mort back in the 1970s when he appeared at a local Boston club. Every year I'd do an annual birthday tribute to bandleader and musical innovator Stan Kenton. I'd read somewhere that Kenton had a major impact on Mort's early career and that Mort was a great lover of Stan's music. With that in mind, I invited him to be a guest on my show. It turned out to be a revelation! He knew the names of every member of every addition to the Kenton band from the early days in Balboa, California, to the final years up to Stan's death.

Since Mort pioneered his style of stand-up in night clubs that showcased primarily jazz music, it was only natural that he adopted some of that free-flowing jazz form as well as the dry, ironic wit of jazz musicians. He was fluent in jazz lingo I like to call "Sahl Speak": gasser, chick, drag, cool it, bugged, the most, dig it, weirdo, wild, shakin', and wigged. Jazz musicians loved him. Sahl cites jazz pianist and bandleader Stan Kenton as his most important performing influence: "Stan, of course, was a great artist, but he was a voice of defiance, and did it on his own terms."

During our interview, Mort recalled the first time he met Stan: "The band manager approached me and said, you always come to see the band, would you like to meet Stan? I was scared to death, totally intimidated." The fact was he'd routinely skipped classes at USC after staying up all night following Kenton's band. Soon after Mort appeared in San Francisco, Kenton invited him to go on the road with the band. Mort was incredulous; he asked Stan, "What if I bomb?" Stan replied, "Don't worry...I'll have the band play louder!"

Mort told me, "In the end, Stan became like a father to me...he had expectations but he always knew how to talk to you; he'd say to me: God endowed you with ideas: value them. Or if there was a problem at a gig and he was talking to a club owner, he'd say: we have a bit of discord; how are *we* going to solve this. He included you."

Stan Kenton's band had a wild, frenzied sound that roared onto the scene during the staid, Ozzie and Harriet, Eisenhower years in the 1950s. I asked Mort his theory of why the band took hold the way it did: "Because of Stan's conviction. He hired fourteen young arrangers for the Innovations band. When you heard Kenton, you knew it was him. He'd say again and again, the purpose of the band isn't to knock the audience out, it's to knock ourselves out. He was a man on a mission. But keep in mind, the East coast really pilloried the band, it was too much for them at first...June Christy and Stan, and they were like heretics...and though some people thought the band was frenzied or stentorian, when they did the ballads like 'Here's That Rainy Day' or 'Lush Life' they had one of the most romantic sounds."

From everything I'd heard about Kenton, he loved being on the road. Mort laughed and said, "A reporter interviewing him on his bus said Stan, you've been all over the world; what's your favorite place? He said 'You're sitting in it.' Back east, down south, out west and due north, we went everywhere and a lot of nowhere. The buses were also segregated in the sense that the intellectuals—guys who wanted to read—sat up front, while the partiers hung out in the back. Also, Stan made two seats for musicians because he said they were never treated right. And a Kleenex box in the ceiling. He said it would straighten out your head to get on the bus after a gig."

Mort continued: "Stan was a way of life; he changed everybody that came after him, and he did things for people. When Lee Konitz joined the band and it wasn't working out, Stan said I have a guy in Los Angeles you're going to study with; he's a classical player. Lee studied for six months, six hours a day, just blowing; then he took over the section and he was lead alto. One night Stan woke him on the bus and asked him: how do you feel now? How are your chops? Lee flexed his biceps and said, 'Stan, I feel like King Kong.'"

We also discussed Mort's relationship with Frank Sinatra during the Kennedy era. Sahl had become one of Kennedy's speechwriters, and Sinatra had called on him to assist his efforts in promoting JFK and his ascendancy into the White House. Mort said, "I'll never forget meeting him for the first time. We were in Beverly Hills at an Italian restaurant and he walks in with his entourage. He sat down next to me and said, 'You want to go on my label? I want you on my label. Money's no problem.' He could enthuse you; he was like a tidal wave. He said, 'My life is terrific; it's the envy of everybody.'"

Sinatra, always the loyalist, stuck by his friend and hired Mort to record a comedy album for his new label Reprise, called "New Frontiers." Their years-long friendship blew hot and cold, but Mort told me he had the opportunity to attend many historic sessions at Capitol Records. Mort said Frank liked to have friends around when he was making those classic albums.

I asked for Mort's take on Sinatra's acting career: "He thought Marlon Brando was pretentious. Frank knew every line of every script he was assigned, and he knew it before the first day of rehearsal. He thought the most energy was in the first take, which some saw as lazy, but that was his view. He did a diverse number of roles...he came out of a generation that thought chicks were the prize...you ran the race and if you won you got the princess. He believed that movies were our literature. That romance was the background music.

"But when Frank sang about lost love it was never whining, it was real; he thought love was essential. The man would give you a house or a car or pay your hospital bill...then the demons would move him and he'd go the other way. Nancy always protected him; she loved him. Frank had to be moved emotionally or he wouldn't get involved with you. If he thought you were a jivey artist he just wouldn't be there. But it was all him, don't forget, He was invested in the tunes...think of him as an artist giving credit to the composers right up till the end. When I worked with him during the Kennedy campaign I never introduced him; he'd come out while I was wrapping up and stand behind me and smile as if to say: isn't he incredible...and that would make me a hero. Then he'd come to the mic and just start singing."

Following the election, Mort got on the wrong side of the Kennedy Democrats by going after the new president. Mort said, "I only have a few months to tell these jokes before they become treason."[121] Peter Lawford told the comic, "You're going to get it, you'll see...you made lots of enemies. Nobody wants you!"[122] The assumption was that Sahl was the Democrat's boy, but as Gerald Nachman said in *Seriously Funny*, "Mort was nobody's boy,"[123] with a personality that over time cost him "friends, colleagues, club dates, managers, wives, and girlfriends."[124] His claim that the assassination had been a conspiracy nearly cost him his career: Ed Sullivan among others refused to have him on his show. Sahl's tirades against the Warren commission's findings on the JFK assassination combined with early anti-Kennedy jokes alienated him from much of his audience. It seemed he'd lost that critical distance between himself and his material.

In Sahl's 1976 memoir, *Heartland*, he vents about his dating past, veering into misogynistic rants: "I used to go out exclusively with actresses and other female impersonators."[125] Gerald Nachman cuts him a little more slack: "He's not a misogynist: he's a totally disappointed romanticist."[126] To me he said, "I agree with Paul Osborne, the screenwriter who said 'men marry women hoping they'll never change and women marry men hoping they will.' Each is understandably inevitably disappointed." *Newsweek*'s August 9 review said the book portrayed him as a "double casualty of the Kennedy years,"[127] outlining the alleged attacks on him by the Kennedy Mafia, followed by his inability to get work and an income that plunged from a million to $13,000.

Mort has appeared at such venues as Mr. Kelly's in Chicago, the Village Vanguard in New York City, and the Crescendo in Los Angeles. His fans ranged from James Jones, Saul Bellow, Leonard Bernstein, Marlena Dietrich, and Woody Allen.

Allen once said, "He was the best thing I ever saw…he was like Charlie Parker in Jazz. Mort was the one. He totally restructured comedy. A great genius who appeared and revolutionized the medium."[128] Allen was just coming up as a shy, nebbishy comedy writer when Sahl owned the crowds at the Hungry i. Before he saw Sahl, Allen hadn't committed to doing stand-up, but after he did, it was either commit or drop the idea entirely. About Sahl's approach he said, "It wasn't that he did political commentary—as everyone kept insisting. It's that he had genuine insights."[129]

Mort celebrated his eightieth birthday at a 2005 appearance at Jimmy Tingle's Comedy Club in Somerville, Massachusetts. Still shocking the system as he has for over half a century, he was as sharp and incisive as ever. He had the audience in the palm of his hand and received a standing ovation.

The next day over lunch at a cozy Italian restaurant in East Boston, Mort seemed relaxed and reflective. We talked mostly about jazz, Stan, Dizzy, Bird, and his early days on the road. Afterward, when I dropped him off at his hotel in Cambridge, he said, "Hang in there babe, and keep swingin'."

Favorite Quotes

"I'm for capital punishment. You've got to execute people. How else are they ever going to learn?"[130]

"A Yuppie believes it's courageous to eat in a restaurant that hasn't been reviewed yet."[131]

Re: Larry King's book, "I read parts of your book all the way through."[132]

On Ed McMahon after Johnny Carson retired: "Ed is still laughing in case Johnny has said anything funny at home."[133]

"The Democrats don't want anyone to be born, while the Republicans don't mind if you're born, they just don't want you to live long enough to collect Social Security."[134]

Sahl recalled a meeting with George Bush, who said to him, "This is a dirty job, but that's what you elected me to do." Sahl's retort: "We didn't elect you that much."[135]

RECOMMENDED READING
Seriously Funny...The Rebel Comedians of the 1950s and 60s

By Gerald Nachman
Published by Pantheon Books, NY

One of the best books written about some of the most revolutionary comics of our time. Mort is on the cover and is the subject of the first chapter, "A Voice in the Wilderness." I had the pleasure of interviewing Gerald Nachman about this and his other book entitled *Raised on Radio*, a marvelous history of radio's golden age.

Mort Sahl's America, audio CD by Eugene McCarthy and Mort Sahl, June 1997

The Importance of Being Ernest

Ernest Borgnine with Joyce Della Chiesa

To my delight, there were only two degrees of separation between myself and Ernest Borgnine. My ex-wife Jackie's husband, Charlie Brown, who has since passed, met Ernie in Las Vegas about twenty-five years ago. Talk about separated at birth! Both down-to-earth outdoorsmen, they loved to hunt, fish, race cars, and drive RVs. Charlie even invited Ernie and his wife Tova to his lodge in Alaska, where he'd built a special room he named the Ernest Borgnine room, which was completely dedicated to the man, his movies, and their incredible friendship.

It was my great fortune to interview Ernie in 2008. I'd just finished reading his memoir, *Ernie*, in which he revels in his love of acting and movie-making. In it he summed up his personal philosophy, which was inspired by an old sign he saw dangling from a street vendor's chestnut cart on a wintry day in Manhattan: "I don't want to set the world on fire," the sign said, "I just want to keep my nuts warm."[136] Though I enjoyed quite a few laughs reading the book, I confessed to him that many passages moved me to tears. Ernie said, "That's okay, Ron, a man shouldn't be afraid to cry. I've read the book over a few times and some things in there leave me teary-eyed too. People cry—men, women—except maybe cowboys...but I'll bet when they get out there in the wilderness with their horses under a moonlit night, who knows, they probably bawl their eyes out."

Ernest was born Ermes Effron Borgnino in 1917 in Hamden, Connecticut, to Camillo and Anna, Italians who immigrated to America at the turn of the century. He joined the navy as an apprentice seaman right out of high school and spent a decade in the service. Back at home he found himself directionless, casting about for what to do next and applying for dead-end factory jobs he never really wanted. He told me, "One day I'd come back from looking for work feeling completely fed up. I remember thinking, forget it, I'll just go back to the service another ten years, get my pension, and call it a life. I said all this to my mother. She was quiet a minute, then out of nowhere she said, 'Have you ever thought of becoming an actor? You like to make a damned fool out of yourself in front of people; why don't you give it a try?' And it's like a light went off and I said, 'Mom, that's what I'm gonna be,' and by God, ten years later Grace Kelly was handing me an Oscar. And it was like falling off a log."

As his book attests, Ernie's mother Anna was no ordinary woman. He shared with me, "She was a countess in real life, and it was frowned upon for royalty to go on the stage, so maybe there was something satisfying for her to see me act. We were so close—she used to take me everywhere; we did everything you could imagine together. She showed me things I never even thought of exploring, took me to Italy, La Scala, Milano. When we came back she started getting this illness no one could diagnose. For years the poor soul suffered...there were times I had to move away from the house to my uncle's, but she had the idea she couldn't do enough for me...we learned later she had tuberculosis. But she was tough, too...the epitome of cleanliness. You could eat off the floors; I know because I used to scrub them. She'd show up with a white glove, and if it wasn't done right I didn't go to the movies that week."

Ernie attended the Randall School of Drama in Hartford, then moved to Los Angeles in 1951, landing supporting roles right away, most notably as a male nurse in the play *Harvey*. His husky voice, boxer's face with his signature gap-toothed grin, and stout build made him a natural to play the heavy. It was as the ruthless sergeant 'Fatso' Judson, Frank Sinatra's killer in 1953's *From Here to Eternity,* that Borgnine found real traction in his career, and he was signed to a seven-year contract.

Ernie said, "It was the first time I got to work with Frank Sinatra, never mind Burt Lancaster, Deborah Kerr, and Montgomery Cliff. I'll never forget the first hour of shooting...I'm up on a platform playing piano, badly, and they're all below me dancing. Sinatra looks up and says, Knock it off, Fatso, we're trying to dance down here. I got up from the stool *very* slowly. Frank looked up and said, 'Jesus Christ, he's ten feet tall!' Anyway, from then on, Frank was the dearest person I've ever known in my life.

"When you hear Frank sing you really feel he's telling you a story, and it's the most beautiful thing in the world. We don't have that any more. Unintelligible racket and screaming and suddenly it's over? Where's the song? When Frank sang, he sang to *you.*"

I asked Ernie what it felt like to constantly play the heavy: "You think that was bad, have you seen *Emperor of the North Pole?* I used to say to my wife Tova, Am I really that bad? And she'd say, Of course not, you're acting. But still, it was frightening. The nasty things I had to pull out of me to become these people... and the next day I'm playing Mr. Nice Guy."

Though briefly typecast as a brooding villain in *Johnny Guitar* and the West-ern *Vera Cruz*, Ernie landed an against-type role as a lonely butcher looking for love in Paddy Chayefsky's 1955 film, *Marty*. His performance won him an Acad-emy Award as well as top honors from the New York Film Critics' Circle as well as Cannes. Ernie reminisced about his experience and the relative simplicity of movie-making at the time: "It was shot in black and white in the Bronx. Remem-ber, there were no computers then, and we made it on a shoestring. There was something so natural, just intuitive about the process then. I remember Fellini— what a wonderful filmmaker—he'd take anybody and put them in. He'd grab a guy on the street and say, 'Hey buddy, what are you doing? Come over here, viene qui, we're gonna put you in a movie, we're gonna put you on a bicycle and teach you how to do this.'"

Ernie continued appearing in movies (a jaw-dropping 201 films are listed on his IMDB page) until landing his signature role as a boat-skipper on the wacky TV series *McHale's Navy*, reprising the role in 1964 for the show's film. The bum-bling crew of PT-73 became an instant hit, solidifying a lifelong friendship with Tim Conway who played Ensign Charles Parker. After the show's cancellation, Ernest quickly made his way back to the big screen, taking on the role of General Worden in 1967's *The Dirty Dozen*.

In the seventies and eighties, Borgnine appeared in a number of acclaimed television movies including *The Trackers, The Ghost of Flight 401,* and *The Poseidon Adventure*; as "Dutch" in Sam Peckinpah's *The Wild Bunch*; and as a helicopter pilot in the hit series *Airwolf*. He even reprised his *Dirty Dozen* character in a series of TV movies: *The Next Mission, The Deadly Mission*, and *The Fatal Mission*.

In 1995 he was introduced to a whole new generation as doorman "Manny Cordoba" on the NBC sitcom *The Single Guy*. During a relative slowdown in his career in 1996, he took the time to indulge his passion for travel, and took off in a customized motor home, finally seeing the country and meeting and spending time with friends, family, and fans. This tour became a 1997 documentary called *Ernest Borgnine on the Bus*.

His gruff, expressive voice made him a natural for voice-overs; he could be heard in *All Dogs Go to Heaven* and *Small Soldiers*. In 1999 he took on the recur-ring voice role of "Mermaid Man," a superhero admired by the absorbent phe-nomenon *Spongebob Squarepants*, the top rated cable cartoon (where he re-teamed with friend Tim Conway as Mermaid Man's sidekick, "Barnacle Boy.") Perhaps the hardest working nonagenarian in show business, Ernie shows no sign of stopping. As I write these words he's working on two movies: *The Lion of Judah* and *Night Club*, and has just won the Screen Actor's Guild Lifetime Achievement Award.

I asked Ernie how he felt about the mind-blowing evolution of movies and movie-making over the past sixty years: "What can I say? I tend to always go back to the Turner Classics, though every time I watch one of my movies I say: you dummy, you could have done better! Movies then had a moral; they were realistic in their own way. Today it's all explosions and sex; to me it's not entertainment. It seemed as though we said so much more with less—it's sexier not showing the sex. We did more with an ankle those days than you can imagine...Bette Davis, Kay Francis, Joan Crawford...to me they were everything.

"Mickey Rooney said when studios collapsed, we just lost it. A director used to really watch your expression—the look in your eyes, your stance, everything; do as many takes as needed, *then* he'd say good, print. Today it's hurry up and shoot and let's go; the clock and money are ticking away. We're overdoing computer graphics, the noise level is insane, and what's with the commercials?"

I asked who he admired in his younger days, who influenced his career, and if there was any newer talent that had caught his eye:

"Gary Cooper, hands down, and Wallace Beery, he was it for me. You know, I'm proud to have won an Academy Award as a character actor; behind the scenes they're the ones that make the picture, a lot of the time. They make the leading actors look good. You give a character actor a chance, and they'll steal it away from you.

"Walter Brennan was a character actor par excellence, he won three Oscars; he almost did away with Bogey in *To Have and Have Not*.

"Orson Welles—what a sweetheart—met him in a bar in New York. My eyes were as big as plates when he walked up and shook my hand. He said, 'Ernie, if you don't win this Academy Award, there is no justice. You deserve it for *Marty*.' I said, th-th-th-thank you Mr. Welles!

"Every time I see Clint Eastwood, I say, Clint, you still haven't used me—come on—I'm right here! I think he's marvelous, same with Ron Howard; but Clint calls his own shots, and he hits two out of three times, and that's not bad. His brilliance is that he's *paid attention*, he knows his stuff; he's become a great director and actor because of it. Nothing's left hanging in his work; he creates well-defined, complete movies with a beginning, middle, and an end.

"Johnny Carson was a man unto himself; few people will approach his standards; he was a gentleman, a man for all seasons, the world was his oyster and everybody loved that oyster.

"In terms of younger talent, I'm certainly not watching it like I should, but I like Gary Sinise—terrific actor—and Kevin Kline when he gets the right parts. These days you have to take what you can get. It's tough, the choices are pitiful, so this younger pool of talent is left stranded in a way."

Though happily married to his present wife, Tova, for close to forty years, Ernest does leave four other wives in his wake. He was previously married to Rhoda Kemins, who he met while in the navy, Mexican actress Katy Jurado ("beautiful, but a tiger"[137]), Ethel Merman, and Donna Rancourt; he has one daughter with Kemins and two children with Rancourt. All in all, Borgnine hasn't spent much more than a year since 1949 unmarried.

He spoke to me frankly about married life: "It's been a wonderful life, it's brought me some wealth...if I didn't have those five wives to worry about I'd have been a *very* wealthy man. I always wanted a family with kids I could do things with, just the normal things, and we did for a while, but my first wife...it seemed like everything was fine as long as we were poor. The minute I got the Academy Award she put on the dark glasses and became Mrs. Ernest Borgnine. She kept saying I gotta go have my hair straightened—she had this beautiful curly hair—it was one thing after another.

"Once during my first marriage I called my wife—I was so excited, and tired— and said I'm done with the picture, I'm coming home. She said you can't come home. I said, what do you mean, I can't come home? She said there's no room for you...I said no room for me in my own house? Well...my family's visiting, she said. I'd been making a picture with Allan Ladd—a great actor—so I took him home with me, probably for moral support, who knows. At home I got a very weak 'hello, how are you'; I felt like a stranger in my own home. One thing led to another and that was the end of that."

Ernie called his month-long marriage to Ethel Merman in 1964 "the worst mistake of my life. I thought I was marrying Rosemary Clooney."[138] Riding high on the success of *McHale's Navy* at the time, Ernie said things started coming unglued during the honeymoon when he received more fan adulation than she did. Merman was loaded for bear. "By the time we got home, it was hell on earth," Borgnine recalled in a 2001 interview. "And after thirty-two days I said, 'Madam, bye.'"[139] Merman remained single after her divorce, devoting a chapter in her 1978 autobiography to the marriage which consisted of one single, blank page.

Ernie said, "I've always had this image of the ideal family in my mind...and I pretty much have it now, but the kids are scattered around, and even though they visit occasionally it's not like I always envisioned it, you know? But Tova's been incredible, so I'm thankful for her."

Borgnine has worked with countless greats including Helen Hayes, Clark Gable, Joan Crawford, Spencer Tracy, Gary Cooper, Montgomery Cliff, Bette Davis, Jimmy Stewart, and Kirk Douglas. He's appeared in comedies, westerns, war dramas, horror films, Biblical epics, even a musical. He's been a good guy, cop, crook, murderer, mob boss, Western villain, an Amish farmer; he's been Jewish, Asian, Irish, Swedish, Mexican, whatever the part called for. Now he's the oldest living person to have won an Oscar, and told me that "acting is still my greatest passion."

I said, Ernie, you're ninety-three years old and bursting with energy and life, what's your secret? He laughed and confided, "Well, I got into trouble on Fox News answering this one...I leaned over and whispered my secret in this guy's ear, and it went around the world and back again, got something like six-hundred thousand hits, and so I'm not going to tell you now, but I think it's the idea of thinking young. You can't just sit in your chair and read the paper and nod off. Old man, my foot! Think and be young, and as long as you do that, you got it made. In terms of work, as long as they need me, I'm ready."

FAVORITE MOVIES

Marty (1955)
Ernie won his Oscar for best actor that year.

From Here to Eternity (1953)
Two classic performances by Borgnine and Sinatra.

The Wild Bunch (1969)
Ernie teams up with an all star cast in this landmark Sam Peckinpah Western.

What's Up, Doc?

Chuck Jones

Permission by www.ChuckJonesGallery.com © Warner Bros.

Creator of more than three hundred animated films over a span of sixty years—
three of which won Academy Awards—Chuck Jones helped shape the humor of
three generations. During the golden age of animation from the mid-thirties
to the early sixties, he helped breathe heart, action, soul, and life into some of
Warner Brothers' most famous characters: Bugs Bunny, Daffy Duck, Elmer Fudd,
and Porky Pig. Those he created himself included: Wile E. Coyote, Pepe lePew,
Michigan J. Frog, and Marvin Martian. Many of these cartoons still enjoy worldwide recognition every day. He also produced, directed, and wrote the screenplay
for *Dr. Seuss' How the Grinch Stole Christmas* as well as the feature length film
The Phantom Tollbooth.

The minute I learned Chuck Jones would be in Boston for an exhibit at a Newbury Street gallery, I leapt at the chance for an interview. How could I miss this? If you can place a value on joy and laughter, then you can estimate the importance of Chuck Jones' life's work. My entire childhood was marked by those thrilling moments when the Warner Brothers logo appeared on the screen at the Adams Theater in Quincy. It was then that I knew, burrowing into my seat with popcorn and Raisinettes, that the bad B movie was over and I could finally see what Bugs was up to.

Jones looked like a man who made cartoons: with his wispy mustache and impish quality he could have been one of his own creations. He was a delight to interview. Born in Spokane, Washington, in 1912, he grew up in Hollywood and was shaped by its wonders. As he explained in our interview,

"We lived on Sunset Boulevard, right across from Hollywood Hills, and my father had an orange grove, which he sold eventually. Charlie Chaplin's studio was two blocks from us, so we'd walk over and watch him work right through a wire fence. These were silent movies, remember, so they didn't need the sound protection. We were friends with a very popular comedy team called Ham and Bud. Bud was a midget and I'd run around in his costumes when I was six years old, and he came to visit us. We saw Mary Pickford during the war—she came riding her white horse down Sunset at the head of the 160th infantry.

"We got to watch lots of stunt work done over the ocean. A guy doing wing-walking was much more likely to live falling sixty feet from these planes that flew at a very slow pace over the ocean; in any case it sure beat landing on the ground. Anybody who happened to be there could be in the crowd scene, and the pay was lunch. I was far too young to be an actor. On the other hand, they tried out my six-month old brother to play a baby, but he failed; he really was one odd-looking kid."

In his autobiography, *Chuck Amuck* (the follow up was *Chuck Reducks*), Jones credits his father, an unsuccessful businessman, for instilling in him his artistic tendencies. For every new enterprise his dad started, he'd order reams of stationary, envelopes, and business cards. As the failed endeavors piled up, so did the paper, which his dad insisted Chuck and his siblings make use of as soon as possible. They drew constantly. Later, in one of Jones's art school classes, a professor proclaimed that each student had one hundred thousand bad drawings in them that they must first get out of their systems before the good stuff could appear. Jones remarked with some relief that since he was well past the two hundred thousand mark, he hoped that he'd purged himself of the dreck.

After graduating from what is now called the California Institute of the Arts, Jones drew pencil portraits on the street for a dollar apiece. He "blundered into animation" in 1932, as a cel washer for former Disney animator Ub Iwerks. It was there he met Dorothy Webster, who he married the same year.

Chuck spoke in detail about the earliest days of animation: "In the twenties we lived on *Felix the Cat, Alfalfa,* the early *Terry Tunes.* William Randolph Hearst actually had a studio at the time called the Metropolitan; he put out *Mutt and Jeff* and *Maggie and Jigs.* Now, keep in mind: they didn't do much; just walked and ran and jumped up and down…but the big deal was that no one had seen characters move before, so it was a delight just to see a still picture move, just like when sound came out. You didn't have to do much, just make some kind of noise or speak, and people were in awe.

"The kind of animation we did then was inspired by Disney's *The Three Little Pigs*: their actions were very much alike with small differences that revealed their character. We may have been young but we weren't dumb: we saw something we could grab hold of. Disney went on to make *Snow White and The Seven Dwarves*, all who looked mostly alike except for Dopey, but again, they were characterized by how they moved and whether they sneezed, things like that. (Disney's) golden age in short subjects was from 1933–41 when their best people went on to make features like *Fantasia.* We didn't feel in competition exactly, we were just learning from what we saw. So by the middle of the war we'd begun to really understand how to animate characters.

"The personality of our characters became more irreverent, more—how can I say this—perky? Definitely insouciant. By post-war everyone was doing that; everything was breaking wide open."

By 1936 Jones had been hired by Fritz Freleng as an animator for the Leon Schlesinger Studio, working under Tex Avery. Along with animators Bob Clampett, Virgil Ross, and Sid Sutherland, space grew tight, so they moved into an adjacent building on the lot they christened the "Termite Terrace." Jones' very first cartoon was *The Night Watchmen* featuring a cute kitten later called Sniffles. His work was called overbearing and lacking in humor at the time; Jones admitted he finally "learned to be funny" with his cartoon *The Dover Boys* in 1942.

In the late forties and fifties he created much of his best-regarded work including Claude Cat, Marc Antony and Pussyfoot, Charlie Dog, Michigan J. Frog, and his three most beloved creations: Pepe lePew, the Road Runner, and Wile E. Coyote. The Road Runner cartoons in addition to *Duck Amuck, One Froggy Evening*, and *What's Opera, Doc?* are considered masterpieces.

Of Pepe lePew, Jones said, "Pepe is the individual I always wanted to be, so sure of his appeal to women that it never occurs to him that his attentions might be unwelcome, or even offensive. I tried to make Pepe's confidence a part of my own personality, hoping to share in his sexual success. On the screen it worked."[140]

Jones explained in our interview how he believed the quality of the cartoons went up along with a deepening understanding of each character. I tended to view Bugs as a tough character, with an urban quality almost like the Bowery Boys. Jones explained: "The Bowery Boys were a take-off on the Dead End Kids; they were definitely tough. Bugs is more...capable. He's the type of character I'd like to have been, personally...but he's not the way I am. He's an extension. I'd like to be a male Dorothy Parker. Hell, I'd like to be a male Burt Reynolds. Someone with that kind of charisma. Most of our characters are failures or prone to making a mistake, like Wile E. Coyote or Daffy Duck or Yosemite Sam. I think that's one reason people respond, because we're all much more familiar with mistakes than triumphs. Anybody's lucky to get one triumph a year...if I made ten pictures a year and one was outstanding in the public eye, then I'd be thrilled. Historically, more have become endearments to the public than I ever expected.

"When Bugs came out, took a bite of the carrot and said, 'What's up, Doc?'—well, that was a breakthrough in character, this attitude he took on. This was when Tex Avery did the *Wild Hare,* when Elmer Fudd was introduced. Mel Banks, (who was the voice of Bugs), said Bugs was a little stinker, but that's wrong; he's urbane, sophisticated. He didn't waste words.

"He could befuddle Daffy when trying to decide whether it was duck season or rabbit season. Daffy said: 'I know what the trouble is: pronoun trouble!' The point is this: we never made pictures for children—we never made pictures for adults! We made them to entertain ourselves. And there was no such thing as a Nielson rating. The only feedback we ever got was from the exhibitors."

As I thought back to all the wild, far-out situations Jones created for his characters, I wondered about the extent of his artistic freedom at the time of Jack Warner and Louis B. Mayer. Evidently, indifference fostered and unfettered their creativity. Jones said, "In the beginning, when we worked for Leon Shlesinger and sold (the cartoons) to Warner Brothers, our shorts were sold bundled with the features: they were sold before they went out, which is why we could experiment so much. Later that changed, but at the time, Jack Warner knew nothing about the animation department. I didn't even meet him until I'd been directing for fifteen years, in the business for twenty-five.

"One day they invited us for lunch in the so-called executive dining room where we'd never before set foot. By that time we worked under producer Eddie Selzer, who hated laughter; a great person to put in charge of an animation studio! Anyway, they knew money was coming from somewhere...Harry Warner said to me: 'I don't know a thing about our cartoons except we make Mickey Mouse.' That showed how little they thought about the short subject, till TV came along and then they realized, hey, there's money here..."

I asked Jones about critics and if they had an influence on what he created. He said, "We could make very public mistakes because there really wasn't anything to compare us to; we were lucky that way. No one knew how to critique animation; the first real critics came along in 1962."

What did curtail creativity were some strict editing requirements for short subjects. Jones said, "It's very specialized work. We were bound by a tough discipline; Spielberg, Scorsese, and Lucas were always surprised to hear that we edited our work to the second. The editor had to learn to time the picture, do the key drawings for an entire film, then send it to the animators, recording the dialogue first. It had to measure out at exactly five hundred and forty feet, which is six minutes, because the exhibitor needed exactly that to build out their program to two hours, which would be a feature, newsreel, and short subject, perhaps a coming attraction. We did thirty cartoons a year for fifteen years this way.

"I think it's true of all creative work that you have to operate within a discipline, and in the end, that becomes an advantage. It forced us to come up with an ending that worked; with a Pepe lePew or Bugs story, it took a lot of artifice to make it work. We always started Bugs out in a natural rabbit environment: him burrowing through the earth in a carrot patch or in the forest; he's provoked by someone and he fights back, which is something we'd all like to do, with the style he does it."

In the early sixties, Jones and his wife Dorothy wrote the screenplay for the animated feature *Gay-Purr-ee*, featuring the voices of Judy Garland, Robert Goulet, and Red Buttons as Parisian cats. The final cartoon Jones created before the cartoon studio closed in 1963 was *The Iceman Ducketh*.

With business partner Les Goldman, Jones wasted no time ramping up again. He began Sib Tower 12 Productions, pulling in most of his gang from Warner Brothers; soon MGM contracted with Jones and his staff to produce new Tom and Jerry cartoons. His short film *The Dot and the Line* won an Oscar in 1965 for best animated short.

Jones stepped into television as his Tom and Jerry series lost steam, producing and directing *How the Grinch Stole Christmas* and *Horton Hears a Who*, though his main focus was *The Phantom Tollbooth*. Though MGM closed their animation division in 1970, Chuck once again struck out on his own with Chuck Jones Productions, producing children's television series as well as the 1979 compilation film, *The Bugs Bunny/Road Runner Movie*. After the death of his first wife, Jones met and married Marian Dern.

In the eighties and nineties, Jones sold cartoon and parody art through his daughter's company, Linda Jones Enterprises. Though not much of a fan of contemporary animation, he never stopped evolving and adapting, even creating new cartoons for the Internet based on his character Thomas Timberwolf. In 1999 he established the Chuck Jones Foundation to recognize, support, and inspire excellence in the art of character animation.

The Wagnerian mini-epic *What's Opera, Doc?* was inducted into the National Film Registry for being "among the most culturally, historically, and aesthetically significant films of our time."[141] To me, *What's Opera, Doc?* explained Wagner in a way that had never been done before on film. Jones outlined some of what went into extracting a cartoon from an opus-length opera:

"We had a wonderful musician named Carl Stalling, who helped us lay out the story on score sheets; he wrote in all the musical accents we should be aware of. All of our pictures needed to be laid out in musical terms, so we had to be thinking musically all the time.

"We took the fourteen hours of Wagner's Ring Cycle and squashed it down to six minutes. A picture like that or the *Rabbit of Seville*, the music has to be just right. We had an eighty-piece orchestra playing Wagner. But I also added lots of timpanis; they gave a wonderful feeling, especially for that guttural roll just before a character is shot out of a cannon."

I told Jones that my best musical analogy for Bugs and his gang was a tight yet loose-knit swinging jazz ensemble, like what Benny Goodman did with Lionel Hampton. Chuck said, "You're the first one, Ron, who's noticed that similarity to swing music and early jazz. These cartoons are orchestrated, but you had to make room for the funny, you know?"

I asked Chuck what he was most proud of. Without a doubt, it was the characters he created, or helped to develop: "The fact that an ordinary person who's not just big muscles—Bugs—can go and handle matters with cleverness and intelligence is very important, and I think the coyote's a hero because he never stops trying. The sympathy is with him, not with Road Runner—you know he's invulnerable—but the coyote represents the multiplication of all the problems everybody has.

"I guess it's pretty simple: to find that people get joy out of something that you got joy doing is the greatest accolade that can happen."

As Bill Schaffer stated so brilliantly in his article for *Senses of Cinema*, "Whaddya Know, It Dithintegrated" published after Jones' death in 2002:

> "Like the rest of us, Chuck Jones, the man, was born at a definite date into a mortal body; one destined to die at an equally definite time and place. Unlike most of us, however, Chuck Jones, the animator, was able to isolate and revivify selected aspects of his personality, endowing them with a completely different, elasticised, effectively immortal kind of life."[142]

The mother of a four-year-old put it much more simply. Upon hearing that Chuck Jones had died, her child asked through her tears, "Does this mean the bunny won't be in the barber chair any more?" The answer was, "No, sweetie, the bunny will be in the barber chair forever."[143]

FAVORITE CARTOONS

The Carl Stalling Project: Music from Warner Bros. Cartoons from 1936–1958

Stalling was the man behind the scenes at "Termite Terrace" who composed and arranged the music for the golden age of animation at Warner Bros. Selections include:

"Dinner Music for a Pack of Hungry Cannibals"
"Beep Beep"
"Nutty News"

"Gorilla My Dreams"
"Hot Cross Bunny"
"Behind the Meatball"
"What's Cookin' Doc"
"I Got Plenty of Mutton"

Warner Bros. CD 926027-2

Looney Tunes: Golden Collection

A DVD that includes 60 of the finest and funniest cartoons from Warner Bros.
Fully restored and uncut. As it says on the cover "A 24–Carrot Gem of a
Collection. Anything less would be DETHPICABLE!"

Warner Bros. DVD 31284

5. ROBERT B. PARKER

Dean of American Crime Fiction

Robert and Joan Parker

Photo courtesy of Joan Parker.

I'll never forget reading Robert B. Parker's novel *Ceremony* and quite literally stumbling upon a mention of—myself. Spenser was on a stakeout in his car listening to *MusicAmerica* on the radio to pass the time. What an odd and wonderful feeling to be part of a quintessential Boston scene. My show had suddenly become immortalized under the masterful pen of the dean of American crime fiction! I began to wonder about the role music played not only in Parker's life, but in his writing and creative life as well, and invited him for an interview on my show.

Parker was a prolific best-selling writer who churned out more than sixty books including Westerns, historical fiction, young adult novels—even a marriage memoir—but it was his detective fiction for which he'll be best remembered: specifically for the thirty-seven novels that star Spenser, Parker's signature creation: the soft-hearted bruiser with a taste for doughnuts and the Red Sox. In fact, Parker gave Spenser a number of his own traits: he was a great cook, boxer, weightlifter, jogger, and dog lover—both Parker and Spenser owned a series of short-haired pointers, all named Pearl.

Born in Springfield, Massachusetts, in 1932 to working-class parents, Parker went to Colby College in 1954, then served as a radio operator with the U.S. Army in Korea. I asked him about his earliest musical influences: "I grew up in New

Bedford listening to Bob and Ray. Also Fred B. Cole, Norm Nathan, Dave May- nard, Norm Prescott, Stan Richards, and Bill Marlowe. There was a brief flourish of Benny Goodman and swing from 1938 to the advent of Elvis in the fifties; it all seemed to pass so quickly! I think keeping this kind of music alive—swing, big band, jazz vocalists like Jimmy Ricks—has always been a struggle. I came back from Korea and thought: who's this guy with the funny haircut and the shoes? I'd never heard of Elvis. And he was the king.

"Both my sons are performers; my oldest, David, is a choreographer in New York, my younger, Dan, is an actor and singer in Los Angeles. They both dig this music. They know it well, in fact David has choreographed to it and Dan sings it in cabaret; it endures with people who like music. Duke Ellington said: 'there's two kinds of music, good and bad.' I'd say a lot is just plain bad."

Parker earned his M.A. in English from Boston University, then took work as a technical writer, copy writer, ad exec, and briefly as a state cop before returning to academia in 1962, finally earning his PhD in detective fiction from Boston Univer- sity in 1971. His dissertation, called "The Violent Hero, Wilderness Heritage and Urban Reality," discussed the exploits of fictional private-eye heroes created by Dashiell Hammett, Raymond Chandler, and Ross Macdonald. Parker became a full professor at Northeastern but retired in 1976. By that time he'd already published five Spenser novels and it was clear that fiction was his true calling. That year Parker's *Promised Land* won the Edgar Allen Poe award from Mystery Writers of America.

Parker once observed that he created Spenser because Chandler was dead, and he missed Philip Marlowe. So much so that in the eighties Parker was chosen to com- plete *Poodle Springs*, a novel that Raymond Chandler had not finished at his death in 1959. He added thirty-seven chapters to Chandler's opening four, "(sounding) more like Chandler than Chandler himself,"[144] as the novelist Ed McBain once remarked. A year later Parker published *Perchance to Dream*, a sequel to *The Big Sleep*.

One of the best ways to understand Robert Parker the man is to look at the iconic characters he created. Spenser is named after Edmund Spenser, a contem- porary of Shakespeare's who examined knightly virtues. He was never given a first name; the rumored reason being that Parker couldn't choose between the names of his two sons: David and Dan. Spenser's longtime love was psycholo- gist Susan Silverman, who one could argue is a stand-in for Joan, Parker's wife of fifty-two years, also a therapist. Where Susan represents Spenser's rational side, Hawk, Spenser's asocial, violence-prone partner and hit man, is another exten- sion of Spenser's personality. The narrative friction that resulted from reconciling Spenser's domestic, rational side with his penchant for brutality resulted in this constant stream of creation that was Parker's life work.

The first few pages of *The Godwulf Manuscript*, the book in which Spenser debuts, reveal the heart and soul of what readers came to love about him: his self- confidence, impatience with grandiosity, and sharp wit:

"'Look, Dr. Forbes,' Spenser says to the long-winded college president who is hiring him. 'I went to college once. I don't wear my hat indoors. And if a clue comes along and bites me on the ankle, I grab it. I am not, however, an Oxford don. I am a private detective. Is there something you'd like me to detect, or are you just polishing up your elocution for next year's commencement?'"[145]

Parker even dealt with his marital problems indirectly in his books. He separated briefly from Joan in 1982 just when Susan left Spenser. Later, in *A Catskill Eagle*, Spenser rescues Susan from captors and they reconcile their differences. Susan wants Spenser to move in with her, but Spenser had come to like having his own place. After a two-year separation from Joan, they reunited with a new arrangement—they bought a fourteen-room 1869 Victorian home with independent apartments. Robert took over the ground floor where he kept up his prodigious five-page-a-day, four-novel-a-year output. "It comes easily," he told the *Wall Street Journal* in 2009, "and I don't revise because I don't get better by writing a new draft."[146] Afterwards he would hand the manuscript over to Joan for her thoughts. Parker never planned how the story would turn out until he'd written it, making the writing process an adventure both for the characters and the author.

Another groundbreaking element of Parker's work was his inclusion of characters of varied races and sexual persuasions, perhaps influenced by his openly gay sons. Hawk and Chollo are African American and Mexican American; there are Chinese, Russians, even a gay cop and a gay mob boss, Gino Fish. This modern sensibility, in my mind, counts almost as much as the pleasure he gave to his millions of readers for the stories he told.

To help prepare for our interview, Parker ticked off a list of his favorite artists: Nat King Cole, Sinatra, Mel Tormé, Carol Sloane, Ella Fitzgerald, Carmen McCrae, Stan Kenton, Ben Webster, Dave McKenna, Bobby Hackett, and Dave Brubeck. He was especially enraptured with Ella: "She was the first lady of song. I'll never forget going to the movies when I was a little kid and watching her sing 'A-Tisket, A-Tasket.' She was probably seventeen, eighteen years old: tall, gangly, with the purest voice that's ever sung popular music; it was like a flute—amazing what she did with that voice. To me she seemed eternally young, the same at sixty as twenty, and she could sing anything, jazz, ballads, novelties."

I asked him whether he listened to music as he wrote his books. "Absolutely not. One of the things a writer does is listen to the way the words sound in his head. I listen before I write, or after. I drive across the country a couple of times a year with Pearl the wonder dog, because we have a house in Los Angeles and I won't fly her out, so I drive out with her every winter. I listen constantly on the way out, nonstop. You'd be amazed at all the music-of-your-life stations there are across this country! Still, there are fewer and fewer places to hear this kind of music any more. In any case, I like the simple, strong, melodic lines that resonate with the way I write. There is a noir music: the blues, lots of saxophones. Ben Webster *is* noir with that guttural sax that he plays."

To help him picture Spenser in different situations, Parker loved to listen to Lee Wiley among others. He said, "Some singers just call up Spenser's Boston for me: he's in black tie, she's in an evening gown...Lee Wiley has a smoky, sophisticated, urban café society sound to her. I remember getting a 45 one Christmas...she sang with Bobby Hackett...I thought that was one of the great albums of all time. Late thirties to fifties female singers had that quality, not now...now they all sound like Joni Mitchell with that soprano hoot, as opposed to Anita O'Day, June Christy, Chris Connor...these women just sounded to me like they'd lived more.

"But don't forget: Spenser also digs the big band stuff; also jazz greats like Stan Getz, J. J. Johnston, Stan Kenton. I prefer vocals, but that's what I grew up on.

"Hawk's musical tastes, believe it or not, are a bit more sentimental. He's a Ben Webster or Coleman Hawkins guy; he loved a smoke-filled jazz club, Charlie Parker, Miles Davis. But he also dug Olatunji, Afrocuban drums."

Parker also talked about the astounding popularity of his books in Japan: "For reasons which are a complete mystery to me, I'm a cult figure in Japan. There are Japanese couples who name their children Spenser. I was there in '89 with Joan and the kids; four hundred people lined up for my book signing. I felt like a rock star. My wife said it's because they think I'm a sumo wrestler. Thanks, Joan! Anyway, there's a great deal of entrepreneurship around Spenser in Japan; there's a cosmetic line called Spenser's Tactics. I've written endorsements for various products over there.

"There's even a Spenser jazz book out there—a collection of all of Spenser's jazz. They went through all the books, took note of every piece of music that's mentioned, and compiled it. They sent me five copies, but I can only read the title and my name."

I asked him how he felt about the *Spenser for Hire* TV series. "Mixed, I guess. I didn't like everything about the show but I thought it was well shot. Tourism in Boston really exploded because of it, any location tie-in will do that; look at *Cheers.* Japanese nationals who wanted to see Spenser's Boston really came in droves. We spent a million dollars a week, did twenty-two shows a year for three years plus the pilot, so sixty-seven shows in all. Four were shot in Toronto, where we pretended we were in Boston."

Parker claims to have met Joan at a party when she was three years old, remembering her when they met again at Colby College in Maine, and marrying her in 1956. I asked if they shared any musical history. He explained, "Before we were married—a long time ago, we've been married for thirty-nine years—we used to listen to Matt Dennis, and 'Eager Beaver' by Stan Kenton. Sinatra's 'Violets For Your Furs' still bring a lump to my throat.

"I also loved Jimmy Ricks' deep bass voice—he played with The Ravens. It's the best I've ever heard, and it seems to emanate so effortlessly from him. They sang 'Love is the Thing.' If Joan and I do have a song, that's it. It was playing the night I proposed. She said, oh, all right."

Robert Parker was just the man I'd imagined him to be: charming, unflappable, and of course an incredible storyteller. He liked beer and baseball but knew the key to his success and happiness was to sit at his desk and spin out his daily pages, which is what he was doing up to the moment of his death in January of 2010. I don't know of any other author who not only captured the essence and spirit of Boston, but imbued such a masculine character as Spenser with such class and heart.

"He was a master of the genre, as many have noted," said Helen Brann, who represented Mr. Parker for forty-two years. "And he was the most fun, the most real, highly intelligent, witty, down-to-earth, warm, endearing guy I've ever known. I adored him."[147]

Parker visited *MusicAmerica* toward the end of its eighteen-year tenure, and I cherished his support at what had been a bittersweet time for me. "This music formed me," he said, "my sensibilities, Spenser's...it colored the backdrop of these books. It's been fun talking about what my characters listen to; in fact, in some cases I didn't consciously think about it until today. Thanks for including me in celebrating this country's musical heritage and everything this show has been about."

FAVORITE BOOKS

> *Ceremony*
> *Poodle Springs*
> Also: the movie *Appaloosa*, a 2005 Western Parker wrote that stars Ed Harris.

Fabulous People/
Simple Food

INTRODUCTION

Through the years, Ron and I have been fortunate not only to witness countless performances, but also to actually spend time with celebrities just talking and relaxing together in our home over a good meal. That said, there were times I'd get butterflies in my stomach while I whipped up a sauce or frosted a cake in the kitchen. It was the role reversal: suddenly I became the entertainer, while they became my audience.

Such pressure! But as a chef, I felt pretty confident.

The fact is, we all have to eat, and Ron and I are passionate about what we eat and love to share that enthusiasm with others.

Making simple, delicious food for the likes of Tony Bennett, Ben Heppner, Stan Getz, Dizzy Gillespie, Dave McKenna, and Eileen Farrell was a thrill. When musicians are on the road and traveling, it's no surprise that they relish a home cooked meal in a quiet setting with no gawkers in the background. It was a joy to be able to set a hearty table for these performers and, in the process, call them our friends.

—Joyce Scardina Della Chiesa

Dizzy Gillespie: Braised Short Ribs and Key Lime Pie

One night when Dizzy was working a late gig in Harvard Square and was afraid he wasn't going to have time to eat, I delivered ribs and pie to him. I slow cooked the ribs with a hot, tart sauce. They were at the "falling off the bone" stage and finger-licking good by the time they reached him. His lime pie had a flaky golden "blind baked" crust with a hint of ginger, a sweet–tart creamy custard, and fresh whipped cream. Delightful, he says!

Dave McKenna: Chicken Provencal

Cooking for Dave was one of my great joys. He was the most enthusiastic audience I could imagine: he loved everything I made for him, but this dish was one of his favorites. I sautéed the chicken, then simmered it with a touch of garlic, anchovies, capers, beautiful tomatoes, fresh parsley and basil, a touch of dried oregano, salt, and pepper and served it with penne, rigatoni, or maybe even spaghetti and always freshly grated Parmesan. For wine: Always a hard decision...the red or the white?

Eileen Farrell: Veal Scaloppini Marsala

Eileen would never start a meal without first enjoying a nice cocktail of top shelf vodka with one rock! Maybe followed by another...only then would we segue into veal scaloppini marsala with angel hair alfredo on the side and lots of grated cheese. Tiramisu and Sambuca would top it all off. Eileen had countless funny, provocative stories about her time at the Met. After she left the Met and the legendary Maria Callas had been fired by General Manager Rudolf Bing, Madame Callas was quoted as saying, "What is the Met anyway...they don't have Farrell!"

Tony Bennett: Simple, Classic, Italian Food

A little pasta, usually penne or rigatoni. A simple sauce of chopped tomatoes sautéed with a touch of garlic. Fresh herbs, salt and pepper...not too spicy. Add the boiled pasta to the saucepan and toss thoroughly. Shave the beautiful Parmesan on top! Served with an arugula salad and hours of talking about the great artists, from Michelangelo, John Singer Sargent, Daniel Chester French, and David Hockney to his own work. Tony lives and breathes art. "Vissi d'arte!" For wine: a glass of red, perhaps Tuscan.

Ben Heppner: Spaghetti all'Amatriciana

In our dining room with the horned old victrola, Ben and his agent Bill came for dinner on an evening when Ben had a night off from his Boston engagement. I served spaghetti with bacon, sweet onions, crushed red pepper, and chopped tomatoes and basil followed by a lightly dressed, lemony Caesar salad. When I brought out the second course: crispy chicken cutlets with sautéed spinach, Bill exclaimed, "Oh my God, I thought that was it!" For wine: Pinot Noir and a Sardinian white.

Stan Getz: Surf & Turf

On our roof deck one evening in the South End of Boston, Stan and Charlie Lake, aka "The Whale," enjoyed the antics of our cat Radames as I served surf & turf: grilled sirloin steak and large marinated grilled shrimp with sautéed mushrooms, zucchini, onions, and herbs, with oven-roasted potatoes coated lightly with extra virgin olive oil, fresh rosemary, tomatoes, toasted pine nuts, and crumbled gorgonzola. After our meal, as if on cue, Radames jumped into his wicker basket and Stan picked him up. Standing there holding the cat in his basket, Stan looked at him and said, "I dig you, man." We all laughed as the two hip cats stared at each other, just grooving away. We have a little snapshot of that moment.

Illinois Jacquet, aka Jean Baptist "Illinois" Jacquet: Fried Chicken with All the Fixings

Illinois danced up a storm when I served him crispy succulent fried chicken with mashed potatoes and brown gravy, butternut squash puree with a touch of cinnamon, and long green beans cooked with diced onions and tomatoes. His feet did this crazy dance imitating all the mashing and squashing the meal involved, all the while sharing musical history with the embellishments of a seasoned performer. Lemon meringue pie and coffee capped off the meal.

Richard Cassilly and Patricia Craig: A Christmas Feast

We shared so many memorable evenings and holidays with this famed opera couple. Dick loved to cook, and while some meals took elaborate planning and preparation, others were spontaneous and whimsical. One Christmas we had fresh oyster stew with hand-made star- and snowman-shaped oyster crackers, whole poached salmon with lemon caper hollandaise sauce, Potatoes Anna, fresh green beans with toasted almonds, all washed down with lots of champagne. Desserts were pumpkin pie with whipped cream flavored with maple syrup and apple cranberry crisp with peppermint gelato.

Robert Merrill: Lobster Savannah

Marion and Bob Merrill loved to come to Boston, mostly I think to have lobster Savannah with us. This dish is prepared by baking the lobster, removing the tail meat and adding to it sautéed confetti-diced sweet peppers and shallots, cooked down with brandy and finished with cream. Replace combined mixture in the shell, sprinkle with cheese, and bake until hot and bubbly. A person could just pass out with happiness after a meal like that!

Ruby Braff: Dorchester Bouillabaisse

Turns out, the impudent man likes the impudent oyster! Ruby was an angel when he held a coronet to his lips, but look out if he had an ax to grind and you were there; few were spared! But the irascible Ruby showed his loveable side when it came to dining. He believed nothing could beat a certain Cape Cod fish house not too far from his cottage. We ended up going there with him and it wasn't bad for a local fish place, but of course I thought I could do better. When he visited us in Boston I served him up a pot of seafood I learned to make in Marseilles many years ago. Ruby flipped! He went on and on, stammering while he slurped everything down with crusty French bread with rouille (a fiery sauce of hot peppers, garlic, olive oil, and breadcrumbs). It wasn't exactly a Bouillabaisse, but it was my New England version of it.

Ernest Borgnine: Fresh Baked (and Caught!) Halibut

Ron and I met Ernie in an odd way. Ernie's best pal was a man named Charlie Brown. Ron's former wife Jackie and Charlie were partners and had a lodge in Alaska where they spent their summers, mostly fishing for halibut and salmon. Jackie and I had become great friends; she was more like a sister-in-law and often invited us to spend time up there. How lucky we were! Not only did we learn how to fish, but we met this wonderful actor with roots in Connecticut and Italy, and now Hollywood. These people adored each other. There was no pretense; just fish, tall tales, and movie and race car stories. And nothing could beat freshly filleted halibut on a white-hot charcoal grill. I brushed the fish with olive oil, coarse salt and pepper, Tabasco, and lime, then placed it on the grill with corn in the husk with the silk removed and big baked potatoes. I served mushrooms sautéed in butter along with the fish, corn, and potatoes. And as the Northern Lights began to glow in the sky, it was time to serve the Baked Alaska!

Norman Kelley: A Summer Table of Earthly Delights

Norman loved to entertain at his house in South Easton, Massachusetts. After a few of his meals of "Loaf Surprise," usually with crushed potato chips mixed in or garnished with canned onions rings, I told Norman I would help him with his parties. One Fourth of July there was a gathering at one of his friend's houses with Norman insisting we have whole salmon as was traditional in Maine. "I'll bring the salmon...having it flown down you know!" When we all came together at his friend's eighteenth-century farm house; the day was hot but promising, an elaborate table set in a beautiful low-ceilinged room for the celebration. People had brought various items and dropped them somewhere near the kitchen...his friend seemed oblivious to this. Nothing was happening to forward the dinner. Everyone was having a marvelous time with cocktails and talk. By the time I inquired as to how we were going to proceed, the friend was ossified! I look in the kitchen: disaster! I looked in Norman's cooler...a huge whole salmon, head on, not scaled and very slippery. Something had to be done and fast. With Patton in command, in less than two hours, the serving table groaned under the weight of the following: poached salmon with dill sauce; orzo with cucumber, tomatoes, parsley, and feta; bruschetta with baby grilled eggplant and zucchini; and fresh mozzarella with basil and the greenest of extra virgin olive oil; and fresh strawberries, shortcake biscuits, and whipped cream. Norman was in his glory. "Come on...there's nobody like us!" was his constant toast!

Harry Ellis Dickson: Roofdeck Lazy Lasagna

We enjoyed several dinners with Harry, many of them at our house. From our roof deck overlooking the South End, we would sip red wine while Harry regaled us with stories of the classical music world, Arthur Fielder, and the Pops. A typical meal that delighted Harry was pasta, an assortment of antipasti including grilled calamari, baked ziti with fresh mozzarella and tiny meatballs...a kind of lazy man's lasagna, and a lemon tart with blueberries, which we ate with a delicious Auslese wine.

Gunther Schuller: Pot Roast with Sauerbraten

When Gunther Schuller arrives at your house, he's usually armed with a small jar of pickled onions for the Gibson he hopes you will provide. He did each time he came to ours, though I tried to stock up on onions as soon as I caught wind of how much he loved a "Sapphire" Gibson. As Ron showed Gunther his studio, I busied myself with the pot roast with sauerbraten, which was finally baking in the oven after days of marinating in red wine. To go with the meat were dumplings and noodles, and red cabbage sautéed with toasted caraway seeds. It was beautiful to behold, and Gunther seemed to relish the meal and enjoy himself thoroughly. We topped it all off with snifters of brandy while we listened to our guest's wonderful adventures and insights.

Jean Shepherd: Picnics at Blueberry Rock

We visited Jean and his wife Leigh Brown in Sanibel Island, Florida, as well as their summer home in Maine, where we would cook in as often as eat out. They also came to my restaurant, the Turtle Café, or our home, when Jean was shooting one of his movies in Boston. I soon learned that even though Jean was in one way an everyman, he had strong opinions about food. One evening at the Turtle, we not only closed the place but stayed after all the help had gone home while Jean finished the cheesecake and another pot of coffee. That night we dined on fresh made gnocchi with tomatoes, oregano, basil, and parmesan, roasted local cod with butterbeans and greens, sautéed chicken marsala with shitake mushrooms, and pork tenderloin with a ginger five-spice rub and sweet potatoes. I believe a bottle or two of Italian wine disappeared along with this feast. On a visit to Waterville, Maine, I compiled a picnic to take to Jean and Leigh's favorite spot, Blueberry Rock, a huge boulder we climbed to enjoy an incredible vista of mountains and ocean. I brought pate with toast points and cornichons, hummus with pita bread, mini-tuna and egg triangles with olive toothpicks, sliced salami and breadsticks, prosciutto wrapped around cantaloupe, and chunks of Parmesan followed by local strawberries and homemade biscotti. We toasted the great Blueberry Rock with a bottle of Italian Prosecco.

Dick Johnson: The Man Loved Everything!

Dick Johnson was the most ebullient man. He could turn a room on just by walking in—upbeat, suave, impeccably dressed, smiling...always excited to do the gig. He might have come from another late night gig hours away, but he was always just happy to be there. He loved to play, he loved his work, and he loved to eat. His dear wife Rose is a legendary cook, and I could never go toe-to-toe with her meatballs! That said, I had the pleasure of cooking for Dick a few times, and it was a joy. The cat was always so appreciative, and we enjoyed every meal together. We shared a variety of foods: grilled sausages, mounds of seafood spaghetti, penne ala vodka, buttered mushrooms, and always a dry martini or two!

Bobby Short: Chateaubriand with Béarnaise Sauce

A beautiful glow in a soft pink light. That is how Bobby appeared to me when I first saw him at the Carlyle in New York City. The most sophisticated and urbane man, he was a delight to watch and a joy to have as a friend. He often worked in Boston and would extend his stay to visit with many of his New England friends. Bobby loved taking his friends out on the town, but I finally got him to come to our house for dinner. Though he said he preferred the simple life, he also loved great food and wine. That evening I prepared gravlax and served it with iced Veuve Cliquot champagne. For our main course, we segued into Chateaubriand with classic Béarnaise sauce and broiled portobello mushrooms with baby leeks and individual potatoes gratinee. This course was served with a Chambolle-Musiney, which was as over the top as the meal. Bobby was glowing; he was so happy to have a home-cooked dinner and one that was so memorable. He was gracious and so grateful, it almost makes me cry when I think of it. But hold on, for dessert, we had a Grand Marnier soufflé with fresh raspberry sauce…and oh, was it grand!

Luciano Pavarotti: A Post-Concert Feast

Several years ago, when the great tenor first came to Boston, there was an after concert reception at the Wang Center, which was at the time known as the Metropolitan Center. I was so excited not only to hear him sing, but to attend the reception afterwards. Knowing he loved to eat, I was bold enough to send some food to his dressing room earlier that day. I kept my fingers crossed, hoping he would get it. After the concert, I stood at the end of a long line of admirers waiting to meet the maestro. I could see that he was seated at a long table, signing programs and exchanging pleasantries with his adoring public. But I discovered, as I drew closer, that there was something else he was doing. Twirling spaghetti with one hand as he signed programs with the other! Amazing! When my turn finally came I asked if he'd received the goodies I send him. He immediately put down his fork, wiped his mouth, stood up, and exclaimed: "Amore! You are divine…and so delicious too!" as he hugged and kissed me on both cheeks. I totally swooned, and I believe Ron had to pull me away. Here's what I sent to Luciano: grilled shrimp marinated in fresh garlic, olive oil, oregano, and lime juice; tiny tomatoes stuffed with creamy smoked eggplant and olives; chicken wrapped in prosciutto drizzled with aged balsamic vinegar; and a healthy chunk of Parmigiano-Reggiano, sliced hard salami, and homemade breadsticks.

acknowledgments

I am so fortunate in my over fifty years in broadcasting to have worked with some of the most talented and creative people in the industry. Wrapping up this book, I thought it only fitting that I mention many of the colleagues, friends, and relatives who have contributed in some way to my life.

I'll never forget my childhood teachers in Quincy: Miss Frances Mahoney who instilled in me a love of history; Arnold Rubin, my science teacher; and Steve Goodyear, who taught me the basics of the Italian language. To classmate Gerry Dempsey: thanks for sharing your copy of *Variety* with me—it changed my life! Many professors at Boston University's School of Public Communications were an inspiration: especially Victor Best, who instilled in me the importance of good diction and losing my regional accent.

I don't know where I would be if Arnie (Woo Woo) Ginsberg and General Manager Ralph Weinman of WBOS hadn't taken a chance and hired me for my first radio gig in 1959. I owe the same debt of gratitude to Don Otto for my stay in the '60s at WBCN, where I was privileged to work with Peter Wolf, Al Perry, Charles Laquidara, Jack Kearney, and my old BU friend, Bill Wayland, among others.

In the world of opera: I thank Milton Cross for bringing opera live from the Met to countless rapt listeners on Saturday afternoons. To Francis Robinson, Assistant Manager of the Metropolitan Opera, and John Tischio, President of the New England Opera Club: my heartfelt thanks and admiration. And of course, kudos to Arthur Puopolo at Court Square Styling, the opera barbershop where you could listen to Pavarotti and get a trim at the same time.

At WGBH, many thanks to David Ives, Henry Becton Jr., Jon Abbott, Marita Rivero, Emily Rooney, and Ben Rowe. To my on-air colleagues, present and past: Robert J. Lurtsema, Bill Cavness, Eric Jackson, Steve Schwartz, Laura Carlo, Kathy Fuller, and Greg Fitzgerald; and from the world of television: Fred Barzyk, who was instrumental in bringing Jean Shepherd to public television; Dick Robinson, founder of the Society for the Preservation of the American Songbook; and Dick Golden: thanks for sharing in this wonderful journey together.

I am grateful to the unmatched professionals at the Boston Symphony Orchestra including Mark Volpe, Managing Director; Tony Fogg, Artistic Administrator; Bernadette Horgan, Director of Public Relations; Gregory E. Bulger of the Gregory E. Bulger Foundation, underwriters for our BSO broadcasts; Brian Bell, producer of our BSO broadcasts; Jim Donahue, sound engineer; Judge Francis J. Larkin for securing underwriting for our early Tanglewood broadcasts from the International

Laborers Union of North America; Jamie and Ethan Berg at the Winthrop Estate in Lenox; and of course the men and women of the BSO.

It's not easy writing about music. Here are a few scribes who have made their words sing: Jack Thomas, Ernie Santosuosso, Ed Symkus, Bob Blumenthal, Richard Dyer, Lloyd Schwartz, and Joe Fitzgerald.

In the culinary world, there are so many friends to thank: From the Turtle Café days, Spider Landevin, his son Reuben and wife Gabriella; Leo Romero and his partner Iory Allison at the Casa Romero; Anita Baglaneas of Jules Catering in Somerville; Elio Richie and his son Frank of Raphael's South Shore Country Club in Hingham; David Colella, General Manager of the Colonnade Hotel; Lefty, Tony, Pat and Rockie at Santarpio's, one of the world's best pizzerias; Joe Baker's Sugar Bowl on Dot Ave; Kevin Tyo and his restaurant 224; Sal and Joe Sconamiglio of Patsy's restaurant in New York City—Frank Sinatra's favorite!—John Chan of Chan's restaurant in Woonsocket, RI; Gordon and Fiona Hammersley of Hammersley's in Boston; and Tommy and Pat Floramo of Floramo's where, of course, the meat falls off the bone!

More dear friends who have made my life richer include: Judge Francis J. Larkin and his wife Virginia; Liz Muir; Frankie Dee of GMMY radio; Dr. Michael Goldberg and his wife Fran; attorney Ron Itri and his wife Maria; movie producer and film scholar Dale Pollock and his wife Susan; singers Renee and Maria Rancourt; Chris Sarno and Janet; Jay and Kate Rooney; sculptor Lloyd Lilly; Arthur and Louise Gobbeo: thanks for the wonderful nights spent listening to opera at your home; Bob and Justine Graham; Carolina Tres Balsbaugh, Al Vega, Dr. Arthur Wills and wife Hannah, John Gillespie, Bob and Suzanne Lobel, Gary and Michelle Cohen; Bob Merwin; Terri Anthony and wife Karen Carbone: thank you for introducing me to Frank Sinatra, Jr.! opera lover Ruth Wells; John and Betsy Henning: our dear friends and traveling companions; Paul Nash and Mark McLaughlin; and Ed Pelletier who just turned 90 and doesn't look a day over 39!

For keeping me in Steve Reeves shape, I tip my hat to Chris and Greg at Gold's Gym on Broadway; thanks also to Dr. Harry Anastopoulas; Dr. Bert and Hannah Wills; and Dan and Norma Frank at the Price Rehabilitation Center.

I am so grateful for my friends at the magnificent Cathedral of the Holy Cross in Boston's South End where I've been privileged to be a lector for the past 25 years.

For their unflagging kindness and support: Mayor Tom Menino; Keith Lockhart; Joan Bennett Kennedy for her friendship and inspiration to write this book; Jonathan Soroff of *The Improper Bostonian*; opera diva Melanie Campbell; June and Dan Weiner of Galaxsea Travel, sponsors of our annual Sinatra cruise; Lawrence (Cha Chi) Loprete; Art Singer, founder of the Massachusetts Broadcasting Hall of Fame; Bill Russell and his partner Bruce Bossard; jazz promoters Sue Au Clair, Ted Belastock, Al Julien, and Fred Taylor; Mary Toropov, former coordinator of the WGBH Learning Tours and Peter Strauss of The Grand Tour; WPLM General Manager Alan Anderson and his staff; DeeDee Rose; Nick Muscato; Pam Donnaruma and staff at the Post Gazette; Vita Paladino, managing director of the Gottlieb

Archive Center at Boston University; my manager and partner Paul Schlosberg; Paul Kelly of Kelly Communications; David Mugar of Mugar Productions; Jordan Rich and Ken Carberry at Chart Productions; Joe Chinzi of *Ontray Magazine*; Chuck Sozio; attorney George Handran; and sports legends Gino Cappelletti of the New England Patriots and Sam Mele of the Boston Red Sox.

For early inspiration and help recording interviews for this book, many thanks to Sue Asci and Jeanne Horos Denizard. I thank attorney Lucy Lovrien for her legal wisdom and guidance, and publicist Jennifer Prost for getting the word out. At Pearson, I am indebted to Bill Barke, Ziki Dekel, Jeanne Zalesky, Kay Ueno, Karon Bowers, Daryl Fox, Sally Garland, Mary Dalton-Hoffman, Wendy Gordon, Phil Olvey, Bayani DeLeon, and Stephanie Chaisson, and Jessica Werley at Integra-Chicago, for their top notch professional guidance on this project.

To my son Aldo, Mary, and my dear grandchildren Tia, Gabby, Nico, Dominick, and Donovan, you have my love always. Thanks also to Robert Chiesa and his wife Madeleine; Joe Breken; and to my aunt Jane Wotton for taking me to one of my first operas at the Boston Opera house when I was 12 years old.

Love and gratitude to my extended family: Tony and Stephanie Treco; Dr. Gail Cave; Uncle Ken Treco and his daughter Yvonne; Aunt Dolores Wells who makes the best jam in the world; John and Lynn Scardina; Richie and Rosie Scardina; Joyce's sister, Donna; and the Lasorsa family of Staten Island.

Ditto for Giacomo, the world's greatest cat, who loves opera.

For the incomparable but not overly ostentatious Erica Ferencik who I discovered thanks to Jordan Rich. Collaborating with Erica has been one of the highlights of my life on this planet: I couldn't have done it without her. Thanks for the peanut butter sandwiches, and to her husband George for letting us sit there for hours in the living room reminiscing, laughing, and finally sorting it all out.

To my many fans and friends, if I have missed mentioning you, my deepest apologies.

This book is dedicated to the memory of my mother and father, Aldo and Florence Della Chiesa, for giving me life and inspiring in me my abiding love of art, music, and culture.

Finally, to the love of my life, my wife Joyce. You're all the world to me.

Chapter 3

1. Nat Hentoff, *Jazz Is*, 54.
2. Bryan Marquard, *Boston Globe*, "Radio Legend Jess Cain Is Dead at 81," February 14, 2008.
3. Jack Thomas, *Boston Globe*, "The Gentle Voice of the Night," October 31, 1996.
4. Robert A. MacLean, *Boston Globe*, "Channel 7's Henning Reassigned," June 4, 1981.

Chapter 4

5. www.ThinkExist.com
6. http://wbghalumni.org/profiles/c/cavness-bill/

Chapter 5

7. Joe Fitzgerald, *Boston Herald*, September 13, 1995.
8. Globe Staff, *Boston Globe*, "The Day the Music Dies?" August 31, 1995.
9. Edward Grossman, *Harper's Magazine*, "Jean Shepherd, Radio's Noble Savage," January, 1966.
10. Joe Fitzgerald, *Boston Herald*, September 13, 1995.
11. Rob Hoerburger, *New York Times,* "Eartha Kitt, A Seducer of Audiences, Dies at 81," December 25, 2008.
12. Whitney Balliett, *The New Yorker*, 1973.

Chapter 6

13. Globe Staff, Boston Globe. "The Day the Music Dies?" August 31, 1995.
14. Joe Fitzgerald, *Boston Herald*, September 13, 1995.

Chapter 7

15. Joyce Curel, *Post-Gazette*, "Ron Della Chiesa, Mr. MusicAmerica," December 25, 1992.

Chapter 8

16. Matheopoulos, *Domingo, My Operatic Roles*, Foreword.
17. Ibid.
18. Anthony Tommassini, *New York Times*, "Richard Cassilly, American Tenor, Dies at 70," February 4, 1998.

19. Donal Henahan, *New York Times*, April 4, 1986.

20. Institute of Jazz Studies, Rutgers University Libraries, http://newarkwww.rutgers .edu/ijs/bc/index.html, "Benny Carter: Eight Decades in American Music," 2009.

21. John Twomey, http://www.jazzsight.com/jazzsightprofiles.html, "The Troubled Genius of Stan Getz."

22. Ibid.

23. http://www.buddyrich.com/index.php

24. Whitney Balliett, *American Musicians II: Seventy-One Portraits in Jazz*, 263.

25. http://www.jazzprofessional.com/interviews/Ruby%20Braff_1.htm, "Ruby Braff: I've Always Hated the Trumpet."

26. *Associated Press*, George Shearing obituary, February 15, 2011.

27. Jake Coyle, *Chicago Sun-Times*, "Jazz Pianist George Shearing Dies at 91," February 15, 2011.

28. Ellington, Edward Kennedy, *Music Is My Mistress*, 265.

29. Tony Bennett, Will Friedwald, *The Good Life*, 55.

30. John Lewis, *AARP Magazine*, "Tony Bennett," July–August, 2003.

31. John J. O'Connor, *New York Times*, "Tony Bennett and MTV: Talk About Bedfellows," June 1, 1994.

32. Lynn Elber, *Associated Press*, "Clint Eastwood tells Tony Bennett story for American Masters," September 5, 2007.

33. James Gavin, *Intimate Nights-The Golden Age of New York Cabaret*, 211.

34. Terry Gross, National Public Radio website, "A Conversation With Bobby Short," March 21, 2005.

35. Short, *Black and White Baby*, 65.

36. Ibid.

37. Stephen Holden, *New York Times*, "Sounds Around Town," June 1, 1990.

38. Whitney Balliett, *The New Yorker*, "New York Voices: Fourteen Portraits By Whitney Balliett," 1970.

39. http://www.mckuen.com

40. Howard Reich, *Chicago Tribune*, "Magic in Music for Frank Sinatra, Jr.," February 12, 2010.

41. Ibid.

42. Hat Nat Hentoff, *Wall Street Journal*, "The Other Frank Sinatra," September 1, 2009.

43. Wil Haygood, *Washington Post*, "Come Fly With Me," July 9, 2006.

44. Nat Hentoff, *Wall Street Journal*, "The Other Frank Sinatra," September 1, 2009.

45. Wil Haygood, *Washington Post*, "Come Fly With Me," July 9, 2006.

46. Jerry Fink, *The Las Vegas Sun*, "Frank Sinatra, Jr. will play to a Vegas unlike his father's," September 2, 2009.

47. Wil Haygood, *Washington Post*, "He's Got a Big Heart and his Pop's Voice but Just a Shadow of His Success," July 9, 2006.

48. Nat Hentoff, *Wall Street Journal*, "The Other Frank Sinatra," September 1, 2009.

49. Ibid.

50. Ibid.

51. Howard Reich, *Chicago Tribune*, "Magic in Music for Frank Sinatra, Jr," February 12, 2010.

52. Josh Getlin, *Los Angeles Times*, "Finally, a show with standards," July 18, 2006.

53. http://www.spaceagepop.com/torme.htm

54. NPR Biography, Nancy Wilson, http://www.npr.org/people/2101390/nancy-wilson

55. *Time Magazine*, "Singers, the Great Pretender," July 17, 1964.

56. "Footsteps of Civil Rights Leaders Placed in International Civil Rights Walk of Fame at Martin Luther King, Jr. Historic Site," http://www.prweb.com/releases/2005/9/prweb280109.htm

57. Richard Harrington, *Washington Post*, "Singer Rosemary Clooney, finishing on a high note," July 1, 2002.

58. Rosemary Clooney, *Girl Singer*, 86.

59. Richard Harrington, *Washington Post*, "Singer Rosemary Clooney, finishing on a high note," July 1, 2002.

60. http://www.rosemaryclooney.com/biography.html

61. Stephen Holding, *New York Times*, "Recalling Rosemary Clooney, Fondly and Lyrically," January 9, 2007.

62. http://www.rosemaryclooney.com/tribute/index.htm, Rosemary's Friends Remember.

63. Joan Merrill, *National Public Radio*, Jazz Profiles: Rosemary Clooney, http://www.npr.org/programs/jazzprofiles/archive/clooney.html

64. Sammy Cahn, *I Should Care*, 23.

65. Ibid.

66. Ibid.

67. *Sammy Cahn Songbook*, Warner Brothers Publications, Inc., 1986.

68. Robin Armstrong, "Sammy Cahn," www.enotes.com

69. Conati et al., Marcello, *Encounters with Verdi*, 303.

70. Sachs, Harvey, *Reflections on Toscanini*, 154.

71. Kimmelman, Michael, *New York Review of Books*, "Music, Maestro, Please!" review of *The Letters of Arturo Toscanini*, November 7, 2002.

72. Ibid.

73. Ibid.

74. Ibid.

75. Sachs, Harvey, *Reflections on Toscanini*, 9.

76. Ibid.

77. Lebrecht, Norman, *The Book of Musical Anecdotes*, 245.

78. Joan Anderman, *Boston Globe*, "'Where the word ends,' he keeps on," February 1, 2009.

79. Ibid.

80. Ibid.

81. *Los Angeles Times*, obituary, "Harry Ellis Dickson, 94; Boston Violinist and Pops Conductor," March 31, 2003.

82. Anne Midgette, *New York Times*, obituary, "Harry Ellis Dickson, 94, Violinist and Conductor in Boston," April 2, 2003.

83. *Los Angeles Times*, obituary, "Harry Ellis Dickson, 94; Boston Violinist and Pops Conductor," March 31, 2003.

84. Dickson, Harry Ellis, *Gentlemen, More Dolce Please: An Irreverent Memoir of Thirty-five Years in the Boston Symphony Orchestra*, 87.

85. Ibid.

86. Ibid.
87. *The Rest is Noise*, blog by Alex Ross, the music critic of the New Yorker, "David Raksin, 1912–2004," http://www.therestisnoise.com
88. Ibid.
89. Paul Zollo, *American Songwriter*, "American Icons: David Raksin," January 1, 2008.
90. *The Telegraph*, Obituaries, David Raksin, August 12, 2004. http://www.telegraph .co.uk/news/obituaries/1469196/David-Raksin.html#
91. *The Film Music Society*, http://www.filmmusicsociety.org/resources_links/ composers/raksin.html
92. Andrew Druckenbrod, *Pittsburgh Post Gazette*, "Music Preview: PSO, Van Hoesen to premiere Previn's Harp Concerto," March 6, 2008.
93. Bernard Holland, *New York Times*, "One Couple Fulfilling Three Musical Roles," March 12, 2005.
94. *Publisher's Weekly*, November, 1991.
95. Ibid.
96. http://www.andre-previn.com
97. David Mermelstein, *New York Times*, "Recordings; Emulating the Romantics in a 'Love Song,'" March 28, 2004.
98. Gerald Nachman, *Seriously Funny*, 266.
99. Ibid, 271.
100. Ibid, 277.
101. Ibid, 267.
102. Ibid.
103. Ibid.
104. Donald Fagen, *Slate*, "The Man Who told A Christmas Story: What I Learned from Jean Shepherd," December 22, 2008.
105. Jean Shepherd, CD: "Will Failure Spoil Jean Shepherd?" Collector's Choice, 2002.
106. Gerald Nachman, *Seriously Funny*, 269.
107. Ibid.
108. Ibid, 270.
109. Ibid, 273.
110. Ibid, 275.
111. Ibid, 268.
112. Ibid, 279.
113. Ibid, 281.
114. Larry McShane, *Seattle Times*, "'First Radio Novelist' Jean Shepherd Dies—Indiana Native was Multimedia Performer," October 17, 1999.
115. Gerald Nachman, *Seriously Funny*, 51.
116. Ibid.
117. http://www.mortsahl.com
118. Ibid.
119. Gerald Nachman, *Seriously Funny*, 53.
120. Ibid.
121. Ibid, 81.
122. Ibid.

123. Ibid, 80.

124. Ibid.

125. Mort Sahl, *Heartland*, Houghton Mifflin Harcourt, 167.

126. Gerald Nachman, *Seriously Funny*, 78.

127. *Newsweek*, review of *Heartland*, August 9, 1976.

128. Gerald Nachman, *Seriously Funny*, 95.

129. Ibid.

130. http://www.mortsahl.com

131. Ibid.

132. Steven Winn, *San Francisco Chronicle*, review: Mort Sahl's America, October 9, 1996.

133. Gerald Nachman, *Seriously Funny*, 93.

134. Ibid.

135. Amy Kaufman's Interview with Mort Sahl, *Los Angeles Times*, October 17, 2008.

136. Ernest Borgnine, *Ernie*, 35.

137. IMDB biography, http://www.imdb.com/name/nm0000308/bio

138. Ibid.

139. Ibid.

140. Chuck Jones, *Chuck Amuck: The Life and Times of an Animated Cartoonist*, 153.

141. http://www.animazing.com/gallery/pages/bio_chuckjones.html

142. Bill Schaffer, *Senses of Cinema*, "Chuck Jones," http://www.sensesofcinema .com/2002/great-directors/jones/

143. http://www.chuckjones.com

144. Ed McBain, *New York Times*, "Philip Marlowe is Back, and in Trouble," October 15, 1989.

145. Robert B. Parker, *The Godwulf Manuscript*, 45.

146. Sarah Weinman, *Los Angeles Times*, "Robert B. Parker left a mark on the detective novel," January 20, 2010.

147. Bryan Marquard, *Boston Globe*, "Mystery Novelist Dies at 77," January 19, 2010.

text credits

Steber, Aprile Millo, Dizzy Gillespie, Benny Carter, Illinois Jacquet, Stan Getz, Buddy Rich, Joe Venuti, Lionel Hampton, Ruby Braff, George Shearing, Dick Johnson, Joe Williams, Tony Bennett, Bobby Short, John Pizzarelli, Mel Tormé, Nancy Wilson, Rosemary Clooney, Sammy Cahn, Arturo Toscanini, Gunther Schuller, Harry Dickson, David Raskin, André Previn, Jean Shepherd, Mort Sahl, and Carlo Bergonzi.